Multimedia & CD-ROMs For Dummies

My _____ plugs in here.

My _____ plugs in here.

My _____ plugs in here.

← Joystick or MIDI box always plugs in here.

Use this space to write down which cable plugs into which jack on your sound card. (See Chapter 3.)

Important Settings to Remember

Whenever you install a new card, write its settings down in this table. By doing so, you avoid later quarrels if another card tries to use the same setting. (Use a pencil in case you change the settings. This paper is thick, so you can do a lot of erasing.)

The Gadget	IRQ (Interrupt)	DMA	Address	Other (Port #)	Notes
Sound card					
Internal modem					
Scanner					
Video capture card					

What to Look for When Shopping

Here's a quick shopping list for a multimedia computer, listing the parts and the numbers attached to them.

The Part	The Appropriate Number
Computer	486SX or 486DX
Video card	At least 256 colors; 24-bit (16.7 million colors) is better
Sound card	16-bit
CD-ROM drive	At least doublespeed; triplespeed is better
Hard disk (or hard drive)	At least 200MB; 340MB is better
RAM (Memory or Random Access Memory)	At least 4MB; 8MB is better

. . . For Dummies: #1 Computer Book Series for Beginners

D0796069

Multimedia & CD-ROMs For Dummies

Cheat Sheet

Common Multimedia Files and Their Contents

The Filename	The Contents
AVI (Audio Video Interleaved)	Video. Windows' preferred format for storing video; these files can be played through Microsoft's Video for Windows software or an updated Media Player.
BMP (Bitmap)	Graphic. Windows' main format for graphics; bitmap files can contain photos or illustrations.
CLP (Windows Clipboard)	Information. Windows' Clipboard, which can hold text, sounds, movies, illustrations, and photos; stores its stash in these files.
EPS (Encapsulated PostScript File)	Information. Text or graphics to be printed on special PostScript printers; popular for exchanging graphics between different types of computers, such as Macs and PCs.
FLC	Animation. A series of illustrations from Autodesk's family of software, or one of dozens of other FLC-making packages.
FLI	Animation. A series of illustrations from Autodesk's family of software, or one of dozens of other FLI-making packages.
GIF (Graphics Interchange Format)	Graphics. Photos or graphics stored in a space-saving format started on CompuServe's on-line service; contains no more than 256 colors and can be transferred between different brands of computers.
ICO (Icon)	Graphics. Small files containing icons for Windows.
JPG (Joint Photographic Experts Group)	Photos. High-quality photographs stored by using a special compression format.
MID (MIDI)	Song. A slightly abbreviated version of the standard MIDI format; designed for Windows MIDI programs.
MOD (Module)	Song. A file containing recordings of musical instruments and instructions for arranging them into a tune.
MOV (QuickTime)	Video. Movies originating from Apple's Macintosh computers.
MPG (Motion Pictures Expert Group)	Video. Highly compressed movies requiring special playback hardware and software.
PCD (Photo CD)	Photo. Photographs stored on Kodak's Photo CDs.
PCX	Graphics. A popular format for storing graphics; these files can be read by most major graphics programs, including Windows Paintbrush.
RLE (Run-Length Encoded)	Graphics. A slightly compressed bitmap file in Windows.
TGA	Photos. File format used by Targa's line of high-resolution video products.
TIF (Tagged Image File Format)	Graphics. File format for moving pictures between types of software and computers; popularized by Aldus PageMaker and used by many scanners.
VOC (Creative Voice)	Sound. Sound Blaster format for storing recorded sounds.
WAV (Waveform)	Sound. Windows' preferred format for storing recorded sounds.

...For Dummies: #1 Computer Book Series for Beginners

References for the Rest of Us

COMPUTER BOOK SERIES FROM IDG

Are you intimidated and confused by computers? Do you find that traditional manuals are overloaded with technical details you'll never use? Do your friends and family always call you to fix simple problems on their PCs? Then the *... For Dummies*™ computer book series from IDG is for you.

... For Dummies books are written for those frustrated computer users who know they aren't really dumb but find that PC hardware, software, and indeed the unique vocabulary of computing make them feel helpless. *... For Dummies* books use a lighthearted approach, a down-to-earth style, and even cartoons and humorous icons to diffuse computer novices' fears and build their confidence. Lighthearted but not lightweight, these books are a perfect survival guide to anyone forced to use a computer.

> *"I like my copy so much I told friends; now they bought copies."*
>
> **Irene C., Orwell, Ohio**

> *"Quick, concise, nontechnical, and humorous."*
>
> **Jay A., Elburn, IL**

> *"Thanks, I needed this book. Now I can sleep at night."*
>
> **Robin F., British Columbia, Canada**

Already, hundreds of thousands of satisfied readers agree. They have made *... For Dummies* books the #1 introductory level computer book series and have written asking for more. So if you're looking for the most fun and easy way to learn about computers, look to *... For Dummies* books to give you a helping hand.

IDG BOOKS

MULTIMEDIA

&

CD-ROMs

FOR

DUMMIES™

MULTIMEDIA

&

CD-ROMs

FOR

DUMMIES™

by Andy Rathbone

IDG
BOOKS

IDG Books Worldwide, Inc.
An International Data Group Company

Foster City, CA ♦ Chicago, IL ♦ Indianapolis, IN ♦ Braintree, MA ♦ Dallas, TX

Multimedia & CD-ROMs For Dummies

Published by
IDG Books Worldwide, Inc.
An International Data Group Company
919 E. Hillsdale Blvd.
Suite 400
Foster City, CA 94404

Library of Congress Catalog Card No.: 94-75906

ISBN: 1-56884-089-6

Printed in the United States of America

10 9 8 7 6

Distributed in the United States by IDG Books Worldwide, Inc.

Distributed in Canada by Macmillan of Canada, a Division of Canada Publishing Corporation; by Computer and Technical Books in Miami, Florida, for South America and the Caribbean; by Longman Singapore in Singapore, Malaysia, Thailand, and Korea; by Toppan Co. Ltd. in Japan; by Asia Computerworld in Hong Kong; by Woodslane Pty. Ltd. in Australia and New Zealand; and by Transworld Publishers Ltd. in the U.K. and Europe.

For general information on IDG Books in the U.S., including information on discounts and premiums, contact IDG Books at 800-434-3422 or 415-312-0650.

For information on where to purchase IDG Books outside the U.S., contact Christina Turner at 415-312-0650.

For information on translations, contact Marc Jeffrey Mikulich, Director, Foreign and Subsidiary Rights, at IDG Books Worldwide, 415-312-0650.

For sales inquiries and special prices for bulk quantities, write to the address above or call IDG Books Worldwide at 415-312-0650.

For information on using IDG Books in the classroom or ordering examination copies, contact Jim Kelly at 800-434-2086.

is a registered trademark of
IDG Books Worldwide, Inc.

About the Author

Andy Rathbone

Andy Rathbone started geeking around with computers in 1985 when he bought a boxy CP/M Kaypro 2X with lime-green letters. Like other budding nerds, he soon began playing with null-modem adapters, dialing up computer bulletin boards, and working part time at Radio Shack.

In between playing computer games, he served as editor of the *Daily Aztec* newspaper at San Diego State University. After graduating with a comparative literature degree, he went to work for a bizarre underground coffee-table magazine that sort of disappeared.

Andy began combining his two interests, words and computers, by selling articles to a local computer magazine. During the next few years, Rathbone started ghostwriting computer books for more-famous computer authors, as well as writing several hundred articles about computers for technoid publications like *Supercomputing Review*, *CompuServe Magazine*, *ID Systems*, *DataPro*, and *Shareware*.

In 1992, Andy and *DOS For Dummies* author/legend Dan Gookin teamed up to write *PC's For Dummies*, which was a runner-up in the Computer Press Association's 1993 awards. Andy subsequently wrote *Windows For Dummies*, *OS/2 For Dummies*, and *Upgrading & Fixing PCs For Dummies*.

Andy is currently contributing regularly to *CompuServe Magazine*, a magazine mailed monthly to CompuServe members. (Feel free to drop him a line at 75300,1565.)

Andy lives with his most-excellent wife, Tina, and their cat in San Diego, California. When not writing, Rathbone fiddles with his MIDI synthesizer and tries to keep the cat off both keyboards.

Welcome to the world of IDG Books Worldwide.

IDG Books Worldwide, Inc. is a subsidiary of International Data Group, the world's largest publisher of computer-related information and the leading global provider of information services on information technology. IDG was founded more than 25 years ago and now employs more than 7,000 people worldwide. IDG publishes more than 220 computer publications in 65 countries (see listing below). More than fifty million people read one or more IDG publications each month.

Launched in 1990, IDG Books Worldwide is today the #1 publisher of best-selling computer books in the United States. We are proud to have received 3 awards from the Computer Press Association in recognition of editorial excellence, and our best-selling *...For Dummies*™ series has more than 12 million copies in print with translations in 25 languages. IDG Books, through a recent joint venture with IDG's Hi-Tech Beijing, became the first U.S. publisher to publish a computer book in the People's Republic of China. In record time, IDG Books has become the first choice for millions of readers around the world who want to learn how to better manage their businesses.

Our mission is simple: Every IDG book is designed to bring extra value and skill-building instructions to the reader. Our books are written by experts who understand and care about our readers. The knowledge base of our editorial staff comes from years of experience in publishing, education, and journalism — experience which we use to produce books for the '90s. In short, we care about books, so we attract the best people. We devote special attention to details such as audience, interior design, use of icons, and illustrations. And because we use an efficient process of authoring, editing, and desktop publishing our books electronically, we can spend more time ensuring superior content and spend less time on the technicalities of making books.

You can count on our commitment to deliver high-quality books at competitive prices on topics consumers want to read about. At IDG, we value quality, and we have been delivering quality for more than 25 years. You'll find no better book on a subject than an IDG book.

John Kilcullen
President and CEO
IDG Books Worldwide, Inc.

WINNER
*Eighth Annual
Computer Press
Awards ≥ 1992*

WINNER
*Ninth Annual
Computer Press
Awards ≥ 1993*

IDG
BOOKS

Acknowledgments

(The publisher would like to give special thanks to Patrick J. McGovern, without whom this book would not have been possible.)

Credits

Executive Vice President, Strategic Product Planning and Research
David Solomon

Editorial Director
Diane Graves Steele

Acquisitions Editor
Megg Bonar

Brand Manager
Judith A. Taylor

Editorial Managers
Tracy L. Barr
Sandra Blackthorn

Editorial Assistants
Tamara S. Castleman
Stacey Holden Prince
Kevin Spencer

Acquisitions Assistant
Suki Gear

Production Director
Beth Jenkins

Project Coordinator
Cindy L. Phipps

Associate Pre-Press Coordinator
Tony Augsburger

Associate Project Editor
Kristin A. Cocks

Editors
Barbara L. Potter
Andy Cummings

Technical Reviewer
Ronald R. Dippold

Production Staff
Tony Augsburger
Valery Bourke
Mary Breidenbach
Chris Collins
Sherry Dickinson Gomoll
Drew R. Moore
Dwight Ramsey
Kathie Schnorr
Gina Scott

Cover Design
Kavish + Kavish

Illustrations
Accent Technical Communications

Proofreader
Henry Lazarek

Indexer
Sherry Massey

Book Design
University Graphics

Contents at a Glance

Introduction 1

Part I: The Multiple Parts of Multimedia
(or How to Buy Everything) 7

Chapter 1: What is Multimedia? 9

Chapter 2: The Computer That Holds Everything Together 21

Chapter 3: Sound Cards (Those Sound Blaster Things) 37

Chapter 4: Your Monitor and Video Cards 53

Chapter 5: Grabbing Movies with a Video Capture Card 65

Chapter 6: CD (Seedy) ROM Drives 79

Chapter 7: Those Tempting Multimedia Bundles with Everything 93

Chapter 8: Your Plain Ol' TV Set (Computerized Channel Surfing) ... 99

Chapter 9: Those Other Computers 103

Part II: Setting Everything Up (or That Cable Plugs in Here) 109

Chapter 10: Installing a Card 111

Chapter 11: Installing CD-ROM Drives 121

Chapter 12: Installing a New Monitor 131

Chapter 13: Hooking Up Everything to Your Stereo 135

Chapter 14: Hooking Up a Camcorder or VCR to Your Computer 141

Chapter 15: Hooking Up Stuff to a TV 147

Chapter 16: It Doesn't Work! 153

Part III: Doing Stuff! (or How to Start Playing) 163

Chapter 17: Making Windows Scream and Flash! 165

Chapter 18: Recording and Playing Sounds on Your PC 189

Chapter 19: Putting Photos on Your PC (That Kodak CD Stuff) 201

Chapter 20: Video for Windows, Camcorders, and Movies 213

Part IV: Making Custom Setups (or Doing Some Serious Work) 231

Chapter 21: Setting Up a MIDI Music Studio 233

Chapter 22: Building the Ultimate Game Machine 239

Chapter 23: Making Video Presentations 247

Part V: The Part of Tens 253

Chapter 24: The Top Ten CDs (or Which Are the Good Ones?) 255

Chapter 25: Ten Cheap Ways to Try Out Multimedia 267

Chapter 26: Ten Ways Manufacturers Try to Confuse You 271

Chapter 27: Ten Thousand File Formats 277

Chapter 28: Ten Solutions to Common Problems 281

Chapter 29: Ten General-Purpose Tips 289

Chapter 30: Ten Legal Do's and Don'ts 295

Part VI: Glossary 299

Glossary 301

Index 311

Cartoons at a Glance

By Rich Tennant

Table of Contents

Introduction 1

About This Book 1
How to Use This Book 2
How This Book Is Organized 2
    Part I: The Multiple Parts of Multimedia (or How to Buy Everything) 3
    Part II: Setting Everything Up (or That Cable Plugs in Here) 3
    Part III: Doing Stuff! (or How to Start Playing) 3
    Part IV: Making Custom Setups (or Doing Some *Serious* Work) 3
    Part V: The Part of Tens 4
Icons Used in This Book 4
Where to Go from Here 4

**Part I: The Multiple Parts of Multimedia
(or How to Buy Everything)** 7

Chapter 1: What is Multimedia? 9

What Does "Multimedia" Mean, Anyway? 9
What Makes Multimedia So Special? 12
What Do MPC and MPC2 Mean? 13
Technical Details about Details 16
What Parts Should I Buy? 17
Do I Need a New Computer? 18

Chapter 2: The Computer That Holds Everything Together 21

The Computer's Role in Multimedia 22
    The central processing unit (CPU, or See-Pea-You) 22
    Cards, slots, and the expansion bus 23
    Do you have enough slots? 27
A Fast (and Big) Hard Drive 28
    So what does all this stuff mean? 28
    Hard drive lingo 29
A Whole Lotta Memory 30
The Mouse 31
The Joystick 32
SCSI Ports (and SCSI II Ports) 33
Last Minute Questions 34
    I don't wanna buy all this new stuff! 34
    Can a laptop work for multimedia? 34
    Can I run my computer and CD player on its side? 35

Chapter 3: Sound Cards (Those Sound Blaster Things) 37

Do I Need a Sound Card? 38
Which Sound Card Should I Buy? 38
    What sounds can a card make? 39
    What other things can a sound card do? 43
Hey, Cut the Tech Talk: Which Sound Card Should I Buy? 45
What's This MIDI Stuff? 46
Why Does My New 16-Bit Sound Card Sound Just Like My
    Cheap 8-Bit Card? 47
What's That VOC, WAV, MID, CMF, and MOD Nonsense? 48
The Buzzwords of Sound 49

Chapter 4: Your Monitor and Video Cards 53

What's a Video Card? 54
Buying the Right Monitor 54
Defrosting Shrimp in the "Video Mode" Zone 55
    Resolution 56
    Colors 57
Choosing a Video Mode 58
Speeding Things Up with an Accelerator Card or Local Bus ...58
The Movies on CDs Look Jerky When Played Back! 61
The Movies Are All Postage-Stamp-Sized! 61
My Computer Doesn't Have A Video Card! 61
What Do All Those Funny Video Words Mean? 62

Chapter 5: Grabbing Movies with a Video Capture Card 65

What Is a Video Capture Card? 65
What Equipment Do I Need to Capture Videos? 66
Why Does My $500 Card Make Postage-Stamp-Sized Videos? ...67
Uh, What Is This "Codec" Stuff? 69
Why Can Other Cards Capture Video Faster Than My Card? ...71
Why Does the Picture Seem Jerky and Then Smooth Out? 72
What Is This PAL, SECAM, and NTSC Stuff? 72
Why Is S-Video Better Than Composite? 74
Should I Bother with MPEG? 74
Video Capture Buzzwords 75

Chapter 6: CD (Seedy) ROM Drives 79

What Do Double-and Triple-Speed Mean? 80
My Friend Says That I Don't Need a Fast CD-ROM Drive 80
What's the Easiest Way to Buy a CD-ROM Drive? 81
Is an Internal Drive Better Than an External One? 82
What the Heck Is a Drive Controller? 83
    Is "proprietary" better than "SCSI"? 83
Can I Really Listen to B.B. King on My Computer's CD-ROM Drive? ...84
What Numbers Should I Look for on My CD-ROM Drive? 85
Will a Kodak CD Fit in My Camera? 86

What Else Do I Need to Buy? 86
    Caddies 86
    Those cheap plastic CD cases (jewel boxes) 87
Simple Answers to Seedy (CD) Questions 87
    What's that MSCDEX file stuff? 87
    All the CD movies look so jerky! 87
    How can I make my own CDs? 88
    Does sound come from the CD-ROM drive or the sound card? 88
Using Hypertext in Multimedia CDs 89
Dirty CDs 90
The Buzzwords 90

Chapter 7: Those Tempting Multimedia Bundles with Everything **93**

What Is Included in a Multimedia Upgrade Package? 93
    Will an upgrade kit make me open my computer? 94
    How do the multimedia upgrades differ? 95
Watch Out for This Stuff 96
Should I Upgrade or Buy a New Multimedia Computer? 97

Chapter 8: Your Plain Ol' TV Set (Computerized Channel Surfing) **99**

Using the TV as a Monitor 99
Watching TV on a Computer 101
Understanding This PAL, SECAM, and NTSC Stuff 101
TV Buzzwords 102

Chapter 9: Those Other Computers **103**

Amiga 103
Macintosh 104
Atari 105
Silicon Graphics Indy 106
Phillips CD-i 106

*Part II: Setting Everything Up
(or That Cable Plugs in Here)* *109*

Chapter 10: Installing a Card **111**

What Multimedia Cards Do I Need? 111
Which Card Goes in Which Slot? 113
How Do I Install a New Card? 114
Uh, I Dropped a Screw Inside There Somewhere 119

Chapter 11: Installing CD-ROM Drives **121**

Should I Hook Up My CD-ROM Drive to My Sound Card? 121
How Do I Install a CD-ROM Drive? 122
    Installing an external CD-ROM drive 122
    Installing an internal CD-ROM drive 124
Sending an External CD-ROM Drive's Sound to the Sound Card 128

MSCDEX.EXE and Other Pesticides 129
A Friend Sold Me His Old CD-ROM Drive, But There's No Driver! 130

Chapter 12: Installing a New Monitor **131**
Installing a New Monitor 131

Chapter 13: Hooking Up Everything to Your Stereo **135**
Playing Your Sound Card through Your Home Stereo 135
Playing Your Home Stereo through Your Sound Card 138

Chapter 14: Hooking Up a Camcorder or VCR to Your Computer **141**
Choosing the Correct Cables 141
Connecting a Camcorder or a VCR to Your Computer 144

Chapter 15: Hooking Up Stuff to a TV **147**
Choosing the Correct Cables 147
Watching PC Programs on a TV Set 149

Chapter 16: It Doesn't Work! **153**
Irritating IRQ and Interrupt Conflicts 153
Addresses and DMA Stuff 155
Jumper Bumping and DIP Switch Flipping 156
Moving jumpers around 157
Flipping a DIP switch 159
My Card Doesn't Work! 161

Part III: Doing Stuff! (or How to Start Playing) *163*

Chapter 17: Making Windows Scream and Flash! **165**
Working with Media Player 165
Playing a file in Media Player 167
Playing videos in Media Player 169
Upgrading Media Player to play movies 170
Adding Windows Drivers 171
Making Media Player play CDs 172
Adding other drivers to Windows 173
Switching to Different Video Modes 173
Using Windows Setup to change video modes 174
Switching video modes through a card's software 176
Objecting to Object Embedding and Linking 176
Embedding an object 177
Customizing your embedded clips 178
Linking an object 179
Packing an object in Object Packager 180
Wading through MIDI 181
Making do with MIDI Mapper 182
Making a Multimedia Postcard in Write 184

Chapter 18: Recording and Playing Sounds on Your PC **189**

Finding the Volume Knob 190
Setting Up Software to Record Sounds 190
    Should I record in mono or stereo? 191
    Should I record in 8-bit or 16-bit? 191
    Should I record in 11, 22, or 44 kHz? 191
    Get to the point already! 192
Recording in Windows' Sound Recorder 192
Playing Sounds in Windows 195
Editing Sounds and Adding Special Effects 195
Making Windows Explode When It's Angry 197

Chapter 19: Putting Photos on Your PC (That Kodak CD Stuff) **201**

What is Kodak Photo CD? 201
What's All This Kodak Stuff Going to Cost Me? 202
Will My CD-ROM Drive Work with Kodak Photo CDs? 203
What Software Do I Need for Photo CDs? 204
Where Can I Get Photo CDs Made? 205
What Format Does a Photo CD Use? 206
Making a Multimedia Family Album on Your Hard Drive 207

Chapter 20: Video for Windows, Camcorders, and Movies **213**

What Is Video for Windows? 213
Recording Your Videos with VidCap 214
    Setting the capture file 215
    Adjusting the audio format 216
    Adjusting the video format 217
    Adjusting the video source 219
    Previewing the video and other options 219
    Capturing options 220
Editing Out the Bad Stuff in VidEdit 222
    Changing videos in VidEdit 223
Making a Video (and Editing Out the Bad Parts) 227

Part IV: Making Custom Setups
(or Doing Some Serious Work) *231*

Chapter 21: Setting Up a MIDI Music Studio **233**

Hardware You Need 233
    The computer 234
    The sound card, microphone, and speakers 234
    MIDI instruments 235
    Tape recorder 236
Software You Need 237
What to Watch Out For 238

Chapter 22: Building the Ultimate Game Machine 239

Hardware You Need 239
  The computer 239
  The sound card and CD-ROM drive 240
  Joystick overload 241
Memory Problems 242
General-Purpose Tips 243
  Know your brand of sound card 243
  Know how to change the volume 243
  Using on-line services 244

Chapter 23: Making Video Presentations 247

Using a Computer for Presentations 247
Understanding Presentation Software 248
  Multimedia isn't always better 249
  Get the right package for the job 249
  Is it easy to use? 249
  Does it come with clips? 250
Setting Up a Computer for Presentations 250
Making Successful Presentations 251

Part V: The Part of Tens 253

Chapter 24: The Top Ten CDs (or Which Are the Good Ones?) 255

Arthur's Teacher Trouble 255
JFK Assassination: A Visual Investigation 256
Your Own Photo CD 258
Encarta 1994 258
The San Diego Zoo Presents . . . The Animals 260
The 7th Guest 261
Street Atlas USA Version 2.0 262
Musical Instruments 263
Berlitz Japanese for Business 265

Chapter 25: Ten Cheap Ways to Try Out Multimedia 267

Using the Windows Speaker Driver 267
Connecting Your PC's Speaker to a Bigger Speaker 268
Starting with an Inexpensive Sound Card 268
Spending a Lot of Time Shopping 269
Checking Out a Friend's Machine 269
Looking for Free CDs 269
Hooking Up Your Sound Card to Your Stereo 270

Chapter 26: Ten Ways Manufacturers Try to Confuse You 271

Full-Motion Video Isn't Always Full Screen 271
Full-Screen Video Isn't Always Full Screen 272
Quarter-Screen Video Isn't Always Quarter Screen 272
CDs Aren't Always Multimedia..274
CD Boxes Aren't Easy to Open 274
Your Computer Can Talk and Listen to You 275

Chapter 27: Ten Thousand File Formats 277

Deciphering File Types 277

Chapter 28: Ten Solutions to Common Problems 281

I Need to Move a 67MB File to Another Computer 281
The Files Are Too Big for My Hard Drive 282
    CD-ROM WORM drive 283
    Tape-backup unit 283
I Can't Find All My Clips 283
I Switched Video Drivers in Windows, and Now It Doesn't Work! 284
The Movies Don't Work Right 285
    My video capture card doesn't record sound 285
    All my captured videos are black and white 285
    The people stutter in my Windows videos 285
    The sound and video look awful on my $4,000 system 286
    Nobody else can play my videos...287

Chapter 29: Ten General-Purpose Tips 289

If It Works, Don't Fix It 289
Copy Favorite Files from Compact Discs 290
Make a Permanent Swap File in Windows 290
Defragment Your Hard Drive 291
Quick and Dirty Windows Browsing 291
Don't Use Programs Like Stacker or DoubleSpace 292
Don't Be Intimidated by Camcorders 293
Upgrade to PCI or Local Bus Video 293
Buy Plenty of Caddies for Your Favorite CDs 293

Chapter 30: Ten Legal Do's and Don'ts 295

Don't Fiddle with Things You Don't Own 295
Do Copyright Your Work 296
Do Understand Public Domain 297
Do Understand On-Line Law 297
Do Get Model and Property Releases 298
Do Find Out More Information 298

Part VI: Glossary *299*

    Glossary 301

Index *311*

Reader Response Card .... *Back of Book*

Introduction

● ●

*F*or years, computers and sound just didn't mix. In fact, sound often signaled an impending catastrophe. A dull beep meant you pushed the wrong button. A crackling sound meant the paper had jammed itself in the printer again. A high-pitched whine meant Scotty had only minutes to repair the transporter before the whole landing party was lost.

But with today's new multimedia computers, sound isn't scary anymore. It has added a fresh novelty to computing, giving boring old technology a facelift. For example, stereo compact discs began earning yawns at least two years ago. But attach a compact disc player to your computer, and it's suddenly *fun* to listen to those old Otis Rush CDs while you're word processing.

Or, when you bought that new camcorder last year, nobody wanted to watch your video of the cat sniffing the couch. But store that snippet of video on some *floppy disks*, pass 'em out in the office, and your coworkers will stumble over each other in the hallways to get a copy.

Unfortunately, multimedia still can't cover up all the dry, boring parts of computing. In fact, multimedia makes some parts of computing even *worse*. Where does that camcorder plug in? Why does a computer need a sound card *and* a compact disc player? And are words like *dither* and *DAC* supposed to make everybody feel like a dummy?

That's where this book comes in. It's an informational arsenal against weird words and difficult decisions. And, after you've discovered which cord plugs in where, it'll help make computing fun again.

About This Book

This book is a reference, just like a dictionary or encyclopedia. But you won't find detailed discussions about electromagnetic spectrum physics or resonant frequencies. Instead, you'll find clear-cut answers to subjects like the following:

✔ Buying the right sound card

✔ Installing cards and compact disc players

> ✔ Adding sound and video to Windows
>
> ✔ Putting photographs and movies on your computer
>
> ✔ Sorting through the 7,346 compact disc titles
>
> ✔ What's a *double-speed, multisession* CD-ROM drive?
>
> ✔ How much is all this stuff going to cost me?

In certain chapters, budding musicians discover how to set up an inexpensive recording studio in their garage. Kids (and adults) find out how to make the ultimate game machine. Business people learn whether computerized presentations are "there yet."

And everybody learns how much fun a computer can be when it's letting you ride noisy roller coasters, travel through exploding galaxies, or breed on-screen wiggling fish.

How to Use This Book

Treat this book like any other reference: look up the problem, find the answer, close the book, and get back to work. Your nose won't sit between this book's pages one more minute than necessary.

Don't bother reading the book from cover to cover — unless it's a rainy afternoon, the power is out, and all your novels are still boxed up in the garage.

When a multimedia problem has you scratching your head, narrow down your search by looking in the book's table of contents; then read the short section containing the information you're looking for. If you're looking for a simple micro-nugget of information — the definition of *DAC*, for example — head for the glossary in the back. Need a little more information? The index lists other helpful areas to check out.

By moving around, you'll be able to extract the maximum amount of information with the minimum amount of work.

How This Book Is Organized

This book is divided into six parts. Each of those six parts is divided into several chapters, and all those chapters are divvied up into even smaller sections. There's no right or wrong way to begin reading — just jump into the section that currently interests you (or confuses you) and start absorbing.

Part I: The Multiple Parts of Multimedia (or How to Buy Everything)

This part of the book describes all the special parts you'll need for a multimedia computer. It shows what the parts are called, what little buzzwords the manufacturers use to describe them, and which little buzzwords should be on the part's box before you buy it.

Part II: Setting Everything Up (or That Cable Plugs in Here)

Unfortunately, buying a sound card doesn't immediately unleash Gorgar's voice in your computer games. You need to *install* the sound card. These chapters describe how to install sound cards, video cards, CD-ROM drives, and other multimedia goodies. Plus, you learn how to connect your computer to your stereo, VCR, TV, or camcorder.

None of that stuff seems to work? Then keep reading. As a no-charge, added bonus, one chapter explains some quick fixes to try when none of this new stuff seems to work right.

Part III: Doing Stuff! (or How to Start Playing)

When all the expensive multimedia toys are bought, installed, and ready to go, it's playtime. Chapters in this section explain how to jazz up Windows so it gives you pep talks as you work, all the while playing soothing sounds of migrating gray whales in the background. Other chapters show how to record sounds, movies, and photographs onto your computer's hard disks. Make a multimedia scrapbook for the grandchildren to laugh at in 20 years!

Part IV: Making Custom Setups (or Doing Some Serious Work)

Ready to turn this book into a tax deduction? Then turn to these chapters. Musicians learn what computer parts they need to plug in that guitar and start noodling some cool Metallica/George Benson riffs. Another chapter shows parents how to set up their computers for games — er, educational uses. Looking for an edge at the office? Check out the chapter on presentations. And real estate brokers learn how to dump pictures of mansions onto their hard drives — there's a little bit for everybody.

Part V: The Part of Tens

A tradition in ...*For Dummies* books, this section includes lists of *bunches* of stuff. Included are the 10 best ways to store these new 60 megabyte files of camcorder movies, the 10 (or 32, to be exact) most common file formats you'll encounter in multimedia, 10 cheap ways to try out multimedia before shelling out any serious cash, 10 ways to retrieve a tortilla chip that fell behind the desk — you get the idea.

Icons Used in This Book

Thumbprints aren't the only things living in this book's margins: you'll spot little pictures called *icons*, each pointing out different tidbits of information.

Looking for hints or shortcuts? Keep an eye out for this icon.

Forgot what you were supposed to remember? Then look for this icon.

The stuff marked with this icon is a definite no-no.

Don't bother reading any of this stuff. This icon warns you of nerdy, technical discussions of stuff that's already covered more simply elsewhere.

Where to Go from Here

Chances are that some part of multimedia has already caught your eye or ear. So head for the table of contents, scoot for that particular chapter, and dig in.

The other chapters are ready for you whenever you are.

Be sure to crank up the volume and disturb the neighbors at least once with your new multimedia computer.

"EXCUSE ME – IS ANYONE HERE <u>NOT</u> TALKING ABOUT THEIR MULTIMEDIA COMPUTING?"

Part I

The Multiple Parts of Multimedia (or How to Buy Everything)

In this part . . .

People don't want to read a boring introductory paragraph— especially when they're rarin' to check out Alice Cooper's cole slaw in their new *Lifestyles of the Rich and Famous Cookbook* compact disc — so this will be short and sweet.

This part of the book describes what your computer needs in order to earn the Official Multimedia label: a CD-ROM drive, a sound card, the right video card, and a few other goodies — even a joystick.

You'll find out which computer buzzwords mean *good* stuff — words like *multisession* and *44 kHz* — and which buzzwords mean yesterday's moldy technology — words like *8-bit* and *FM synthesis*.

Plus, here's the best news of all: you don't have to read this whole section. Each multimedia goody, from sound cards to CD-ROM drives to TV sets to video cards, gets its own specific chapter later in the book. You don't have to be bored by *multisession* when you're really just scratching your head over *FM synthesis*.

(Alice Cooper left out his cole slaw, but you will find Eva Gabor's Hungarian Goulash.)

Chapter 1
What is Multimedia?

In This Chapter
- ▶ What does multimedia mean?
- ▶ What does a multimedia program do?
- ▶ Why the fuss over multimedia?
- ▶ What is MPC?
- ▶ What computer parts do I need?
- ▶ Will I need a new computer?

*N*ot sure what multimedia is all about? Don't feel bad; nobody else knows, either. Stuffy computer scientists are *still* writing elaborate papers analyzing the subject, and nobody can reach an absolute conclusion. But everybody agrees on one thing: multimedia is *fun*.

This chapter merely tackles that same "What is multimedia?" stuff, so feel free to skip it — it's only here for the computer scientists to argue about. Instead, skip ahead to the fun chapters about joysticks and sound cards.

What Does "Multimedia" Mean, Anyway?

Let's start off with a secret: you already own a multimedia computer.

The word *multimedia* simply means being able to communicate in more than one way. For example, if you rub your stomach while describing Ben and Jerry's ice cream to a friend, you're making a *multimedia* presentation: you're communicating verbally *and* visually. You're also smearing sticky stuff on your T-shirt, but that's beside the point.

Your computer can communicate in several ways, too. When you turn it on in the morning, it flashes text on the screen (visual communication) and beeps (audio communication). That's multimedia, plain and simple.

Anything else is a matter of degree. The better your computer can handle sound and graphics, the better your multimedia programs will look — and the more impressive your computer will be when the neighbors drop by to see why you haven't left the house recently.

Of course, the computer industry defines *multimedia* as something much more elaborate. That way, people have to buy lots of expensive new parts to beef up the way their computers communicate.

- ✔ For example, the computer's little built-in speaker needs to be beefed up with a sound card and speakers, costing anywhere from $50 to $500. (See Chapter 3.)
- ✔ The computer's boring old text needs to be spiffed up with fancy color graphics from a fancy video card, so you can see exotic pictures of tree frogs and hot-air balloons. (See Chapter 4.)
- ✔ Also, files containing high-fidelity sound and graphics consume a *lot* of disk space. Because multimedia programs are so huge, they're often stored on compact discs. That means you'll also need to buy a computerized compact disc player — a CD-ROM drive. (See Chapter 7.)
- ✔ In fact, the computer industry is very specific about what computer parts you'll need for multimedia. You'll find a complete description a little later in this chapter.

Even if your CD-ROM drive can play Stevie Ray Vaughan CDs, you *still* need a sound card. That's because a CD-ROM drive can either grab computerized information or play back a musical CD, but not both at the same time. When you're running a program, the CD-ROM drive merely hands the sounds over to the sound card for playback.

Table 1-1 shows what a multimedia computer is able to do, as well as the parts responsible for doing that stuff.

**Table 1-1   A Multimedia Computer Can Do These Things
            with These Parts**

A Multimedia Computer Can Do This	When You Add This Part	Comments
Recreate the sounds of musical instruments (or *synthesize music*)	A sound card and a speaker	Sound cards vary widely in quality when creating music.
		Some can sound like *real* instruments, like violins, pianos, or tubas. The cheap ones sound like Pic 'n' Save toy pianos. (See Chapter 3 for more information.)
Play back recorded sounds	A sound card and a speaker	When playing back recorded sounds, sound cards don't vary nearly as much in quality. The more-expensive cards — called *16-bit* cards — will sound clearer, however. (See Chapter 3 for more information.)
Show pictures and movies on the monitor	A color monitor and a fancy graphics card	If your computer is under two years old, its video card and monitor can probably already handle this. (Chapter 4 covers video cards and monitors.)
Access information stored on a compact disc	A CD-ROM drive	These discs fit inside your computer (*internal* and less expensive) or come in a box that sits next to your computer (*external* and more expensive because you're paying for the box).
		Your stereo's compact disc player won't double as a CD-ROM drive, unfortunately.
Run Windows	Microsoft Windows Version 3.1	Just about every computer comes with Windows already installed, so this requirement is no big deal. (Actually, some computers *don't* run Windows and they can run even *better* multimedia programs. These are described in Chapter 9.)

What Makes Multimedia So Special?

Back in the dark ages when people started buying their first television sets, people also stopped listening to sports on the radio. Football tackles were much more impressive when you could see the helmets fall off. The same goes for multimedia programs. A program that can flash pictures and play sounds is much more exciting than a program that just puts words on the screen.

For example, computer programs have taught foreign languages for years. Unfortunately, most programs were merely computerized sets of flash cards. Yawn.

But a *multimedia* language program makes learning much more fun. Instead of trying to recall the French phrase for "roasted boar ear broth," you can watch as the on-screen French waiter mouths the correct pronunciation for each entry on the menu.

Are you *sure* you want to order "bien cuit filtre à café"? Push the button to hear it pronounced again. And again and again, until you've got it right. Multimedia computers might look and sound more *human*, but they're still as patient as ever.

The computer science professors say that multimedia programs all have several basic things in common, which are explained in Table 1-2.

Table 1-2	Elements of a Multimedia Program
This Part of Multimedia	*Allows for This*
Text	This part of multimedia — displaying words on the screen — is the base layer of almost all programs. Text is still a quick way to spread information, so programs will always use it.
Pictures	Multimedia computers can display photograph-quality pictures on the monitor. Seeing a shiny garden slug on the screen carries a *lot* more impact than just reading about one.
Movies	With a multimedia program or part, your computer can turn into a TV set, letting you watch *Bewitched* reruns. Or the computer can store snippets of your own home movies onto disks, letting you mail baby-food movies to the relatives on a floppy.
Animation	Sometimes animation (cartoons) can express a point better than movies. Without animation, for example, nobody could show footage of dinosaurs biting each other.

This Part of Multimedia	Allows for This
	Some industry folks use the word *animation* to describe any type of moving picture, including movies.
Sound	A biting dinosaur isn't much unless you can hear the bones crunch as well.
Increased control	Best yet, multimedia lets you jump around. Bored with the biting dinosaurs? Click on a button, and switch to the flying Pterodactyls, instead.
	Unlike a normal, television-style movie, a computerized multimedia program lets you skip past the boring parts and watch the fun stuff, over and over. Plus, there's no delay while the VCR rewinds; multimedia programs can jump quickly to different areas.

✓ By itself, multimedia is nothing new. Recorded sound, movies, and pictures have been around for years. The new part is the way computers can *intertwine* these things. A multimedia program can describe a cat, show a movie of it playing with yarn, play a meow sound, and let you print out a 50-cents-off coupon for a ten-pound bag of Jonny Cat — all at the same time.

✓ Some skeptics say multimedia is a glorified word for expensive computer games. And they're partly right. But what's wrong with computer games, anyway?

✓ In fact, an educational program that mimics a computer game will be used more often than one that mimics a textbook.

✓ Whether the skeptics like it or not, all new computers will soon be sold with multimedia equipment built in. New technology inevitably replaces old. Stereo sound replaced mono. The telephone replaced the telegraph. And today, even country farmers can take advantage of satellite technology — they no longer predict the weather solely by observing a leech in a jar.

What Do MPC and MPC2 Mean?

Because nobody really knows what the term *multimedia* means, a group of confused computer companies banded together to create their own definition. They called their definition *MPC*, short for Multimedia PC, and created a little logo to go with it, as seen in Figure 1-1.

Crusty old bores

The computer industry is all excited about multimedia for several reasons, but not for the reasons you may expect.

First, multimedia computers cost much more than those boring, nonmultimedia computers. The more computer goodies everybody buys, the more money goes into the industry's pocket.

Plus, multimedia computers encourage people to spend more money on frivolous stuff, not just standard business programs. Remember when Jeff at the office installed those icons that burped?

Finally, software companies *love* to release their programs on a compact disc: then it's harder for people to make free copies of the programs for their friends.

That's not to say that multimedia is a hoax, however; the move toward multimedia computers is inevitable. Five years ago, color monitors were an expensive, gimmicky fad. Today, everybody has one. In a few years, every computer in the store will come with a CD-ROM drive and a sound card.

So, if you're buying a computer today, be sure to take a flying leap into the multimedia fray. Your computer will last a few years longer. Poor Dennis Cushman in Mira Mesa, California, bought a monochrome monitor a few years ago, and he's still cursing himself. (So is his wife.)

Figure 1-1:
This symbol appears on the boxes of parts and computers that meet the standards set by the Multimedia PC Marketing Council, Inc.

If you have a computer that's been designated *MPC* (Multimedia PC), it can run any of the multimedia software that has the MPC logo on the side of the box.

As fancier parts and computers hit the shelves, the MPC creators realized that their first set of standards weren't good enough. So they released a *new* set of guidelines, as well as a new logo, seen in Figure 1-2.

Figure 1-2:
This newer symbol appears on the boxes of computers, parts, and software that meet more-demanding multimedia standards.

What' the big difference between MPC and MPC2? An MPC2 computer can run larger and more elaborate multimedia programs and can run them much faster.

Table 1-3 shows the parts that your computer needs to meet the MPC standards, as well as the newer MPC2 standards.

Table 1-3	Requirements to Meet MPC and MPC2 Standards		
The Part	*MPC*	*MPC2*	*Real Life Recommendations*
CPU	16 MHz 386SX	25 MHz 486SX	At least a 50 MHz 486DX
Hard disk	30MB	160MB minimum	340MB
RAM	2MB	4MB	8MB
CD-ROM	Yes, please	Yes, please, but make it work twice as fast (*doublespeed*)	Yes, please, but make it work three times as fast (*triplespeed*)
Video card	VGA	640 × 480 with 65,536 colors	1024 × 768 with 65,536 colors
Floppy disk	3 ½-inch, high-density	3 ½-inch, high-density	Same
Joystick	Yes, please	Yes, please	Two, please
Sound card	8-bit with 8-note synthesizer	16-bit with 8-note synthesizer; MIDI playback	Same

- ✔ If your computer has mostly MPC2-level parts but has a few MPC-level parts as well, then it's still considered an *MPC* computer.

- ✔ Many computer companies ignore the MPC and don't bother to stick its logo on their boxes. So don't automatically think that your PC isn't up to snuff with the MPC simply because you didn't see the MPC logo on the box.

- ✔ In fact, the MPC standards are set so low that just about every computer sold in the past two years is able to meet them, provided you add a cheap CD-ROM drive and sound card.

Technical Details about Details

The computer industry is particularly picky about the words it uses to describe sound cards and CD-ROM drives. Table 1-4 shows some of the technofine print, edited down to minimum levels of common decency. Don't worry about absorbing all this stuff now; all these fancy buzzwords are explained in more human terms in chapters farther down the road.

Table 1-4	Specific MPC and MPC2 Computing Standards	
Part	*MPC*	*MPC2*
CD-ROM drive, also called "Optical Storage" unit (explained in human terms in Chapter 6)	Sustained 150 kilobytes-per-second transfer rate; average seek time of one second or less; 10,000 hours MTBF	Meets MPC levels but *doublespeed;* offers a sustained 300 KB-per-second transfer rate, using less than 40 percent of processor time
	Recommended 64K of read-ahead buffering	Average seek time of 400 milliseconds or less; multisession-capable and XA ready
	Volume knob on the front and audio (music) outputs	
Sound card (covered in more human terms in Chapter 3)	8-bit *Digital-to-Analog Converter* (DAC) and *Analog-to-Digital Converter* (ADC); a sample rate of 22.05 and 11.025 kHz	Meets MPC levels but adds 16-bit DAC and ADC; a sample rate of 44.1, 22.05, and 11.025 kHz
	Microphone input	Must be stereo
	Internal synthesizer hardware with multi-voice, multi-timbral capabilities and six simultaneous melody notes plus two simultaneous percussive notes	

Part	MPC	MPC2
	Internal mixing capabilities to combine input from three sources (CD Red Book, synthesizer, and DAC) and present the output as a stereo, line-level audio signal at the back panel	
	Each input has at least a 3-bit volume control (8 steps) with a logarithmic taper	
Video (Video cards and monitors are covered in Chapter 4)	VGA compatible display adapter, and a color VGA compatible monitor capable of 640 × 480 in 16 colors.	Color monitor with display resolution of 640 × 480 with 65,536 (64K) colors.

What Parts Should I Buy?

A multimedia PC is like an electric toothbrush. The fancy ones clean plaque from the rear molars better than the less-expensive ones, but both types of toothbrushes still clean your teeth. And if you can remember to floss after every meal, you can probably get by with an inexpensive toothbrush.

To get out of this weird toothbrush analogy, here's the simple truth: the more money you spend, the better your multimedia PC will perform. Choose multimedia parts like you choose a toothbrush. Only you can decide the level of acceptable performance.

✔ For example, some people will be happy with mono sound; others want stereo. Some don't mind if their PC's movies fill a small corner of the screen; others want their PC's movies to fill the entire screen.

✔ If sound is important to you, spend the extra money for a 16-bit sound card and avoid the less-expensive 8-bit sound cards.

✔ For multimedia that looks and sounds the best, choose the *fastest* parts you can find. For example, because the newer, double-speed CD-ROM drives are faster than the old ones, they can display movies more realistically than the first drives that hit the market.

✔ Buy a new toothbrush when the brushes start to bend outward and no longer form a straight ridge.

Do I Need a New Computer?

You may not need to buy a sparkling new multimedia PC, no matter how cool the roller coaster demo looks in the store.

To see if your current computer is up to snuff, first look at its CPU, or *central processing unit*, as described in Chapter 2. The CPU is the brain of your computer, and it controls how well everything else can work. If you're going to be working mainly with sound, you can get by with a 386 computer. But if you want to add any fancy video — movies or animation — you need a 486 computer.

Second, how many multimedia parts does your computer already have? Check out Table 1-3; you'll need a CD-ROM drive, a sound card, a fast video card, a large hard drive, and plenty of memory.

Third, are you handy with a screwdriver? If not, ask the kid at the computer store how much the store charges to install everything and then add that to the price.

Finally, compare that total "upgrade" price to the cost of a new computer with all the multimedia stuff already installed. Which sounds like the better deal? If you haven't decided yet, keep reading.

- For people who don't like fiddling with their computers, the answer's easy: buy a new computer with everything installed.

- Sometimes different parts don't get along when installed inside the same PC. For example, one company's sound card may not work right when connected to another company's CD-ROM drive. When buying a part, make sure the store will let you return it without charge if the part doesn't work in your particular computer setup.

- Because multimedia parts sometimes fight with each other, consider buying a multimedia upgrade kit (see Chapter 7) from a single company. These bolt-on boxes come with a CD-ROM drive, a sound card, and speakers, with everything already installed and singing in harmony.

- Still haven't decided? Then check out the handy Fiddle Factor table, Table 1-5. That should clinch it.

Table 1-5	Fiddle Factor
Your Level of Fiddling	*Verdict*
I *love* fiddling with my computer! Gimme my static-free gloves!	Buy the current rage in multimedia parts and install them all yourself. Beware, however: the latest, greatest technology almost always has problems that haven't had time to work themselves out.
I *like* to fiddle with my computer.	Buy the parts separately and install them yourself. Buy parts in the middle price range and avoid the cheapest stuff.
I fiddle a *little* bit.	Buy an upgrade kit. Because these parts already get along, the installation is a lot easier.
Get that thing away from me!	Buy a new computer with everything already installed. Sure, it's hard saying good-bye to the old one, but keep reminding yourself of all those *free* compact discs that come with a new computer.

Chapter 2

The Computer That Holds Everything Together

• •

In This Chapter

▶ A computer's role in multimedia

▶ The central processing unit (CPU)

▶ Hard drive

▶ Expansion Slots (or "BUS")

▶ Memory (or "RAM")

▶ Mouse (or "Squeak")

▶ Joystick (or "Wham")

▶ SCSI (or "Huh?")

• •

*A*lthough most people drool over the graphics and sound on a multimedia computer, the real star lives *inside* the computer's case.

Just like stagehands who go unrecognized on the street, the little chips inside your computer coordinate all the flashy on-screen action, making sure that the right scenery hits the screen at the right time and in the right order. Don't forget the sound effects, either — your computer sure can't.

This chapter gives credit to all the internal parts frantically scrambling around inside your computer while you idly watch the action on the screen.

Now if we could just figure out what the "key grip" is supposed to do. . . .

The Computer's Role in Multimedia

Back in 1980, when your computer's innards were first on the drawing board, the engineers decided that computers should simply slap text and numbers onto the screen. Big deal.

Today, that same text-slapping computer is trying to slap full-color *video* onto the screen, and it's buckling under the pressure.

The next few sections explain which parts of your computer may be starting to sag and where you might need to hoist some scaffolding.

The central processing unit (CPU, or See-Pea-You)

Your computer's "brain," or its *CPU*, evolved from those little calculators that cost a bundle years ago and now come free for subscribing to the right magazines.

Also known as a *microprocessor* or *central processing unit*, the CPU simply processes numbers. In fact, your computer translates *everything* into numbers: press the letter *Y* on your keyboard, and the CPU shifts around the appropriate numbers to put the letter *Y* on the screen.

The CPU doesn't work up a sweat when shuffling text around on the screen. But when it's simultaneously shuffling text, showing videos of high-speed chases, and playing back stereo sirens, it's working overtime.

For example, to play a movie, your CPU needs to flash a bunch of pictures (*frames*) onto the screen, one after the other. The more *frames per second* your computer can flash, the smoother and more lifelike the movie looks.

Powerful CPUs can kick out more frames per second then the wimpier ones, as shown in Table 2-1.

Table 2-1	Powerful CPUs Can Produce More Frames Per Second
This CPU	*Can Toss This Many Small Pictures onto Your Screen*
486SX, 25MHz	15 frames per second (fps)
486DX, 33MHz	20 fps
486DX2, 66MHz	30 fps (TV-quality)

First, here's the boring statistical stuff. A CPU comes on a little square wafer called a *chip*. And the *bigger* the numbers on your CPU — 286, 386, or 486 — the faster and more powerful it can act.

Don't bother trying to use an XT or 286 computer for multimedia programs. They're barely powerful enough to display a color picture of a Chevy El Camino, much less a movie of an El Camino crashing through barn doors.

CPUs like the 386 and 486 have another number attached to them — their speed, measured in *megahertz*, or MHz. The bigger the MHz number, the faster the computer can move around numbers and El Caminos. Most 486 computers are rated at either 25 MHz, 33 MHz, or a tire-squealing 66 MHz.

There's more: a chip ending in the letters *DX* can run faster than one ending in *SX*. And a chip that ends in the letters *SL* runs as fast as an SX, but without sucking up as much electricity. (That's why SL chips are popular with laptops and their owners.)

Computers work with sound more easily than with video. Even a lowly 386SX computer can play back stereo, CD-quality sound. To *record* sound with that quality, however, you'll probably want a 486. And you'll definitely want a 486 to record your own videos.

The CPU sits on a flat fiberglass plate called a *motherboard*. Motherboards and CPUs are designed to get along with each other; you usually can't pull out an old CPU and stick in a faster one without replacing the motherboard as well.

If you're stuck with a slow 486 CPU, check your computer's manual for something called *OverDrive*. Vrooom! Some computers let you plug a special OverDrive chip into a special parking place on its motherboard to give your computer's CPU a boost.

- ✔ If you have the money (and a large cooling fan), consider buying a Pentium. A Pentium is a relatively new CPU that's super speedy and super expensive.

- ✔ The new *PowerPC* computers handle multimedia well, too. Because they're a new technology, however, be prepared for a few more problems than with the older, time-tested technology.

Cards, slots, and the expansion bus

The inside of your computer has a special storage area similar to a wine rack. A wine rack lets you slide new bottles of Bordeaux into empty spots; your computer lets you slide new *cards* into its empty slots. This computerized wine rack is called an *expansion bus*.

Cards are where the multimedia action's at. Slide in a *sound card*, for example, to start listening to music and sound effects. Slide in a *video capture card*, and you can copy movies to your computer from your camcorder.

Here's the problem, though. If your wine rack is designed for normal bottles of Bordeaux, a gallon of Gallo simply won't fit. And the same holds true for computers. Not all cards and slots are the same size, leading to much gnashing of teeth.

In fact, computers can use any of *six* types of slots and cards. Some slots accept just about any type of card, while others only accept one. Table 2-2 shows the different slots and cards on the market.

Table 2-2	Cards and Slots Used in PCs		
Name of the Card and Its Slot	**Pros/Cons**	**Compatibility**	**How to Identify the Card**
ISA 8-bit (Industry Standard Architecture)	These old farts are the original design and have been around for years. Most computers use these slots, so ISA cards are easy to find. Because they're an older design, ISA cards and slots aren't as fast or powerful as the others in this chart.	An 8-bit ISA *card* fits into any slot except MCA and PCI. An 8-bit ISA *slot* accepts only 8-bit ISA cards. Sometimes a 16-bit card still works, but not at full capacity.	These simple little guys have a single protruding tab which plugs into a single slot. (See Figure 2-1 for an illustration.)
ISA 16-bit	These newer, 16-bit slots can move information around twice as fast as the older, 8-bit cards. If a sound card says *16* in its name, it probably requires a 16-bit slot. The 16-bit slots started to show up on 286 computers.	A 16-bit ISA *card* fits into any slot but 8-bit ISA, MCA, and PCI. A few 16-bit cards still work in an 8-bit slot, but not as quickly. A 16-bit *slot* accepts any card but MCA, EISA, and PCI.	These cards have two protruding tabs right next to each other; the first tab slides into the ISA 8-bit slot, the other slides into a smaller slot right next to it. (See Figure 2-2.)

Name of the Card and Its Slot	Pros/Cons	Compatibility	How to Identify the Card
EISA (Extended Industry Standard Architecture)	These slots can run ISA cards as well as EISA cards — they're a faster and more powerful breed of cards. EISA slots never really caught on, so EISA cards are kinda hard to find.	An EISA *card* only works in an EISA slot. An EISA *slot* accepts any card but MCA and PCI.	These have two protruding tabs, like the previously described 16-bit cards, but the tabs have funny notches in them. Figure 2-3 shows an example of this card.
MCA (Micro Channel Architecture)	IBM tried to upgrade the old ISA design, but their new card never caught on. MCA slots are only on old "genuine" IBM computers and a few NCR comput- ers. MCA cards are faster than regular ISA cards, but they're harder to find.	An MCA *card* only works in an MCA slot. An MCA *slot* only accepts MCA cards. No strangers allowed.	If you're having trouble finding cards that fit your slots, you probably have MCA slots. Its protruding tabs start a little farther back on the card than the other types. Some MCA cards have two tabs; others have three. (See Figure 2-4.)
VESA Local Bus (Known as *VLB;* the especially long- winded call it the *Video Electronics Standards Associa- tion's Local Bus*)	These cards make video hop onto the screen faster; they don't help much when capturing video, however. Longer than normal, some folks say these cards bend a little easier than other cards, making them easier to break.	A VESA Local Bus *card* only works in a VESA Local Bus slot. A VESA Local Bus *slot* accepts any card except EISA, MCA, and PCI.	This card looks just like a 16-bit ISA card, but it has another notched tab protruding near its back end, as shown in Figure 2-5.
PCI (Peripheral Component Interconnect)	The newest design, these fast little doo- dads work best with Pentium chips.	A PCI *card* only works in a PCI slot. A PCI *slot* only accepts PCI cards.	These cards look much like MCA cards but with some subtle sizing differences. (See Figure 2-6.)

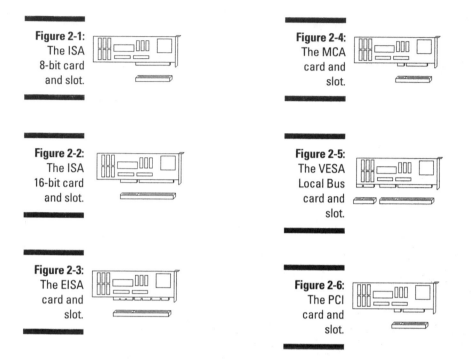

Figure 2-1: The ISA 8-bit card and slot.

Figure 2-2: The ISA 16-bit card and slot.

Figure 2-3: The EISA card and slot.

Figure 2-4: The MCA card and slot.

Figure 2-5: The VESA Local Bus card and slot.

Figure 2-6: The PCI card and slot.

The dreary manual from your computer or motherboard should say what type of slots it uses. It's often hard to tell just by looking inside.

In fact, most computers come with two *different* types of slots. For example, most 386 computers come with some 8-bit slots and some 16-bit ISA slots.

- ✔ Computers with PCI slots almost always toss in a few ISA slots for the kids. (These let you use your old ISA cards until more PCI cards hit the market.)

- ✔ Computers with local bus slots almost always come with 16-bit ISA slots, too.

- ✔ Computers with MCA slots don't have any other types of slots; you're stuck with those expensive, hard-to-find MCA cards.

- ✔ If you can't find multimedia gadgets for your MCA slots, visit a computer store's laptop section. Digital Vision makes a video capture gizmo that plugs into a printer port, for example, and New Media has a 16-bit stereo sound card built onto a PCMCIA card.

- ✔ A card that says *VLB* on the box or in its name is probably a *VESA Local Bus* card. These cards are fast, but only when they're plugged into a specific *local bus* slot. Plugging them into a regular ISA slot just won't cut it.

- Before shopping for cards, open up your computer to see how many slots it has and how many aren't already being used. Otherwise, you might come home with a card that won't fit anywhere.

- Are all your computer's parking spaces full? Then check out the following section for tips on freeing up a slot or two.

Do you have enough slots?

Most wine racks are expandable to handle a good day at the auction. But with a PC, you're stuck with what you get. Most PCs come with eight slots, although a few embarrassed models come with just two.

Eight slots might sound like plenty, but most computers eat up three slots right away. Computers need a *controller* card for transporting information to and from the disk drives, a *video* card for controlling what goes on the screen, and an *I/O* card to supply places to plug in your printer and perhaps a mouse.

Add a fax/modem card, a sound card, a scanner, and a video grabber, and you may not have room for your CD-ROM drive controller. That's why it's just as important to count slots as well as cash before heading to the computer store.

Here are some tips for cramming as many goodies into as few slots as possible:

- Because most PCs have several different types of slots, try moving the cards around. For example, if an 8-bit card is plugged into a 16-bit slot, move that card to a vacant 8-bit slot. This frees up the 16-bit slot for a faster, 16-bit card.

- Some manufacturers now cram *two* goodies onto one card. For example, many sound cards let you plug in a CD-ROM drive. That way your CD-ROM drive won't need a controller card (and its subsequent slot).

- Not all sound cards work with all CD-ROM drives, unfortunately. Some drives prefer something called *SCSI*, described later in this chapter. And some Sound Blaster cards only work with certain Panasonic-endorsed CD-ROM drives. (More about this in Chapter 7.) Plugging an incompatible drive into the wrong place can damage it.

- Some video cards let you plug in a *mouse* as well as a monitor. If you've been using a *bus mouse*, plugging the mouse into the video card can free up a slot.

- If you're using an *internal* modem, buy an *external* modem. Plug the external modem into a vacant COM port, and you've freed up the internal modem's old slot.

✔ Look for odd combinations. For example, Intel's SatisFAXion400i fax/modem comes with a port to plug in a scanner. That can free up a slot formerly used by your scanner. Whoopee!

✔ Most sound cards come with a joystick port built-in, so don't bother buying a game card for its joystick. In fact, pull out your old game card when you buy a sound card. This not only frees up a slot, but keeps your computer from being confused by too many joystick ports. (More about joysticks in Chapter 22.)

A Fast (and Big) Hard Drive

Everybody knows a big hard drive is necessary to store information. But multimedia programs don't need a *big* hard drive. They need an *enormous* one. Table 2-3 shows how much hard disk space is gobbled up by snippets of text, mono sound, stereo sound, and video.

Table 2-3   How Much Space Do Text, Sound, and Video Files Need?

This Type of Information	*Needs About This Much Disk Space*
One page of plain text	3 kilobytes (3K)
Ten seconds of low-quality sound (mono, 8 bits at 11K)	110 kilobytes (110K)
Ten seconds of good-quality sound (stereo, 16 bits at 22K)	880 kilobytes (880K)
Ten seconds of high-quality sound (stereo, 16 bits at 44K)	1,800 kilobytes (1.8MB)
Ten seconds of video (already compressed)	5.5 megabytes (5.5MB)
Ten seconds of video with sound (already compressed)	7 megabytes (7MB)

So what does all this stuff mean?

Because one minute of high-quality sound can eat up 10 megabytes of hard disk space, the answer is obvious: buy a *huge* hard drive — even 340 megabytes isn't considered too much. And if you'll be dealing with lots of video, buy an *obscenely huge* hard drive.

Not planning to record any sound or video? Then you can live with a slightly smaller hard drive. Your computer can grab huge files off the program's compact disc. A compact disc can hold more than 600 megabytes of information.

Don't think that compact discs solve everything, though. Even programs that come on compact discs often copy a few programs to your hard drive, and this can eat a couple megabytes of space.

Some compact disc programs say they work faster if you copy parts of them to your hard drive. For example, Activision's cool Return to Zork game comes on a compact disc, but the manual recommends copying 45 megabytes of the game to your hard drive for the best action. And that's a *lot* of space to give up for faster-flying vultures.

A hard disk and floppy disk are known as *magnetic disks*. Compact discs, by contrast, are called *optical* discs. That's because hard drives use little magnets to process information. CD-ROM drives use little lights to read information. Some people have the best of both worlds: little refrigerator magnets with lights on them.

Stacker, DoubleSpace, and other compression programs can slow down a hard drive's performance. Both programs take extra time to squeeze or unsqueeze all the information as it flows through the hard drive. For best results, ditch the compression programs and buy a bigger hard drive.

- ✔ Never installed a hard drive? Check out *Upgrading & Fixing PCs For Dummies* for the scoop.
- ✔ A hard drive is where your computer *stores* programs; memory is where your computer *runs* programs.

Hard drive lingo

Make sure your hard drive is not only big but *fast*. With hard drives, speed is usually measured as *access time*. Table 2-4 translates the foreign language you'll hear when shopping for a new hard drive.

Table 2-4	Hard-to-Figure-Out Hard Drive Words	
This Word	*Means This*	*Which Boils Down to This*
Capacity	Measured in *megabytes*, capacity is the amount of data the drive can store.	The *more* megabytes, the better. Buy the biggest drive you can possibly afford.
Access time	Measured in *milliseconds*, access time is the speed at which your drive can find a file and read information from it.	The *smaller* the number, the better, and 12ms is pretty good. Surprisingly, the biggest hard drives often have the fastest access times (as well as the biggest price tags).
Data transfer rate (DTR)	Measured in *kilobytes per second*, the DTR is how fast the hard drive can squirt streams of information to your computer.	The *bigger* the number, the better. Unfortunately, manufacturers tend to get a little sneaky with these figures; stick with access time for the best measurement.
Controller card	This card lets your hard drive talk to your computer.	Many newer computers don't have a controller card. The hard drive plugs straight into the motherboard.
"Bare"	When listed in an advertisement, bare means the hard drive is sold by itself.	You'll need your own rails and cables to connect it to your computer.
"Kit"	Kit refers to the hard drive plus the rails and cables necessary to mount the hard drive inside your computer.	Kits cost more because of the cables and rails.

A Whole Lotta Memory

Ever since Windows became as trendy as Sport Utility Vehicles, you've probably heard people telling you to "buy more memory." Unfortunately, the multimedia industry says the same thing. In fact, the echo is growing louder. "Buy more memory-y-y-y."

That's because most multimedia programs today run under Windows, which is a real memory hog. Windows needs at *least* four megabytes just for itself and an occasional round of Solitaire in the background. (Not quite sure what this Windows stuff is all about? Hop ahead to Chapter 17.)

Most multimedia programs run best when Windows loads part of them into memory first, bypassing the slow rumblings of a hard drive or CD-ROM drive. This brings your memory requirements up even more — perhaps 8 or 12 megabytes.

Finally, if you're going to be recording sounds or video, nobody will laugh if you spring for 16 megabytes of RAM. Some programs record your masterpieces to memory before storing them to your hard drive. The more memory you have in your computer, the more you'll be able to record.

In a bizarre change of pace, some brands of video capture cards don't work right if you have 16 megabytes of RAM or more. You have to tweak your computer and bring its memory down to only *15* megabytes. This bit of weird-ness is covered in Chapter 4.

A hard drive is where you computer *stores* programs; memory is where your computer *runs* programs.

The Mouse

Everybody already has a mouse by now, so feel free to skip this section.

Waita sec — some multimedia programs make you do *more* than simply point an arrow at an on-screen button and click the mouse. The program in Figure 2-7, for example, lets you click buttons, slide little bars, and even turn knobs — just like a cat faced with a doorknob. Ecstasy!

Figure 2-7:
In this sound-mixing program, the mouse can turn a knob, move a sliding bar, and click buttons.

✔ Mice come in two flavors: a bus mouse and a regular mouse. The tail of a regular mouse plugs into a COM port. The tail of a bus mouse plugs into its own card. (See the cards and slots section earlier in this chapter.)

✔ If you don't already have a mouse, then for heaven's sake, don't buy a *bus* mouse. These mice require their own *card*, and that card uses up a *slot* that could be used by something more fun, like a video capture card.

✔ Some video cards can do double-duty. In addition to displaying pictures, these video cards let you plug in a mouse. This can free up either a slot or a COM port.

The Joystick

Although multimedia industry professionals testify that multimedia is for serious computing work, something fishy is going on: the Multimedia PC Marketing Council, Inc. says a multimedia PC must have a *joystick*.

The cords from these serious peripherals — joysticks — fit into a special plug on something equally serious known as a *game* port.

✔ Buy a *matched* pair of joysticks — two joysticks from the same company. Whenever Andrew Kleske loses to me in SpeedBall, he always complains that he got the *bogus* joystick, snatching away any thrill of victory.

✔ Joysticks from an old Atari won't work on your IBM-compatible PC. I've already tried. (Same goes with Nintendo and Commodore, too, although old Apple joysticks sometimes work in a pinch.)

✔ Don't buy a game card at the store; just about every sound card already comes with a joystick port built in.

✔ To plug *two* joysticks into *one* port, pick up a Y-cable at the computer store. They're much cheaper at the computer store than in the special-order catalog that came with your sound card.

✔ Most MPC-sanctioned multimedia software doesn't use a joystick, however. That's because most multimedia software runs under Windows, and Windows prefers a mouse and keyboard.

✔ Joysticks get proper respect in Chapter 22.

SCSI Ports (and SCSI II Ports)

The word SCSI (Small Computer System Interface) really *is* pronounced *scuzzy*, but that doesn't mean it's OK to say it at an office party. SCSI ports are a terribly nerdy way to connect gizmos to your computer. SCSI ports are also here to stay: almost all CD-ROM drives want to send their information through a SCSI port.

Where does a SCSI port come from? Like most computer goodies, it usually comes on a *card*, just like a sound card or video card.

The SCSI card plugs into one of your computer's slots, described earlier in this section. Then a thick cable from the CD-ROM drive plugs into the socket on the SCSI card. (This stuff gets a step-by-step treatment in Chapter 10.)

When you buy a CD-ROM drive, the salesperson will probably ask if you need a *CD-ROM drive controller*. He's usually talking about the *SCSI port*. You have two options:

- ✔ Some sound cards come with the SCSI mechanics built in. You can install an internal CD-ROM drive, plug its cable into the SCSI jack on your sound card, and be home free. You won't need to buy a CD-ROM drive controller.

- ✔ Or you can buy a CD-ROM drive controller card along with your CD-ROM drive. (These controller cards cost extra, too.)

Unfortunately, not all sound cards have a *real* SCSI port. Some companies install fake ones that only work with certain brands of CD-ROM drives. How do you know whether a card will work or not? The only way you'll know is by looking in the sound card's manual or calling the card's tech support line and asking if their particular sound card works with your particular brand of CD-ROM drive.

Find out what CD-ROM drives can plug into your sound card *before* you go shopping.

External CD-ROM drives can't plug into a sound card's SCSI port. The card's SCSI port lives inside your computer, out of reach of the drive's cable.

Some people already have a SCSI port in their computers, because some huge hard drives use one. People with SCSI ports usually already know they have one, though. If you don't know whether or not your computer has a SCSI port, then it probably doesn't.

Last Minute Questions

This section is for you, there in the back, with your hand raised.

I don't wanna buy all this new stuff!

If you have a sound card, a 386 computer, and a CD-ROM drive, you don't *have* to shell out all sorts of cash for all these upgrades. Your multimedia programs will probably still work.

Unfortunately, they won't work *well*.

- The sound track will skip, sounding like a bad record the disc jockey put on just before heading down the hall for a fresh cup of coffee.

- The video won't look like *video*. Instead of seeing a video of an airplane taking off, doing a loop-the-loop, and landing, you'll see two still pictures: an airplane on the runway, ready to take off; and an airplane on the runway, just after it's landed. The computer just won't be able to keep up.

The more money you spend for a fast computer, the better your multimedia programs will look.

Can a laptop work for multimedia?

It is much more difficult to get flashy sound and graphics out of a laptop. And in the computer world, the words "much more difficult" translate into "much more expensive."

For the most part, a laptop's only advantage for multimedia is its portability. It's great for lugging around and giving presentations — expensive presentations.

- When shopping for a laptop to make multimedia presentations, look for a powerful CPU and a large, fast hard drive. The rest of the stuff you'll have to add on.

- For example, even the most-expensive laptops don't have large color screens. Make sure your multimedia laptop has a *VGA output port*. That way you can plug a larger, regular-sized monitor into the laptop so the gang in the conference room can see everything.

- When you're buying a laptop to make portable presentations, make sure it can display *two* images — one on the screen and the other through its video output port. Then it's easier for you to see what's going on while you're sending the action out to a larger monitor or overhead projector.

- ✔ Some companies are releasing multimedia products that connect to a laptop's (or any computer's) parallel port. For example, Digital Vision makes an "image grabber" for capturing pictures from a camcorder while you're on the road.

- ✔ MediaVision sells a sound card that connects to the parallel port, adding sound to presentations (or games while you're on the road).

- ✔ Or, if your laptop has a PCMCIA slot, check out the PCMCIA sound card from New Media Corp., at 714-453-0100. They sell a PCMCIA SCSI card, too. With these two, you can finally play killer CD-ROM games on your laptop!

Can I run my computer and CD player on its side?

Many people like to turn their computer on its side to take up less space and look cooler. Can they still do this if they have an internal CD-ROM drive?

Yep. But only if the CD-ROM drive uses caddies — those annoyingly expensive little cages you need to drop the CD into first. These caddy things let the CD player get a firm grip on the disc, even when the player is turned sideways.

If your CD-ROM drive doesn't use a caddy, though, don't mount it on its side.

Don't use a camcorder on its side, either, even to get better pictures of the giraffes at the zoo. You'll know why the first time you watch the videos.

Chapter 3

Sound Cards (Those Sound Blaster Things)

● ●

In This Chapter

▶ Do I need a sound card?

▶ Which is the *best* sound card?

▶ Understanding 8- and 16-bit cards

▶ Recording with a sound card

▶ Those *upgradable* sound cards

▶ All that MIDI stuff

▶ Understanding words like "cardioid"

● ●

*W*ithout a sound card, your multimedia programs can't shake the walls and annoy the neighbors.

But which sound card do you need? How are the cards different? And what do all those weird words mean on the side of the sound card's box?

This chapter explains *all* that stuff, laid out buffet-style. There's a lot of food here, so don't try to eat everything on your first trip. For example, if you just want to know the difference between an *8*-bit and *16*-bit sound card, turn gently to that section, absorb the informational nugget, and put the book back down.

Or, if you find yourself scratching your head, trying to choose between "wavetable" and "FM synthesis," head for that specific section and start chewing.

To avoid that uncomfortable, stuffed feeling, dig into the informational trough slowly, one plate at a time. You have plenty of time to go back for seconds.

Do I Need a Sound Card?

When the sound dies on a TV set, nobody keeps watching it. Somebody gives it a few whacks on the side, fiddles with a few knobs on the VCR, and then calls in the repairman. Sound is a *must*, even for people who don't watch MTV.

Computers never made many sounds, so people never knew what they were missing. But once you've heard your computer make some *real* sound — creaky power-supply fans don't count — there's no going back. You *need* a sound card.

> ✔ Some games can play sounds out of a computer's speaker, but these unsophisticated sounds give the PC's sound capability a bad rap. A sound card is completely different. It's like comparing your car's modern stereo to the AM radios of the 1930s.

> ✔ With a sound card, your computer will sound as good as your home stereo. In fact, some cards sound *better* than some stereos.

> ✔ Your computer's CD-ROM drive can most likely play your Rolling Stones CDs as well, but only through earphones. To hear sound through speakers, you need a sound card. A sound card comes with a built-in amplifier, which makes the CD-ROM drive's sound loud enough to be played back on speakers and not just tiny earphones.

> ✔ Microsoft wrote a Windows PC Speaker Driver that lets you hear sound through your computer's built-in speaker — even without a sound card. Unfortunately, the driver doesn't work for MIDI (described later in this section) music, it freezes up your computer while it's playing sounds, and it sounds like a dying cicada. Other than that, it's great.

Which Sound Card Should I Buy?

There's no way to visit the grocery store and bring home the *best* groceries. Some folks like fresh string beans, while others choose canned. Still others prefer fresh, organic, or even plain wrap. If you're looking for what is considered the *best* of something, there's no simple answer.

Sound cards aren't just fresh or frozen either. Before you can choose the *best* one, you need to know a little bit about what different cards can do. This section points out the basic differences among the current crop of cards.

Don't want to wade through all this sound card stuff? Then buy a sound card that says "stereo," "16-bit," and "wavetable." These cards sound the best and work with the largest variety of software.

What sounds can a card make?

Almost all sound cards can fiddle with sounds in two different ways. First, the cards can act like a musical instrument and *create* sounds — just like the keyboards/synthesizers you've heard the longhairs play on MTV.

Second, the cards can act like a tape recorder and play or record sounds. The following sections explain the various features of sound cards and why multimedia programs expect you to know how the features differ.

Creating sounds (synthesizing) with a sound card

When a sound card creates a sound, musical engineers say that it's *synthesizing* sound. The card is acting as a musical instrument, just like a piano or Bill Clinton's saxophone.

For years, sound cards created musical sounds by using a simple technology called *FM synthesis*. Sounds created by FM synthesis — such as the music from the old Ad Lib and Sound Blaster cards — didn't sound like music created from a *real* piano, for example, and certainly didn't sound like Bill Clinton's saxophone. These sounds still sound computer-generated.

But FM synthesis is cheap and better than no sound at all. In fact, most cards still use FM synthesis. But that technology is slowly being replaced with newer, more lifelike technology called *wavetable*.

Wavetable technology kicks butt over FM synthesis, because sound cards no longer make music with computerized tones. Instead, the sound card looks up the instrument it needs in a *wavetable* (a built-in selection of actual recordings) and creates the instrument sound based on the sample.

To play an acoustic guitar, for example, the computer grabs the guitar sound from its wavetable and plays the note for as long as necessary. No broken strings!

- ✓ When listening to a game's musical sound track (or a MIDI file) on your sound card, you're most likely hearing the card's *synthesizer*.
- ✓ Good news: cards that use wavetable technology aren't hard to use. They automatically replace old FM synthesis sounds with new wavetable sounds. This means that wavetable is still compatible with all the old Ad Lib and Sound Blaster stuff; everything just sounds a lot better.
- ✓ With FM synthesi*s*, your sound card creates various beeps and tones to emulate different instruments. With wavetable technology, the sound card bases its sound on real recordings of instruments.

✔ The point? Wavetable sound cards create more natural sounds. Listen to the depth of sound in both cards before choosing one and let the width of your wallet make the final decision.

✔ The best wavetable cards have all their sounds stored in their own *Read Only Memory* (ROM) chips for easy access. Other cards come with a few sounds in ROM and pick up the rest on-the-fly from your hard disk or RAM. Although this can cause problems for people with limited disk space or memory, these cards often sound better.

✔ Some of the latest cards are *upgradable*. The cards initially use the cheap FM synthesis technology so you can start listening to everything right away. When you have the extra cash, you can buy a wavetable chip that plugs onto the card, adding the cool, new wavetable sounds.

✔ Ancient technology department: The folks who created the Sound Blaster once used technology even lamer than FM synthesis to create sounds. Called *Creative Music System* (CMS or CM/S), this technology could create *stereo* tones. Unfortunately, CMS sounded twice as bad as FM synthesis. (The old Game Blaster card used CMS.)

✔ If your sound card has upgrade options for CMS chips, ignore them. This option is old news.

✔ Some people refer to wavetable technology as *sampling* technology. Other people say the term *sampling* means a little bit more: it lets users record their own sounds and assign them to the card's wavetable.

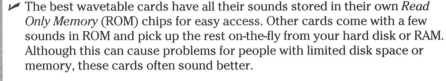

Boring explanation of old technology

FM synthesis comes from *frequency modulation* — the same bit of technology you've been hearing on your radio for years. But instead of manipulating frequencies to send over the airwaves, sound cards manipulate frequencies to send over your speakers.

By fooling with the frequencies — changing pitch and blending tones — the card could create sounds that sorta, kinda resembled musical in-

struments. Listeners weren't fooled, however. The instruments sounded like computer-generated tones.

A company called Ad Lib used FM synthesis when it released one of the first computer sound cards in 1987. The tones sounded like what you hear when pushing buttons on cheap key chains that say "Warp Speed." But hey, even warp speed tones sounded okay for some games.

Playing and recording sounds with a sound card

In addition to *simulating* the sound of a tuba, sound cards can record the sound of a real tuba. Sound cards can act as computerized tape recorders. Fun!

To record a sound, the card converts the incoming sound wave to numbers and then stores the numbers in a file. To play back a sound, the computer grabs the numbers and converts them back into the sound.

Computer numbers are called *digital*, and sound waves are considered *analog*. So, when you record your first belch with a sound card, you're making a *Digital to Analog Conversion*. Technicians call that a *DAC*. Anybody nearby calls it gross.

- ✔ When you're listening to a file ending in the letters VOC or WAV, you're listening to a *digitally recorded* sound.

- ✔ To record a sound, you need a microphone. Sound cards usually don't include a microphone, so Radio Shack has made a fortune by selling inexpensive ones. Make sure the microphone fits into your sound card's microphone jack, which is usually a small, ⅛-inch hole. (Most of the jacks are for mono microphones, too.)

- ✔ Most sound cards come with software for recording and playing sounds. Don't have any software? Then just use the Sound Recorder program software that comes with Windows 3.1. (Check out Chapter 17 for Windows tips.)

- ✔ An 8-bit sound card can't play or record sounds as accurately as the more expensive 16-bit sound cards. But 8-bit sound cards don't sound terrible. In fact, most of the sounds you'll hear on programs today are 8-bit sounds, and they won't sound any better when played through a 16-bit card.

- ✔ You can find more sound card tips in Chapter 18.

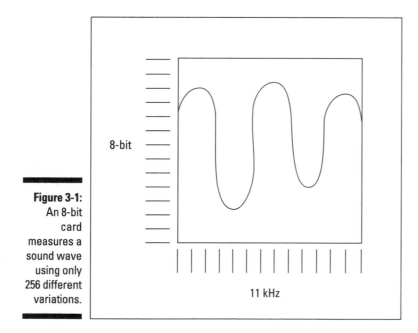

Figure 3-1:
An 8-bit card measures a sound wave using only 256 different variations.

8-bit

11 kHz

Grunt level stuff on sound physics

A computer converts everything into numbers, and sound is no exception. As a sound wave comes down the wire, the computer measures it and stores the measurements in a file.

To play the sound back, the computer looks at the measurements and re-creates the sound. Simple. But there are a few finer points.

First, as the sound wave rolls in (just like a wave from the ocean), the computer measures its size. But how precisely does the computer need to measure? Well, when recording the sound using an 8-bit card, the computer has a small ruler, and it divvies up the sound into 256 possible sizes.

When recording a sound with a more powerful, 16-bit card, the computer has a more precise ruler. It divvies up the sound into 65,536 different possible sizes. Naturally, the 16-bit card does a more accurate job of measuring, and the file will sound much better when played back.

Because sound waves roll in continuously, how often should the computer measure the wave's size? That's where kilohertz comes in. If the computer measures the wave's size 11,000 times per second, it's recording the sound at 11 kHz. If it's measuring the wave's size 44,000 times per second, it's recording at 44 kHz. Its recording rate is also called its *sampling rate*.

Figures 3-1 and 3-2 show a sound wave being measured two ways. Figure 3-1 (as seen on the preceding page) shows how an 8-bit card measures a sound wave's peaks and valleys using only 256 different variations. And when recording at 11 kHz, the card isn't taking measurements very often. Figure 3-2 shows how a 16-bit card measures a sound wave's peaks and valleys using 65,536 different variations. And when recording as 44 kHz, the card is taking measurements 44,000 times each second.

So the sound wave in Figure 3-1 is simply being measured more accurately than the one in Figure 3-2.

The drawback? Because the 16-bit card measures more accurately and more often, it comes up with a *lot* more numbers to describe a sound. And that's why the 8-bit card recording at 11 kHz can stuff its numbers into a 110K file, whereas the 16-bit card recording at 44 kHz comes up with a 880K file. (And if it's recording in stereo, the size doubles, bringing it to 1760K.)

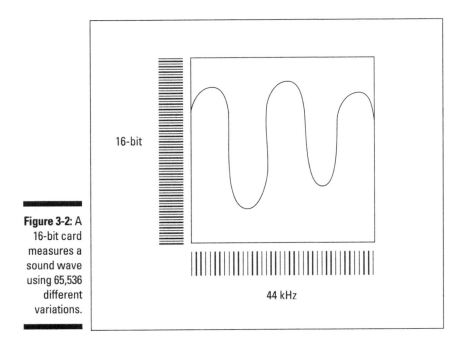

Figure 3-2: A 16-bit card measures a sound wave using 65,536 different variations.

16-bit

44 kHz

What other things can a sound card do?

Sound cards can do more than make noise. Not a whole lot more, but here's the rundown for comparison shopping.

Amplifier

Most sound cards come with a little built-in amplifier. The amplifier takes sound and makes it loud enough to hear.

For example, by connecting a cable from your external CD-ROM drive's Line Out jack to your sound card's Line In jack, you can amplify the sounds coming from your CD-ROM when you're listening to music CDs. No need for earphones, which always get tangled up with the mouse anyway.

- ✔ Amplification is measured in *watts*. You won't need more than four watts for most computing needs.

- ✔ Want something really *loud* for playing Yngwie Malmsteem guitar solos? Then connect a cable from your sound card's Line Out jack to your home stereo's Line In or Aux jack. Doing so makes your computer as loud as your home stereo. (You'll find complete instructions in Chapter 13.)

The game port

The cable from the joystick plugs in here. The game port is the same as the jack found on most cheap game cards. (Joysticks and game cards get more mention in Chapter 22.)

The MIDI port

The MIDI port is the same as the game port described in the preceding section. Plug a special MIDI box into the game port and you can connect MIDI instruments.

MIDI gets its own section later in this chapter, so I won't bore you with details twice. MIDI is simply a way for musicians to connect electronic instruments to their computers.

Musicians don't have to give up their joysticks, though. Most MIDI boxes come with a game port to replace the one they're plugged into.

- ✔ Because most sound card buyers aren't musicians, many manufacturers don't include a MIDI box with their sound cards. They make you buy the box separately for extra cash.

- ✔ Some of the less-expensive sound cards don't have a game port at all. That means that you can't add MIDI keyboards should you get the creative urge down the road of life.

The SCSI port

Described in Chapter 2, a SCSI ("scuh-zee") port is a place to plug in special SCSI gadgets. SCSI gadgets are more popular than you might think: most of the CD-ROM drives sold today must plug into a SCSI port.

Some sound cards come with a SCSI port onboard, where you can plug in a CD-ROM drive. Other sound cards don't come with a SCSI port, and you have to install a separate SCSI card for the CD-ROM drive.

And there's a third alternative. Some sound cards have a CD-ROM port, but it's not SCSI-compatible. These cards only work with special CD-ROM drives made by certain companies.

- ✔ If you want to plug a CD-ROM drive into your sound card, be careful when shopping — not all drives plug into all sound cards.

- ✔ If you have an *external* CD-ROM drive, don't worry about your sound card's SCSI port. You won't be using it, because external drives require their own SCSI controller card.

> ✓ If your sound card and internal CD-ROM drive don't get along, it's not the end of the world. Leave the sound card installed and plug in a second card to control the CD-ROM drive.
>
> ✓ CD-ROM drives get a lot more attention in Chapter 6.

Hey, Cut the Tech Talk: Which Sound Card Should I Buy?

Check out Table 3-1 for a no-nonsense explanation.

Table 3-1	When to Buy What Sound Card
Your Life Story	*Your Sound Card*
I'm broke.	Use Microsoft's Speaker Driver for Windows. It's free and it lets you hear sounds in Windows through your computer's speaker. (If you have a modem, check out *MORE Windows For Dummies* — it shows how to grab it from Microsoft's Bulletin Board System.)
	Cost: Free
I buy dental floss but reuse it.	Buy Disney's Sound Source. It's a cheap little box that plugs into your computer's parallel port and sounds like an old drive-in movie speaker, but it's one step up from nothing.
	Beware: although it works with Windows programs, many DOS programs don't support it.
	Cost: $30 – $50
I have a *few* extra bucks.	Buy a Sound Blaster-compatible sound card. These cards usually have dorky-sounding names, but they sound better than the Sound Source and are compatible with more multimedia programs.
	Cost: $50 – $100
I want something that sounds decent, but I won't be showing it to the world.	Get a 16-bit Sound Blaster-compatible card, like Sound Blaster 16 or Pro AudioSpectrum 16. These cards work with most multimedia software and sound fine.
	Cost: $120 – $150

(continued)

Table 3-1 *(continued)*

Your Life Story	Your Sound Card
I want something that will make all my friends jealous.	Buy a board with wavetable technology. Your music will sound like *music*, not computer-generated tones. If it's Sound Blaster-compatible, the board will work with nearly every multimedia program. Cost: $200 – $250 If you can't come up with the cash just yet, buy a cheaper board that's *wavetable-upgradable*. When the check comes in, you can pop in a wavetable chip for killer sound.
"Fetch me another snifter, James. And none of that cheap stuff."	The goat cheese of sound cards, Turtle Beach's Monterey Multisound packs performance as well as price. It's for professionals (or amateurs with a lot of money), and it sounds great on any Windows programs. But the card has a tragic flaw. Because it is not Sound Blaster-compatible, it's useless when you're trying to play games in DOS. The company's less-expensive models battle it out in the other categories and are Sound Blaster-compatible. Cost: $500 and up

✔ Sound cards rarely come with microphones. Add a mike to the shopping list if you're thinking about recording barf sounds to use with Windows.

✔ Few sound cards come with speakers, so add a pair to your budget. Or you can route the sound through your home stereo, if your family doesn't mind listening to Zork instead of NPR.

✔ Speakers contain magnets that are deadly to the information stored on floppy disks. Unless your speakers say "magnetically shielded," don't put disks next to them. (Compact discs are OK, though.) You can usually put speakers on top of your PC's case.

What's This MIDI Stuff?

Musicians needed a special way to fiddle around with their computers. They couldn't just record their music to the hard disk because the files were too big. A one-minute jam session could eat up ten megabytes of hard disk space. And if the drummer kept the solo going too long . . . well, you can see the problem.

So some smart musician invented *MIDI* — the Musical Instrument Digital Interface. MIDI is a complicated word for a simple concept.

Instead of using a computer to record their actual sounds, musicians use the computer to record their finger action: what note is being played, at what time, in what order, and for how long.

A MIDI file is the resulting list and particular order of musical notes. It's kind of like computerized sheet music, but your *computer* plays back the sound, not your fingers.

- ✔ When a sound card reads a MIDI file, the card plays back each note, at the right volume, and in the right order.

- ✔ Because MIDI is a computer-oriented language, it works best with electric instruments like a keyboard. The gal down the street can't record MIDI files with her bagpipe.

- ✔ Sound cards play MIDI files through the card's built-in synthesizer. Because sound cards use different types of synthesizers, the same MIDI file sounds different on different sound cards.

- ✔ For example, a musician with a $5,000 synthesizer could record an incredibly elaborate song and store it as a MIDI file. The guy down the street could play back the song on his $50 sound card. The song wouldn't sound as good — the instruments wouldn't sound as realistic — but the guy down the street could still hear the tune.

- ✔ Musicians don't *have* to use a sound card's built-in synthesizer for MIDI. They can stick with the better-sounding synthesizer in their electric piano.

- ✔ MIDI gets a lot more attention in Chapter 21.

- ✔ Why does the CANYON.MID file play in Windows, but no other songs do? Hit Chapter 21 for that one, too.

Why Does My New 16-Bit Sound Card Sound Just Like My Cheap 8-Bit Card?

Here's the problem: the 16-bit sound cards only sound better when playing *16-bit* sounds. Because most sounds are recorded at only *8-bit*, your new sound card won't sound any better than your old one.

But when you start hearing your first program with 16-bit sound, you'll know.

What's That VOC, WAV, MID, CMF, and MOD Nonsense?

Sound cards deal with sounds in several different ways. When mixed with several different manufacturers, the result is a jumble of filenames.

Table 3-2 shows which types of sounds are stored in which types of files.

Table 3-2	Files and the Sounds They Contain
Files Ending in These Letters	*Contain This Stuff*
CMF	Songs. A program packaged with some Sound Blaster and Game Blaster cards saves songs in this format.
MFF (MIDI File Format)	Songs. An MFF file is a MIDI file that doesn't necessarily adhere to Microsoft's Windows standards. (See Chapter 17.)
MID	Songs. Short for *MIDI*, it's the most universal way for musicians to store songs for playback on other computers.
MOD	Songs and sounds. A MOD file is a collection of digital sounds and the songs that use them, usually used by Commodore's Amiga computer. MOD files can still be played back on IBM PCs and Macintoshes if you can find a "MOD player" program.
ROL	Songs. A program packaged with the Ad Lib card saves songs in this pseudo-MIDI format.
VOC	Sounds. VOC is a format Sound Blaster uses to store recorded sounds. Used mostly in DOS; Windows doesn't like them.
WAV	Sounds. A WAV file contains digitally recorded sound that's used by Windows and a few DOS programs.

✔ Sometimes sound cards come with programs to translate different file formats, such as VOC to WAV. Other times, you're stuck with a file you can't play.

✔ A few shareware programs can translate formats from one to another. If you have a modem, join CompuServe and head for the MIDI Forum's libraries.

The Buzzwords of Sound

Sound cards come with zillions of terms. Table 3-3 explains a few of the wackier words you'll come across when dealing with sound cards, their boxes, or their scary installation menus.

Table 3-3	Sound Card Terms and Their Meanings
This Word	*Means This*
8-bit vs. 16-bit	A 16-bit card costs more and sounds better than an 8-bit card.
ADC (Analog-to-Digital Converter)	A sound card that's able to record sound.
ADPCM (Adaptive Delta Pulse Code Modulation)	A way to pack more sound into a smaller file (although it won't sound quite as good). Chances are, you'll never have to deal with it.
Analog	Something constantly changing, like a sound wave or political opinion.
Automatic gain control	A sound card that automatically adjusts the volume to record or play at a comfortable level.
Cardioid microphones	Microphones that pick up sound mostly from in front of them. (See Omnidirectional microphones.)
CD Digital Audio (CD-DA)	A CD-ROM is in this mode when it's playing a musical CD. (Also called *Red Book*, for some corporate reason.)
CD-quality sound	A phrase describing sound recorded at 16 bits, 44 MHz. (That's the rate used to record your musical CDs.)
Condenser microphone	These battery-powered guys work best when recording sensitive sounds like pianos and whispers.
DAC (Digital-to-Analog Converter)	A sound card that can play a recorded sound from a file.
Daughterboard	A small card that pops onto a sound card to give it new abilities. For example, plugging a Wave Blaster daughterboard onto a Sound Blaster 16 adds wavetable sound.
Digital	Anything that a computer has converted to numbers.
Distortion	Although electric guitarists spend hundreds of dollars trying to create it, most sound card owners consider it unwanted noise.
DMA (Direct Memory Address)	A way for sound cards to talk to computers. If two cards try to talk on the same DMA, they'll argue, leading to hissing sounds or a frozen computer, especially when you're trying to access a disk. (See Chapter 16.)

(continued)

Table 3-3 *(continued)*

This Word	*Means This*
Drivers	Software that lets the computer talk to a specific part, like a sound card. Different parts need different drivers. (Your computer loads the drivers listed in a special file called CONFIG.SYS.)
DSP (Digital Signal Processor)	A chip on your sound card that takes some of the workload off your computer, especially when fiddling with sound — adding echoes, reverb, and other effects.
Dynamic microphones	The best mikes for recording loud, powerful stuff, such as heavy metal bands or arguments on Larry King's show.
FIFO (First In, First Out)	Information that lines up in order, with the first potato down the chute being the first to emerge from the bottom.
FM (Frequency Modulation)	An older technology to mimic musical instruments from computer synthesized tones.
Frequency	Without getting complicated, an annoying mosquito whines at a *high* frequency; a fog horn rumbles at a *low* frequency.
Frequency response	Most cards don't capture the very lowest or highest frequencies; they cut a little off the ends. A *wide* frequency response, by contrast, results in a more lifelike recording.
GM (General MIDI)	MIDI files with all the instrument sounds lined up in a designated order; nobody's been futzing around, creating "new" instrument sounds. (See MIDI, MT-32.)
IRQ (Interrupt Request)	A computerized "tap on the shoulder" used by sound cards when they need the CPU's attention. Your computer has only a few of these "shoulders," and cards trying to use the same IRQ won't work right. (See Chapter 16.)
MIDI (Musical Instrument Digital Interface)	A way to store music as a series of computerized instructions; the resulting file can be played back on a wide variety of computers and electronic instruments.
MPU-401 interface	A MIDI standard created by Roland Corporation that is used by most professional musicians with their MIDI instruments.
MT-32	A MIDI standard with instruments arranged in a slightly different order than General MIDI. (See GM.)
Multi-timbral	A sound-creation technology with better-sounding instruments than FM synthesis, but it's not as good as wavetable.
Multi-voice	Ability to mimic more than one instrument; found in most cards.
Omnidirectional microphones	Microphones that pick up sound from all around them, not just in front. (See Cardioid, Dynamic microphones.)

This Word	Means This
PCM sampling (Pulse Code Modulation)	The method of recording sound described in the "Grunt level" section earlier in this chapter.
Qsound	A new technology for making 3-D sounds so missiles sound like they're coming from *any* direction. (Packaged with the Sound Blaster 16.)
RCA audio cable	Commonly found on most home stereos, this cable ends with a little round metal "hat" that slides onto a little round metal "head."
Sampling rates	The amount of attention the sound card pays to a sound when recording. Higher sampling rates make for better quality, but larger files. (It's measured in kHz — *kilohertz*.)
SCSI port (Small Computer System Interface)	A special connector required by most CD-ROM drives; found on a special SCSI *card*, as well as some sound cards.
Sound Blaster compatible	This means the card works with any software written for the Sound Blaster card. (That's about 90 percent of the programs on the market.)
Synthesized	Sounds created by computer circuitry.
Timing/ Synchronization	Matching two things, like the sound of a voice to on-screen lip movements.
Voice	Another word for a musical instrument sound. A 20-voice synthesizer won't necessarily produce 20 instruments, however; many cards mix two or more voices when creating more-complex instrument sounds.
Voice annotation	Adding snippets of sound to documents. Click on the Sound icon in the general manager's memo, for example, and hear him apologize personally for the budget cuts.
Voice command	Controlling the computer by voice, not keyboard. For example, say "bold" and the computer will **boldface** a word. Fun! Unfortunately, you need to talk to your computer for several hours before the voice command software can recognize your voice. (Keep the door locked so bystanders won't watch in horror.)
Yamaha OPL2 synthesizer	Found in older sound cards, it's a mono chip with 11 voices. Also called YM3812. (See FM synthesis.)
Yamaha OPL3 synthesizer	Found in most mid-range sound cards, it's a stereo chip with 20 voices. Also called YMF262. (See FM synthesis.)
Yamaha OPL4 synthesizer	A stereo chip with wavetable sound that's now appearing on the market. It works with all software written for the older OPL chips, too.

Chapter 4
Your Monitor and Video Cards

• •

In This Chapter

▶ How to buy the right video card

▶ Understanding the differences among monitors

▶ Matching a video card with a monitor

▶ Understanding video modes and resolutions

▶ What's an *accelerated* video card?

▶ Do I need a video card with a video capture card?

▶ How can I use my TV as a monitor?

▶ Why are the movies so *small*?

• •

*A*t the movie theater, when the dinosaur rumbles across the big screen, everybody marvels at the lifelike technology. But who's responsible for getting the dinosaur on the big screen? The special effects guy? The camera man? The director? Well, it's something much more ho-hum — the movie projector.

Without a state-of-of the art movie projector — and a clean, splotch-free screen — the movie would stay in the can.

This chapter looks at your computer's version of a movie projector and screen: its video card and monitor. If you're in the market for a video card or a monitor, check out this chapter before pulling out the credit card.

And keep this chapter in mind for ammunition when a rude new multimedia program complains that you're running in the "wrong video mode."

What's a Video Card?

A *video card* slides into a slot inside your computer. One edge of the card pokes out at the computer's rear, leaving a place to plug in your monitor's cord.

When a program wants revolving spheres to appear on the screen, it sends a polite request to your video card. The card pieces together the right picture and sends it through the monitor's cord to the screen. Shazzam: the spheres appear and begin to spin.

- Choosing a video card used to be simple: the decision was either black-and- white or color. Today though, shoppers must choose among different *resolutions*, *colors*, *acceleration*, and a handful of other equally irritating choices.

- Plus, a card needs to be matched with the right monitor, or the card and monitor won't work together. Or, the two might work but won't take advantage of all of each other's features. An upcoming section shows how to match cards and monitors so that you don't end up eating soup with a fork.

A *video card* sends pictures to your monitor. A *video capture card,* described in Chapter 5, grabs incoming pictures from a camcorder or VCR. Even if you're going to put a video capture card inside your computer, you'll need a regular video card, too.

When plugging your monitor's plug into the video card, the *wide* edge of its oblong plug faces toward your computer's big round fan hole.

Buying the Right Monitor

Because many multimedia programs look like fun, computerized TV shows, the first impulse is to buy a huge, glamorous monitor — something Eddie Murphy would choose for his home-theater system.

But differences in the price tags between TVs and monitors can be a shocker, as seen in Table 4-1.

Table 4-1 Monitoring Prices of Monitors and Televisions	
Monitor Prices	*Television Prices*
A 15-inch monitor costs about $500	A 15-inch television costs about $300
A 17-inch monitor costs about $1,000	A 17-inch television costs about $350
A 21-inch monitor costs about $2,000	A 21-inch television costs about $400

Notice a disturbing trend? Monitors are a *lot* more expensive. They're more complicated, too, with many more numbers for you to decipher when you're shopping.

Here are a few tips when deciding which monitor to put in the shopping cart:

◆ Choose a *color* monitor, not monochrome (the computer term for black and white). Shades of gray will never make a multimedia sunset look real, no matter how loudly the seagulls squawk in the background.

◆ Look for a monitor measurement called *dot pitch.* This measures the sharpness of the picture.

◆ Buy a monitor with a dot pitch of .28 or smaller, or you'll find yourself squinting when you're trying to read text on the screen.

◆ Unfortunately, monitor prices skyrocket when the size gets larger than 15 inches. But for best results, pick up a 17-inch monitor. (Eddie Murphy would spring for the 21-incher.)

◆ Run your favorite multimedia program on a monitor to see what it looks like; that's the best way to choose between monitors.

Salespeople measure a monitor's size as if it were a TV — they measure the inches diagonally between the screen's top and bottom corners. They measure the monitor *before* its plastic case goes on, however. That's why a 15-inch monitor seems more like a 14-inch monitor when you measure it yourself.

✔ The new flat screen monitors look better than the old ones with curved edges. The picture looks more like a *picture* — not a TV set.

✔ The *video card*, not the monitor, determines how many colors you can see on the screen. Just about any color monitor made in the last two years can display a rainbow — but only if the video card can crank out enough colors to keep up.

✔ The most practical monitors are *multisync* or *multiscan,* meaning they're more versatile when running different programs.

✔ Want to use your TV set as a monitor? It's a lot more difficult — and expensive — than you might think. Look to Chapter 8 for information.

Defrosting Shrimp in the "Video Mode" Zone

It's Saturday afternoon. The multimedia cooking program runs on the computer next to the microwave oven. Your shrimp is marinating nearby on the kitchen counter. Your hands are covered with shrimp-peel gunk.

You push the software's "play" button with the handle of the spatula to watch the "How to Devein a Shrimp" video.

And the program says you need to switch to a different *video mode*. Huh? Better wash your hands before tackling this one. A video mode is a combination of two things: *resolution* and *colors*, each described in the following sections.

Resolution

Just like tiles covering the bathroom wall, tiny dots called *pixels* form a big grid across your monitor's screen.

When the video card tells the monitor to light up certain pixels — bingo — a picture appears on the screen.

The more pixels the card and monitor can light up, the more detail you're able to see in the picture.

- ✔ The computer industry has solemnly decreed that pixels can line up in four possible combinations: 640 rows by 480 columns, 800x600, 1024x768, and 1280x1024.

- ✔ The *bigger* the number of rows and columns, the *higher* the resolution, and the *sharper* your multimedia programs will look.

- ✔ Most cards and monitors can work in several different resolutions. (An upcoming section tells how to switch to different resolutions.)

Boring resolution anti-matter

If pictures look better with more pixels, why not buy the cards and monitors with the most pixels possible? Because they cost so much. Equipment with higher resolutions, like 1024x768, can cost twice as much as stuff that only displays lower resolutions, like 640x480.

So you'll have to pick and choose when shopping, especially because monitors and cards can each display several *different* resolutions. For example, a card and monitor that can display pictures at 1024x768 resolution can still display pictures at 800x600 and 640x480.

Figure 4-1 shows Windows running in 1024x768 resolution. The Eiffel Tower in the bottom-right corner is taking up 640x480 resolution; the Tower in the middle is taking up 800x600 resolution.

It boils down to this: the higher the resolution in Windows, the more windows you can see at the same time.

Figure 4-1:
A 1024x768 monitor can pack three Eiffel Towers onto the screen, each in a different resolution.

Photo courtesy of *Wizardware Multimedia Ltd.*

Colors

A high-resolution monitor and video card can display shrimp veins in minute detail. But there's one more element to the mix: color.

The more colors there are on the screen, the more realistic the shrimp veins look. So computer engineers decided that computers can work with specific amounts of colors. For example, you can run Windows in 16; 256; 65,536; or 16.7 million colors.

- So why not always use the *most* colors possible? Because doing so slows things down. The more colors the video card has to fling around, the more time it takes to fling them.

- By mixing a specific amount color with a specific resolution, the computer industry came up with a new term: *video mode*.

- For example, a 1024x768 resolution with 65,536 colors is one video mode; 640x480 resolution with 16 colors is another video mode. In fact, most cards and monitors can display stuff in at least *four* different video modes.

- So what video mode should you use? Check out the very next section.

Choosing a Video Mode

Confused about what video mode you need? The answer is simple.

To run most multimedia programs today, make sure your video card can display at least 256 colors when running at a resolution of at least 640x480.

✔ Try running your multimedia program in several different video modes. Then choose the mode that makes the program run the smoothest. Sometimes you'll need to make a trade-off, such as sacrificing colors for speed.

✔ Avoid any video mode that's "interlaced" — it has an awful flicker. Because a monitor's highest resolution is usually interlaced, plan on running programs using the monitor's *second* highest resolution.

✔ Don't know how to switch video modes in Windows? Head for Chapter 17.

Because high-resolution equipment packs so much information onto the screen, a large, 17-inch monitor makes everything easier to see.

Speeding Things Up with an Accelerator Card or Local Bus

For years, people bought new video cards simply to add more color to their programs. After you increased the number of colors from 16 to 256, for example, that little green parrot looked more and more like it flew right out of *National Geographic*.

But as the video quality improved, the computer slowed down. Tossing hundreds of thousands of colored dots onto the screen takes a *lot* of video slingshots.

So a clever nerd invented a *graphics accelerator chip* to stick on *accelerated video cards*. The computer no longer had to grunt over all that graphics work — it simply handed the chore to the video card. The chip handled the video, freeing up the computer for more dignified stuff, like moving paragraphs around.

Another technology, *local bus*, can also speed up your video. Basically, the local bus is a special slot on a computer's motherboard that lets you plug in special *local bus cards*, which are described in Chapter 2.

TECHNICAL STUFF

Don't bother with outdated EGA/VGA/CGA stuff

As corporate engineers cranked out new monitors and cards to display more colors at better resolutions, corporate marketing departments kept cranking out new names to put on the packages: CGA, EGA, VGA, and a few others.

Each abbreviation described cards or monitors that could display a certain amount of video modes.

The following table shows the names of the modes and their resolutions and colors:

The Mode	*The Resolution and Colors*
Hercules, CGA (Color Graphics Adapter), and EGA (Enhanced Graphics Adapter)	None of these three cards or monitors works with today's multimedia programs. EGA, the best of the pack, can only display 16 colors. Leave 'em at the garage sale next to the rattan coffee table.
Video Graphics Array (VGA)	This card can work in two modes: 320x200 with 256 colors and 640x480 with 16 colors. Neither mode is good enough for most multimedia programs.
SuperVGA (sometimes called SVGA or VGA+)	SuperVGA is sort of a catch-all phrase for anything more powerful than VGA. Basically, this card covers the following modes: 640x480 with 256 colors, 800x600 with 16 colors or more, and most video modes with even higher resolutions.

Unfortunately, marketing departments stopped cranking out convenient "EGA/VGA" abbreviations after VGA, so the video mode standards are a little hazy.

Today, most people ignore these abbreviations and shop by specific resolutions. For example, they'll look for a card that can display 256 colors at 1024x768 or some other mode. The term SuperVGA doesn't mean as much as the other EGA/VGA terms did during their heyday.

Plug a local bus video card into its local bus slot, and your graphics speed up significantly. There's only one catch, though: if your computer doesn't have a local bus slot, you can't use a local bus video card. But you can stick with an accelerated video card, and they're not bad at all.

- A local bus video card is sometimes called a VESA Local Bus card. (It's also called a VLB card by computer veterans who are truly over the edge.)

- Most motherboards built before 1992 don't have a local bus slot, and there's no way to add one (unless you replace the entire motherboard, that is).

- Yes, there are now *accelerated local bus video cards*. Actually, acceleration chips don't add very much extra oomph to a local bus video card, but the words "accelerated local bus video card" look impressive on the box.

TIP

If you're running Windows or any Windows multimedia programs, upgrade to an accelerated video card or, if your computer is built for it, a local bus video card. You'll notice a speed increase immediately.

TECHNICAL STUFF

Boring details about video card memory

For years, computers have been memory hogs, especially when running Windows. But now, video cards are screaming for memory, too. And video cards want their *own* memory—they won't share what's already there. The term *video memory* refers to memory chips that live on the video card itself, not on your computer's motherboard.

To put out 256 colors, a video card needs at least 512K of memory, and the requirements go up from there. A card needs 1MB of memory to display 1024x768 resolution. Want to see picture with 16.7 million colors in 800x600 resolution? The card will need two megabytes of video memory.

The side of a card's box lists the number of video modes the card can crank out, so you don't have to remember the memory specifications. Just remember that more memory is always better (and more expensive, but that's probably expected by now — sigh).

Finally, some video cards let you plug in additional memory chips to add more colors or higher resolutions. Unfortunately, you'll probably have to buy these chips direct from the folks who made the card — if they're even still selling the chips. So buy the card you want *now*. Don't buy a low-resolution card, thinking you can always add memory later.

The Movies on CDs Look Jerky When Played Back!

Your CD-ROM drive is probably the culprit. It simply can't kick out information fast enough for a smooth movie. You'll want a faster CD-ROM drive, covered in Chapter 6.

The Movies Are All Postage-Stamp-Sized!

Yeah, they look kind of dumb at first. *All* movies are going to be small on your computer. With a few exceptions, computer-video technology hasn't caught up to your basic television set. (These few exceptions are covered in Chapter 6.)

My Computer Doesn't Have A Video Card!

Some computers released in the early 90s pulled a fast one with their video cards. To speed things up, the manufacturers built the video card circuitry directly onto the computer's motherboard. These computers simply don't have a video card.

If there's no video card to pull out and replace, you're left with two upgrade options:

- ✔ Dig out your computer's manual and see how to turn off the internal video card circuitry. Some computers make you move a little *jumper*, described in Chapter 16.

- ✔ Plug in a new, faster video card and see if it works. Some computers are polite enough to turn off their built-in video when they sense that you've stuck a new video card inside.

Some computers with built-in video call themselves *local bus video*. However, this is an early version of the technology; these computers don't have a local bus slot that can hold a local bus card.

What Do All Those Funny Video Words Mean?

Video cards and monitors are full of technical buzzwords. But you don't need to know what they mean. Just trust your eyes to decide what looks best.

Believe it or not, the best way to buy a monitor and card is to head for the computer store and play Windows Solitaire on a bunch of different monitors. Ask to see a movie or two, as well, and then check out a word processing program to make sure the letters are easy to read.

When you decide which monitor looks best, buy it, along with the video card that powers it.

Some sales people will gab about "dot pitch" this and "vertical sync" that. But don't buy a monitor and card unless you've seen it in action. All the technical specifications in the world don't mean anything compared to your own eyeballs.

If you're still curious about what those video buzzwords mean, check out Table 4-2.

Table 4-2	Awful Monitor Terms	
This Word	*Describes This*	*And Means This*
24-bit	Video card	A 24-bit card can display 16.7 million colors, which is about the number of colors that the human eye can differentiate on a screen.
8-bit	Video card	An 8-bit card can display 256 colors. (A 256-color picture still looks OK, if you squint a little.)
8514/A	Video card	A special variety of card that displays 1024x768 graphics.
Accelerated video	Video card	A card with a special chip that helps your computer put pictures on the screen more quickly.
Bandwidth	Monitor, card	The speed at which your card can send information to your monitor. The faster the speed, the better. Bandwidth is measured in *hertz*, and 70 Hz is considered good.
Color	Card	The number of colors a card can display on the screen. (Today's monitors can display any amount of colors.)
Compression	Files	A way of making video files take up less space.

This Word	*Describes This*	*And Means This*
Dither	Software	A way to smooth out differences between colors in a computer picture.
Dot pitch	Monitor	The distance between the little pixel dots on the monitor. The smaller the dot pitch, the clearer the picture.
Driver	Card	A piece of software that helps computers talk with new parts like sound cards or fax modems.
Full-screen video	Card	A way to run movies full-screen, like a TV. Cards with special MPEG technology can display full-screen video. (See Chapter 5.)
Interlaced, noninterlaced	Monitor	Technical stuff that's much too boring to bother with. Just remember that a *non*interlaced display has less flicker and looks better.
JPEG	File	Files containing pictures in a highly compressed format.
Mode	Card, monitor	A combination of resolution and color. For example, a combination of 640x480 resolution with 256 colors. There's no right or wrong mode. It all depends on personal preference and wallet width.
MPEG	File, card	A way to compress movies so that they will fit on discs for quick and easy playback. An *MPEG chip* can play back movies full-screen. (See *Full-screen video.*)
Multiscan, multifrequency, or multisync	Monitor	Versatile monitors that can work in a wide variety of video modes.
Pixel	Monitor	A tiny little dot on your monitor. (Put your nose against the glass and take a peek.)
Resolution	Monitor, card	The number of columns and rows of pixels your monitor and card can display.
SVGA	Monitor, card	A bantered-about term that generally means any video mode greater than 640x480 resolution with 256 colors or more.
True color	Video card	Able to display 16.7 million colors, which is about as many colors as the eye can differentiate on a monitor. (See 24-bit.)

(continued)

Table 4-2 *(continued)*

This Word	Describes This	And Means This
VGA	Monitor, card	A resolution of 640x480 with 16 colors. (Also covers resolutions of 320x240 with 256 colors.)
Video memory	Card	Memory chips that let a video card process pictures. The more memory, the higher the resolution the card can display. (See VRAM.)
Video conferencing	Expensive stuff	A way to talk to people and see them on a computer simultaneously. Requires special cameras, monitor, software, money, and patience with new technology.
VRAM	Card	Especially speedy (and expensive) memory on fast video cards

Chapter 5

Grabbing Movies with a Video Capture Card

• •

In This Chapter

▶ What is a video capture card?

▶ What equipment do I need?

▶ Why are all the movies so tiny?

▶ How do video capture cards differ?

▶ What is a codec?

▶ What are the differences between composite and S-video?

▶ Do I need an MPEG card?

• •

*S*tep right up for the latest in whizbang technology. Yes, you not only can process words on your PC, but now you can process *movies*. Get your friends together, hook up your camcorder or VCR to a video capture card on your PC, and start recording your own MTV videos. Well, at least that's how these video capture cards are *supposed* to work. This chapter explains why they *don't* work that way — and why they're still a lot of fun, anyway.

What Is a Video Capture Card?

Just as a sound card lets you record sounds on your PC, a video capture card (or *video grabber*) lets you record your own pictures — anything from a still shot of desert sheep to a thrill-packed white-water video of your friend who fell in the river last vacation.

Video capture cards come in two basic models. The first is a *still image grabber*, often called a *frame grabber*. Regardless of the name, the card works like film in a camera. You hook up a camcorder to the card and point the camera at the birthday cake. When you see the birthday cake on your monitor — and the candles look just right — push a button on-screen with your mouse. Snap. You've saved the picture to your hard drive.

The more-expensive cards can grab entire movies. Hook up a TV, camcorder, or VCR to the card and preview your video on the computer screen. Everything set up right? Push a button, and the card starts recording the incoming video to your hard drive.

The problem with all this new technology? It's all too new to work very well. Computers translate everything into numbers, and movies take up a *lot* of numbers, many more than your computer can handle. So your computer cheats — it makes the movies tiny and cuts out a lot of detail.

The moral? When it comes to watching reruns of David Letterman, your $2,500 computer can't beat your plain old $250 VCR.

- ✔ Video capture cards cost much more than sound cards. They start at about $350. And the good cards — the ones that perform like you want the *cheap* ones to perform — cost several thousand dollars.

- ✔ Video capture cards don't replace your plain ol' video card. You still need a video card, or you won't be able to see and control the software that grabs the incoming movies.

- ✔ Video capture cards can't capture sound, either. If you want to capture your killer sound track along with your movies, your computer needs a sound card.

- ✔ Many video capture cards come with a copy of Microsoft's Video for Windows to control the capturing and editing of videos. (Video for Windows is covered in Chapter 20.)

Just like sound cards, video capture cards are called *analog-to-digital converters* by the people who write computer manuals.

What Equipment Do I Need to Capture Videos?

If you want to start editing videos, the video capture card probably won't be the most expensive part of the package — unfortunately. A video capture card doesn't work on just *any* old PC. No, it prefers the top-of-the-line models with all the equipment described in the following list.

- ✔ You need a VCR, camcorder, or TV with video output jacks to hook up to the card.

- ✔ Add a *fast* hard drive to the shopping list. Slow drives can't store all the video as quickly as it comes in. If you're recording anything longer than a dozen seconds, you need 30 to 60 megabytes of extra hard drive space. (That's extra space *after* you've installed Windows and all the card's software.)

✔ Are you using DoubleSpace or Stacker? Get rid of it. These compression programs usually slow down the hard drive too much.

✔ A muscular computer needs to oversee the whole process. Many capture cards recommend a *fast* 486; a 386 can't capture video as well.

✔ Most cards require at least 4MB of RAM, but you'll be a lot less frustrated with 8MB or more.

✔ Finally, your video card should display 256 colors — at the least.

But, hey, it was time you upgraded, anyway.

Why Does My $500 Card Make Postage Stamp-Sized Videos?

Welcome to video editing on an IBM-compatible computer! You have entered the technology at its infancy. That's why everything is so small.

Movies are simply snapshots that are strung together in a long line. When the snapshots — called *frames* — are flashed on-screen rapidly, one after each other, they create the effect of a movie.

Now, here's the holdup. On your TV, each second of video is made up of *30* frames that are flashed one after the other. Most computers take a second to put *one* photo on-screen, much less 30. So the computers shrink the video until it's the size of a postage stamp. The smaller the pictures, the easier the computer can flash them on-screen. The smoothest videos are the smallest videos. Figure 5-1 shows the sizes most video cards use for capturing images. The images take up varying room on a 640x480 resolution screen, the biggest using a quarter of a VGA screen.

Now, here's the weird part. If you divide the 640x480 resolution in half, you get 320x240; Figure 5-1 shows a 320x240 window sitting in a 640x480 screen. Because you've divided the resolution in half, some card manufacturers claim that 320x240 resolution is *half-screen*. But as shown in Figure 5-1, the video only fills a *quarter* of the screen!

Or if you divide 640x480 by four, you get 160x120 resolution. You've divided it by four, so some manufacturers call it *quarter-screen* video. But as shown in Figure 5-1, the video only fills *one-sixteenth* of the screen.

Some card makers use this mathematical curiosity to fool you, so look at the card's *numbers* — not the words — when choosing among different capture cards. Otherwise, your postage stamps may look even smaller.

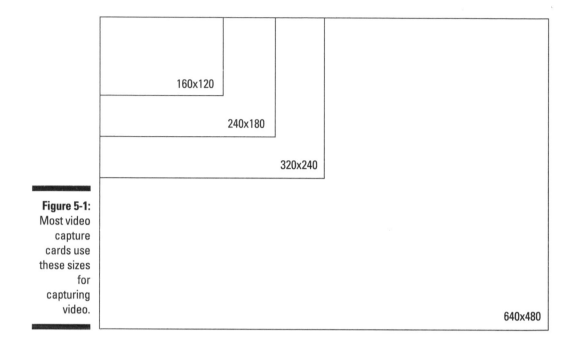

Figure 5-1:
Most video
capture
cards use
these sizes
for
capturing
video.

↙ When grabbing videos at 320x240 resolution, most cards are straining. The video looks jerky when played back, usually because the card can't keep up with the incoming video and skips parts of it.

↙ Do you want to make high-quality videos that can fill your entire screen? Then look to spend a lot more than $1,000 for your capture card. Check with specialty video-editing houses and be prepared to spend four or five thousand dollars. (*Videomaker* magazine carries ads for a wide variety of equipment; to subscribe, call 619-745-2809.)

↙ Some special cards can play full-screen video; they just can't *capture* video at that rate. For example, Sigma Design's ReelMagic card can play back full-screen videos. Of course, there is a catch: The videos must use a certain MPEG formula, which is described in the wild and wacky codec section found later in this chapter.

Bunches of big numbers and small movies

Whenever video-capture buffs talk about video capture, they consider a resolution of 640x480 pixels to be full-screen. To match the colors on your television set, that full-screen must also display about 16 million colors!

A 16-million color picture that fits on a 640x480 screen takes up about one megabyte. Because movies need to display 30 pictures per second, your computer needs to throw around 30 *megabytes* of data every second.

That is a lot more oomph than most of today's computers can handle. Besides, a ten-second snippet of video would completely fill a 300 megabyte hard disk — a scary thought to anybody but hard-drive salespeople.

So, until computer horsepower goes up, the size of movies will stay down.

Uh, What Is This "Codec" Stuff?

Computers must transform everything into a string of numbers before they can stick it in their hats, and movies are no exception. Movies, with all their colors and moving pictures, turn into obscenely huge amounts of numbers when stuffed into a file. A ten-second video of the cat sniffing a lobster can easily fill a 300MB hard drive.

So when storing a movie, computers compress all those numbers into the smallest file possible — often making the file a hundred times smaller than before. How? By various shenanigans much too complicated to discuss here without a sunny patio and an idle afternoon.

But here is the codec part, anyway. Computers *compress* the video while they pack its numbers into a file. Then they *decompress* the movie when they play it back. So somebody took the simple words *compress* and *decompress* and created an ungainly computer word: *codec* (*co*mpress and *dec*ompress — get it?).

Because different companies all think they've come up with the best way to compress videos, they all have their own codecs. (It's pronounced CODE-eck, by the way.) Video for Windows comes packaged with several codecs, including Microsoft's own brand. Some codec's are handled by software, others rely on special hardware built into video capture cards, and still others use both.

Which codec is best? Well, that's like asking what color is best for socks — there is no correct color. Some codecs can make tiny video files, but the video doesn't look so hot. Others make great movies, but the files are still huge. Most fall somewhere in between. You usually won't have much of a choice between codecs, anyway. Most capture cards favor a certain codec, which is packaged with the software that comes with your card.

When choosing between codecs, you need to decide how you want your video to be played back. On a fast computer? A slow computer? A wide variety of computer speeds? From a slow CD-ROM drive? A fast CD-ROM drive? A hard drive? What video quality do you need? How many colors? How much motion is in your particular video? And finally, how much disk space can your video consume? Answer these questions and then experiment with different codecs until you find one that works best for that particular video.

Then repeat the process for your next video.

- ✔ Some people insist that *codec* stands for en*co*der and *dec*oder. But it's certainly not something you want to be seen arguing about.

- ✔ Some codecs can compress and decompress video without losing any picture quality at all. These have earned the nickname *lossless codecs* — which is also a great name for a band.

- ✔ However, most codecs chop out a little detail as they compress pictures. These are called *lossy codecs* — also a great name for a band.

- ✔ Some lossy codecs trim out irrelevant detail so carefully that you can't tell the compressed version from the original movie. In fact, some lossy codec experts say you can cut more than 90 percent of the detail out of a file without anybody noticing. (These folks probably don't dust their shelves, either.)

Complicated codec crud

It's pretty easy to cut extraneous information out of a video file. For example, suppose that the video shows a golf ball sailing through a cloudless sky. When writing the video information to a file, the computer doesn't *really* need to list detailed color information for the top half of the movie; it can just list the color as sky blue. Then when playing back the video, the computer simply puts the color blue in the top half. This shortcut can cut the file's size in half.

Also, most videos don't change much from frame to frame. For example, when the golf ball flies through the air, the background stays pretty much the same. So the computer stores one complete frame with the exact colors of both the golf ball and the sky. For the next few frames, the computer merely notices the golf ball's new location and then stores the *differences* between the frames — not the complete information for each frame — when saving the information to a file.

This idea of storing the differences between frames, instead of the information in the frames themselves, is called *interframe coding*. And it's just one of the ways codecs differ.

Table 5-1 shows some of the codecs you may come across when playing with video capture cards and their software. Feel free to experiment with different codecs — there is no surefire winner.

Table 5-1	Frequently Used Codecs
This Codec	*Does This*
Microsoft Video 1	The default codec, this does a good job for most needs. Because it comes free with every version of Microsoft's Video for Windows, it's quite popular.
Microsoft RLE	Use this for low-detail video to play back on low-end computers (386SX CPUs or 16-color video cards). It works best for talking heads — videos with very little movement.
Intel Indeo	This always captures 16-million colors and then adapts its playback to the computer it's being played back on. Cards with special built-in Intel video-capture chips (i750) can speed up the capture and playback; software-only processing does a slower job.
MPEG	The Motion Picture Experts Group is one of the best compression methods and also one of the most complicated. That's why it takes expensive cards to record with it or play it back.
Motion JPEG	The Motion Joint Photographic Experts Group was first developed for still shots. It's now used for video, as well.
Cinepak	This started on the Macintosh but now works with Video for Windows, as well. It's slow at compressing, but the results look great.
Spigot	These codecs work with Creative Labs' video capture cards.
Ultimotion	IBM's codec for OS/2 multimedia ("Ultimedia") video. Looks very nice, but you need OS/2.

Why Can Other Cards Capture Video Faster Than My Card?

Blame the codec, Captain. Some cards and codecs are designed to capture video faster than others. It all boils down to this point: some video capture cards grab all the incoming video and stash it in a huge file on your hard drive.

When you're done sending video to the card, the card finally turns to the chore it has been putting off: compressing all that video information in that huge file. When the card is done, the video shrinks down to normal size.

This approach causes two problems. First, your finished video may need only 5MB of hard disk space, but you may need *50MB* of hard drive space to capture it all as it comes in. Second, you'll be twiddling your thumbs for 10 or 15 minutes — or even several hours, depending on the video's length — while waiting for the card to compress all that stored footage. When the card is done, you can finally see how your video turned out.

Other cards can compress video as quickly as the pictures come down the wire. For example, Intel's Smart Video Recorder board comes with a super-fast chip that grabs and compresses the video on the fly — no thumb-twiddling and no need to keep such a big chunk of your hard drive free. (That chip is called an i750®, by the way, and Intel is selling it to a few other companies for their cards, too.)

Why Does the Picture Seem Jerky and Then Smooth Out?

The first time you play a movie in Windows, the video may stop and start a little, as if the movie projector had some popcorn in the gears. But after you play back the video a second time, it flows smoothly. This happens because Windows has to grab the movie from your hard drive the first time, and your hard drive isn't very quick about handing over information. After the first showing, Windows keeps a copy of the movie — or parts of it, at least — in memory so that the second time you play it, Windows can spit it out a lot faster.

What Is This PAL, SECAM, and NTSC Stuff?

Most folks know that people in different countries speak different languages. But only video veterans know that countries are using different formats to broadcast their TV shows, too.

There are three formats. If you're living in the United States, simply choose NTSC whenever it appears on a menu and move on to more important parts of the book. If you're not living in the United States, check out Table 5-2.

Table 5-2	Broadcast Standards for Different Countries
If You Live in This Country	*Choose This Video Format*
United States, Canada, Mexico, Central America, Bolivia, Chile, Colombia, Ecuador, Peru, Surinam, Venezuela, Japan, Korea, Taiwan, the Philippines, Bahama Islands, Jamaica, and most of the other Caribbean islands	NTSC
Much of western Europe, including Austria, Belgium, Denmark, Finland, Germany, Great Britain, Holland, Italy, Norway, Portugal, Spain, Sweden, Switzerland; Australia, Malaysia, New Zealand, Thailand, Hong Kong, and Singapore	PAL
France, Bulgaria, Hungary, Monaco, Poland, the former Soviet Union, much of Eastern Europe, Iran, Iraq, and Guiana	SECAM

Unless you're a world traveler, you probably don't have to worry about these differences. Just remember this: your TV set or camcorder probably won't work overseas, even if you *do* find the right power adapter to plug in the wall.

- ✔ Some video capture software lets you grab video using NTSC, PAL, or SECAM formats. Be sure to tell the software what version you're using. You can usually save the option so that you never have to worry about it again (unless you take your computer to Italy over the summer).

- ✔ If you accidentally tell your software to use the wrong format, nothing loathsome shoots from the top of your monitor. If you choose PAL when your country uses NTSC, for example, the picture probably looks tilted at the top half of the screen. If you change the setting to NTSC, the picture straightens up.

- ✔ When buying TV stuff for your computer — capture cards, TV cards, and camcorders — make sure that you're buying the right format for your particular country: NTSC, PAL, or SECAM. (Chances are that the salesperson is stocking the right stuff for the right country, but watch out for those mail-order places — they sell a lot of stuff overseas.)

- ✔ Finally, some capture-card manufacturers wised up: their equipment can switch between *any* country's format. Don't expect that feature on older models, however.

Why Is S-Video Better Than Composite?

Most video capture cards come with two input jacks, generously allowing you to plug in an S-video cable or a composite cable. If you have an S-VHS camcorder or an Hi8 camcorder, use the S-video jacks. The card captures higher-quality pictures. You don't have Super-VHS or Hi8? Then settle for the picture you get with the composite cable. (Most people can't tell the difference in video quality, so don't grind your teeth too hard.)

And if you don't know what sort of cable your equipment uses, head for Chapter 14. It has figures of the little cables and where they plug in.

S-video, also known as Y-C video, transmits an image's luminance and color portions separately, allowing for more control over the picture. In *composite* video, the signals are lumped together. Yawn. S-video just looks better, that's all.

Should I Bother with MPEG?

Somebody finally found a codec that can compress video files thinner than snails on a rainy day. The Motion Picture Experts Group (MPEG), a modest-minded group of broadcast-industry folks, found a way to compress a video file by 100 to 1. A video that normally takes up 1,000K can now fit in a 10K file. Not only that, but MPEG shamed those postage stamp-sized movies; MPEG videos can fill your computer's entire screen with video, making your monitor look like a television set.

Sound too good to be true? It is. Compressing the video takes special equipment and a *long* time. And here is the clincher: to play back the MPEG video full-screen at any decent speed, you need to install a special card with a special MPEG chip.

- ✔ If you buy a special MPEG board — Sigma Design's ReelMagic, for example — you can play special full-screen versions of some of your favorite computer programs. The videos in the MPEG version of Return to Zork look like movies, not computer games.

- ✔ Any new technology takes time getting accepted, however, and only a dozen or two companies are releasing MPEG versions of their software.

- ✔ Buying an MPEG board is like buying into any new technology: You take the plunge and then wonder whether it will catch on. VHS did, but Beta didn't. Cassettes did, but 8-track didn't. V-6 did, but the Wankel Rotary Engine didn't. (Insert your own here: "My _____ did, but my _____ didn't.")

- ✔ If you want an MPEG board, make sure that it's compatible with your computer's VGA card. Some cards don't get along. Also, the best MPEG boards can perform as sound cards and CD-ROM controllers, so you can do *something* with them until MPEG finally catches on.

Video Capture Buzzwords

The video industry comes up with more than their fair share — far too many — of buzzwords. So when you come across a weird word in a manual or a program's menu, look it up in Table 5-3 to see what the word means.

Table 5-3	Video Capture Buzzwords
This Word	***Means This in Real Life***
8-bit	A file containing up to 256 colors
16-bit	A file containing up to 65,536 colors
24-bit or TrueColor	A file with up to 16.7 million colors (which is about as many colors as the eyeball can decipher on-screen)
Algorithm	The scientific formula used for a codec
Aliasing	A fancy word to describe those yucky, jagged edges that make computerized pictures look, well, like they came out of a computer
Analog	Natural things, like waves, sounds, and motion — things that computers have a hard time turning into numbers (see *Digital*)
Antialiasing	Technology used to get rid of jagged edges found in computerized graphics
Aspect ratio	A picture's proportions (If you change a picture's height, some programs keep the *aspect ratio* by changing the picture's width, too, keeping things in balance.)
AVI	Audio Video Interleaved — the format that Windows uses for saving video with sound
Bitmap	A file format in Windows for storing graphics
Codec	A way to compress video into a file and then decompress it when playing it back
Contrast	The range between a picture's lightest and darkest tones
Coprocessed /Accelerated video	Cards with special computer chips for flinging pictures on-screen extra fast
DIB	Device-Independent Bitmap — a file format for graphics in Windows

(continued)

Table 5-3 *(continued)*

This Word	*Means This in Real Life*
Digital	Computerized things; collections of numbers to represent pictures, sounds, video, or internal angst (see *Analog*)
Dithering	A way to blur and change colors, making images look more realistic under different video modes and palettes
Dropped frames	Skipping a particular image but picking up the next one down the line, when a computer can't keep up with the incoming information
Dubbing	Adding new pieces of video or audio to previously recorded stuff to touch it up
Encoding	Compressing a file (When you're translating home movies to computer files, you're encoding them.)
Filter	To remove an undesirable quality, such as removing a hiss from a recording or the wine stains from the picture of the carpet
FPS	Frames Per Second — the number of pictures flashed in a second to give the video the illusion of motion (NTSC uses 30 FPS; PAL/SECAM uses 25 FPS.)
Frame	A single picture that, when pieced together with other pictures and displayed in a certain order, creates movies (Remember the flip-the-pages books where a cartoon guy would skip or jump?)
Full-motion video	A computerized movie — not necessarily filling the screen — showing at either 30 frames per second (NTSC) or 25 frames per second (PAL/SECAM)
Full-screen video	A movie that fills the entire screen, not just a small box
Gradient	Having an area smoothly blend from one color to another, or from black to white, or vice versa
Gray scale	Images using shades of gray instead of color
High resolution	Images with more pixels per square inch than low-resolution images, making them more realistic
Indeo™	Intel's codec for video

This Word	*Means This in Real Life*
Intel's Smart Video Recorder	Intel's video capture card with a special chip for capturing and storing videos on the fly (see Real-time compression)
Interactive video	A program that lets people push buttons to control what videos they want to see
JPEG	Joint Photographic Expert Group — a codec used mainly for still pictures, not movies
Key frame	A video frame containing a complete picture, not just the changes from the previous frame
Lossless compression	Computerized video containing all the original picture information (even the irrelevant parts)
Lossy compression	Computerized video with some of the stuff chopped out to save space
Luminance	A video-geek's word for *brightness*
MCI	Media Control Interface — a part of Windows that lets different brands of multimedia parts work together
MPEG and MPEG II	Motion Picture Expert Group — a group deciding how videos should be compressed (The MPEG standard produces *consumer* quality video; the MPG II standard creates *broadcast* quality video.)
NTSC	National Television Standard Connection — the video standard used mostly in the United States, Canada, and Japan
Overlay	A way to superimpose computer graphics over a video; often used to add titles to videotapes
PAL	Phase Alteration Line — video format used in most of western Europe and Australia
Palette	The variety of colors contained in a video or graphics file
Phono cable	Cable used mostly for connecting stereo equipment but can also work for video equipment in a pinch (Video-specific cables provide better pictures.)
Pixels	Picture element — the little dots on-screen that light up in different colors to make pictures
QuickTime	Macintosh's equivalent of Microsoft's Video for Windows program for processing video

(continued)

Table 5-3 *(continued)*

This Word	*Means This in Real Life*
Real-time compression	A way to compress incoming movies as quickly as they come into the computer — also known as *one-step capture*
RIFF	Resource Interchange File Format — a format for storing sound or graphics files so that they can be played by different brands of computer gear
RLE	Run Length Encoding — Microsoft's codec for videos of no more than 256 colors
S-VHS	Super-VHS — a high-quality videotape format sent through S-video cable
S-video	High-quality video used in Hi-8 and S-VHS — also known as *Y-C Video*
Sampling rates	When computers listen to a sound or watch a video to stick the information into a file, they're *sampling* the information; the *higher* the sampling rate, the better the quality, the closer the computer pays attention to the information, and the bigger the resulting file
SECAM	Séquential Couleur A Mémoire (Sequential Color with Memory) — a video format used mostly in France, as well as parts of eastern Europe
Teleconference	A phone meeting where callers can both see and talk to each other and nobody has to worry about the extra garlic bread they had for lunch
TIFF	Tagged Image File Format — a file for storing high-quality graphics; especially handy for swapping files between PCs and Macintoshes
Tweaking	Fiddling with knobs until everything finally looks right
Y/C	Video format used by S-VHS and Hi-8 — nerds say that the signal is broken into a separate chrominance (color) and luminance (brightness) channel

Chapter 6
CD (Seedy) ROM Drives

• •

In This Chapter

▶ What do double- and triple-speed mean?

▶ What's the easiest way to buy a CD-ROM drive?

▶ Why do I need a drive controller?

▶ Is internal or external best?

▶ Do Kodak Photo CDs work with every camera?

▶ Do I need to know what SCSI does?

▶ What's that MSCDEX file stuff?

• •

*F*ew people try to stick an 8-track tape into their stereo's CD player. And a record doesn't fit into a VCR, either. That's because the entertainment industry doesn't want to confuse people.

The computer industry, on the other hand, does exactly the opposite — the industry bigwigs decided to store programs on compact discs that look *exactly* like music CDs. Your stereo can't play the computer's CDs, but your computer can play the musical CDs.

Now get this: a Kodak Photo CD might not work in your computer or stereo. Add a few more weird computerized formats like CD-i and CD-XA, and the confusion thickens.

This chapter peels back the weirdness to show what discs you can stick where, when, and why on earth you'd want to.

What Do Double-and Triple-Speed Mean?

Your home stereo's CD player isn't a very complicated beast. When you insert a disc, the CD player starts playing the first song. When it reaches the end of the disc, the CD player stops. Unless you tell the CD player to skip some of the dopier songs, it simply plays the disc from beginning to end.

And that's the problem with computers: they *love* to jump around when reading information from a disc. Open a file, and you can hear frantic whirring noises inside your computer as it grabs information.

Because the first CD-ROM drives couldn't jump around quickly (and couldn't transfer information quickly, either), somebody invented a *double-speed* CD-ROM drive. These drives spin twice as fast, letting the computer suck up information twice as fast.

- ✓ The faster the CD-ROM drive can spin the disc, the faster your computer can run programs stored on CDs.

- ✓ The faster your computer can grab programs, the better your multimedia program will look. Pictures hop onto the screen more quickly; the sound isn't as choppy; and the movies don't jerk around so much.

Single speed is how fast your stereo's CD player spins. Double-speed CD-ROM drives can therefore spin twice as fast when accessing data. Triple-speed CD-ROM drives spin three times as fast as original, single-speed drives, and quad speed CD-ROM drives spin . . . well, you guessed it.

A computer's double-speed CD-ROM drive can still play music CDs — the drive slows down to the proper speed when you swap your computerized encyclopedia for an old Led Zeppelin CD.

When shopping for a CD-ROM drive today, don't buy anything slower than a double-speed drive. Buy a triple-speed drive, if you can afford it.

My Friend Says That I Don't Need a Fast CD-ROM Drive

People who say that you don't need a fast CD-ROM are usually trying to sell you their old, slow one after they have upgraded. Here's how their "You don't need a fast CD-ROM drive" argument usually goes:

First, *all* CD-ROM drives are slow. Your hard disk can grab information ten times faster. (That argument is true, by the way.)

Second, many CDs merely contain text, such as phone numbers or the complete works of obscure Latin poets. Because the drive merely grabs words, puts them on the screen, and then stops working, it doesn't need to be fast. *Any* CD-ROM drive can find and display text in a few seconds — much more quickly than you could find it in a book. (That's true, as well.)

Finally, many compact discs contain stuff that's supposed to run off your hard drive: bunches of small programs, Windows wallpaper, and other goodies. Because you copy the stuff to your hard drive and run it from there, the CD-ROM drive doesn't have to be speedy. (True.)

In fact, there's only one reason why you need a fast CD-ROM drive: for running multimedia programs. Because multimedia programs run straight from the disc, your CD-ROM drive needs to kick out information as quickly as possible.

✔ If you're going to use a CD-ROM drive only to grab text or to copy programs to your hard drive, then you won't need a speedy one. Spend that extra hundred bucks on more memory instead.

✔ If you're going run multimedia programs, however, you want the fastest drive you can find.

What's the Easiest Way to Buy a CD-ROM Drive?

From easiest to most difficult, here are your options for buying a CD-ROM:

◆ For immediate CD-ROM drive satisfaction, buy a *multimedia upgrade kit*. Described in Chapter 7, these kits come with a CD-ROM drive, a sound card, speakers, and a way to avoid shopping for all the components separately and trying to piece everything together.

◆ The next easiest method, if you already have a sound card, is to buy a CD-ROM drive that's listed in the sound card's manual as being compatible. Not all drives work with all sound cards — especially the early Sound Blaster cards — so check the sound card's manual *before* you buy the drive.

◆ Buy the CD-ROM drive's *controller card* when buying the drive. By plugging the drive into its own controller card — *not* the port on the sound card — you won't have to worry about compatibility problems.

◆ Finally, if your sound card says it has a *SCSI 2 port* and your CD-ROM drive says it supports SCSI 2, the devices have the best chances of getting along.

✔ Any of the methods described here work. They're just sorted by hassle-factor, with the last one making you hold the screwdriver — and the drive's manual — for the longest period of time.

✔ Because the terms CD-ROM controller card and SCSI sound so scary, they get their own sections later in this chapter.

Is an Internal Drive Better Than an External One?

An *internal* CD-ROM drive fits inside your computer and pokes out from the front. You feed it discs they way you feed a floppy drive.

An *external* CD-ROM drive contains the guts of internal CD-ROM drive mounted inside its own little box. The box can live anywhere on your desk. (It takes discs just like a floppy drive, too.)

Neither type of drive is better than the other; one just fits inside your computer, and the other comes in a little box about the size of a large city's phone book.

✔ External CD-ROM drives cost more because you're paying for the little box and thick cables.

✔ Internal CD-ROM drives are cheaper because the manufacturers can leave out the box.

✔ Internal CD-ROM drives can sometimes be plugged into a *controller jack* on your sound card. By contrast, external CD-ROM drives need their own controller card. (Controller cards are described in the next section.)

✔ Internal CD-ROMs can shoot their sound directly in the CD-ROM connector on your sound card, leaving the sound card's line-in jack free for other things, like your radio.

✔ When it's listed in a catalog, a *bare* CD-ROM drive usually doesn't include the controller card. A CD-ROM drive kit includes the card and cables.

✔ An internal CD-ROM drive needs room to sit inside your computer, usually right below a floppy drive. If you have two floppy drives — and no room for the CD-ROM drive — check out the *combo* drives from Teac. These drives combine a 5 ¼- and a 3 ½-inch drive into the size of one drive, leaving room for your CD-ROM drive.

What the Heck Is a Drive Controller?

On your stereo, the CD player plugs into your amplifier. But where does a CD-ROM drive plug into your computer? The drive needs a *controller* — a place to plug in — so your computer can tell it when to grab stuff off the disc.

Yep — it's Yet Another Thing To Think About when heading to the computer store. You have two choices:

You can buy a CD-ROM controller card and plug it into a slot inside your PC. A cord connects the CD-ROM drive to the card. The card, usually sold separately, is often called a *SCSI Host Adapter*, or a *SCSI card* (described in the next section).

Or some sound cards come with a special CD-ROM drive controller built in. You can plug the CD-ROM drive's cables right into your sound card and start playing.

- ✔ Unfortunately, not all sound cards can control all the CD-ROM players on the market. Some brands don't like each other. Better check your sound card's manual — especially if you have an early Sound Blaster — to see if it supports the drive you've got your eye on.

- ✔ For the most part, a sound card that has a SCSI controller works with more CD-ROM drives than a sound card with a *proprietary* controller. (SCSI and proprietary controllers duke it out a little later in this chapter.)

Is "proprietary" better than "SCSI"?

Although it sounds like something gross found in public drinking fountains, SCSI ("skuh-zee") is a unique way to hook a bunch of toys to a computer.

Basically it works like this. A SCSI card plugs into your computer, and a computer toy — a SCSI CD-ROM drive, for example — plugs into a connector or port on the card.

Then other SCSI toys can be strung along, each plugging into each other. In fact, you can plug up to seven SCSI toys into that card. (Engineers call a string of SCSI gizmos a *daisy chain*.)

Most CD-ROM drives need to plug into a SCSI port. So some sound cards come with a SCSI port built-in, ready for your CD-ROM drive.

Other sound cards and CD-ROM drives don't use SCSI technology. The manufacturers of these cards and drives decided their products would only work with each other's products.

So, they made *proprietary* connectors. For example, the Sound Blaster Pro's connector only works with Panasonic's CD-ROM drives. A SCSI CD-ROM drive won't work.

- ✔ SCSI stands for *Small Computer System Interface*. Yawn.

- ✔ Proprietary connectors are cheaper than SCSI connectors because they control one CD-ROM drive, not a string of computer toys.

- ✔ SCSI isn't perfect, either. The SCSI format comes in several flavors, and not all SCSI CD-ROM drives work with all SCSI-compatible sound cards. You have to check the sound cards' manuals or call their technical support people to make sure they're compatible.

- ✔ The SCSI controller on some sound cards only supports a single CD-ROM drive — you can't daisy chain other SCSI toys along the string.

SCSI-compatible computer toys can plug into other brands of computers, such as Macs. If you're working with both Macs and PCs, you might want to consider a SCSI-based, not proprietary, CD-ROM drive.

Can I Really Listen to B.B. King on My Computer's CD-ROM Drive?

Yep. Most CD-ROM drives sold in the past two years can play music CDs as well as computer CDs.

In fact, you can even embed parts of a B.B. King song into a Write document. (Chapter 17 shows how; Chapter 30 shows how it can be illegal to do so.)

- ✔ If you buy an external CD-ROM drive, make sure it has an *audio output* jack. You want to run a cable from these jacks to your sound card so that you can hear the music through your sound card speakers. (That's all described in Chapter 11.)

- ✔ Internal CD-ROM drives come with two little cables; one connects to its controller, and the other connects to your computer's sound card so you can hear stuff.

- ✔ To play music CDs in Windows, use Media Player.

- ✔ If you stick a Led Zeppelin disc in your CD-ROM drive and try to read the disc in File Manager, you see an ethereal message like the one in Figure 6-1. That's because music CDs don't store their songs in DOS files, so File Manager gets confused.

Figure 6-1:
Windows
File
Manager
can't read a
music CD,
but
Windows
Media
Player can
play it.

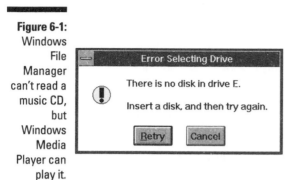

What Numbers Should I Look for on My CD-ROM Drive?

Like anything else associated with computers, CD-ROM drives come with plenty of numbers listed in the fine print. Only two of the numbers are worth remembering.

Access time: This refers to the number of *milliseconds* a drive takes to find and grab a piece of information. The *smaller* the number, the *faster* the drive.

Look for an access time of 200ms or less.

Data Transfer Rate: This number is the most important and refers to the speed a CD-ROM drive can suck information from a disc and shove it into the computer. The bigger the number, the better the drive.

A single-speed drive has a data transfer rate of 150K per second, a double-speed drive can move data at 300K per second, and triple-speed drives are moving information at 450K per second.

A CD-ROM drive's *data transfer rate* should be 300K per second or higher for best results.

Don't be fooled by some advertisements. Some vendors say they're selling a *375ms CD-ROM drive* for an incredibly low price. The letters *ms* refer to *access speed* — and it's the *data transfer rate*, or DTR, that really makes a difference. (Data transfer rate is measured in kilobytes per second, or *KB/sec.*)

Will a Kodak CD Fit in My Camera?

Everybody else jumped onto the computer bandwagon several years ago, and Kodak has finally grabbed the bandwagon's back bumper.

Kodak now lets you take plain old 35-millimeter film and slides to the developer, who later hands you the negatives and a compact disc containing the pictures.

Stick the disc in your computer and you can see the pictures on the screen. (You have to buy Kodak's software first, however.)

The Windows wallpaper possibilities are endless. Chapter 19 has the complete scoop, so just remember one thing here:

To use Kodak Photo CDs on a CD-ROM drive, the drive must be *multi-session* compatible and *Kodak CD-ready*. Most new CD-ROM drives meet those standards, so you probably won't have to worry about it.

What Else Do I Need to Buy?

Just like cars and spouses, CD-ROM drives end up with hidden expenses. This section covers a few.

Caddies

Most CD-ROM drives don't let you slide in CDs as if they were floppy discs. Instead, you need to put the CD inside a *caddy* — a little plastic case with a hinge — and then slide the caddy into the drive.

Opening and closing the caddy can be a colossal pain when switching between several discs, leading to the following tip.

If you're working with several CDs, buy a separate caddy for each of them. This not only makes it easier to switch among CDs quickly, but it keeps the CDs cleaner and out of harm's way.

- ✔ Most caddies are a standard size, usually referred to as *Sony* caddies. Some CD-ROM drives by NEC and Philips use a different-sized caddy.

- ✔ For the best price on caddies, check the backs of computer magazines for a mail-order house and buy a dozen or so.

Don't buy the cheapest caddies you can find. If they fall apart, you might have to open up your CD-ROM drive to sweep out remnants.

Those cheap plastic CD cases (jewel boxes)

The plastic cases on some CDs break when you first open them; others wait until you've dropped them on the floor. And if you order CDs through the mail, the cases are usually broken on arrival.

Your local music store usually sells replacement cases. Or if you're near any computer magazines, check out the pages near the back for a mail-order store. Don't worry about ordering the cheapest ones — they're *all* built cheaply.

Oh, the industry sometimes calls them *jewel boxes*, not *little plastic cases*. Go figure.

Simple Answers to Seedy (CD) Questions

The next few sections cover some of those CD-ROM questions that inevitably pop up after playing with one for the first time.

What's that MSCDEX file stuff?

Basically, the MSCDEX.EXE program lets DOS talk to a CD-ROM drive and grab files from it. But this question can wait until Chapter 11, which shows you how to install a CD-ROM drive.

All the CD movies look so jerky!

The movies probably look jerky because your CD-ROM drive is not spitting out the movies quickly enough. For clean movies, the drive needs to kick out a fresh picture at least fifteen times each second. If your drive can't crank pictures out that fast, you see the delay between each picture. Some solutions follow:

- ✔ Buy a faster CD-ROM drive — double-speed or triple-speed.

- ✔ In Windows, run the movie in an even *smaller* window.

- ✔ If you're using DOS 6.2, try playing the movie a second time, right after the first. DOS 6.2's SmartDrive program copies parts of the movie to memory as it's being played. When played the second time, the computer can play the movie back more smoothly because it won't have to stop and grab bits and pieces of the movie from the CD-ROM drive.

✔ Buy DOS 6.2 if you aren't using it.

✔ Buy an accelerated video card. Sometimes your video card can't keep up with the pictures that your computer is trying to display.

✔ Copy the movie from the CD to your hard drive and run it from there. Running the movie from your hard drive is always going to be a smoother operation than running it straight from your CD.

How can I make my own CDs?

Buy your own CD maker. CD makers — writable CD-ROM drives — cost about $3,000 now, but the price keeps dropping. To have somebody copy your information to CDs, look in the Yellow Pages under *Data Storage Equipment* for a CD Mastering shop.

Does sound come from the CD-ROM drive or the sound card?

When you're listening to a music CD through headphones, you're hearing the sound straight from your CD-ROM drive. The sound card isn't involved.

When you're hearing a music CD from your sound card's speakers, you're still hearing it from your CD-ROM drive. However, the CD-ROM drive is routing the sound through your sound card. The sound card makes the sound loud enough so you can hear it.

Finally, when you're hearing sound from a program, your sound card is kicking it out. The CD-ROM drive is merely delivering the information to the sound card, which puts it all together.

What's all this Red Book and Yellow Book stuff?

Two huge corporate conglomerates, Philips and Sony, invented the compact disc together, and their executives sit in big rooms and decide how to make the most money off their invention.

These companies come up with new *formats* — new ways that different gizmos can read compact discs. So the execs type a format's specifications and stick it in a folder. The color of the folder's cover refers to the specification. I'm not making this up!

For example, your home stereo reads music CDs using a certain format stored in the *red* folder, so a *Red Book*-compatible CD-ROM drive can play music CDs. Computer CDs are Yellow Book. (So is this book.)

Using Hypertext in Multimedia CDs

You've probably heard the word *hypertext* tossed out breathlessly by the same people who murmur *virtual reality, data superhighway, graphical user interface,* and *Hostess Twinkies.*

Hypertext describes a computerized way of searching for things — no more looking stuff up in an index. Most multimedia CDs use hypertext, which is a fancy name for words with special meaning.

When you see a word in a multimedia program that stands out — either because it's underlined or is a different color from the rest — it's considered *hypertext.* Click or double-click on the word, and the program immediately brings up more information relating to that word.

For example, a document about Philadelphia sandwich shops might contain a list of sandwiches with all the ingredients in different colored letters. If you see the word *Cheese Whiz* in a different color, click on it. Doing so brings up more information about Cheese Whiz — like where it's from and how manufacturers make it just the right consistency to squeeze out of those little tubes.

Some multimedia programs have *hypermedia* as well as *hypertext.* When you click or double-click on the word *Cheese Whiz,* a host of options pops up. Click on the movie camera picture to see a video of Cheese Whiz workers stuffing the cheese into little tubes. Click on the little microphone to hear the last remnants of Cheese Whiz leaving the canister. Or click on the camera to see a picture of the cook at Jim's Steakhouse squirting it onto a waiting customer's sandwich.

Here are a few guidelines for using multimedia programs:

- ✔ If a word appears in a different color than the other words, it's probably *hypertext.* Click on the word, and the program brings you more information about that subject. To return to where you left, look for a button that says *Back.*

- ✔ If you search for a word in a multimedia encyclopedia — *esophagus,* for example — and the program brings up more information, the word *esophagus* might be in a different color than the other words. Clicking or double-clicking on it won't do anything, though (except make a click sound). It's just a different color so you can find it easily. After all, you were searching for it.

- ✔ Clicking on little pictures (called icons) in a program usually launches additional features. Clicking on a little camcorder usually brings up a video, for example. Microphones mean sound, and a camera usually means photo.

Dirty CDs

No, not *that* kind of CD. We're talking about discs with an inadvertent peanut butter smear. To remove it, use a drop of dish detergent and lots of running water at room temperature. Don't rub the discs, except for a light push with a finger to get the peanut butter gobs off. Then shake off any water and pat the CD with a soft, clean cloth to remove the extra water.

   ✔ Don't rub a disc with anything, and don't clean it with anything but water.

   ✔ Be extra careful with the *unlabeled* side of the disc — that's the side where the player grabs its information.

   ✔ Handle discs by their edges. Or put your finger through their inner hole like you were a kid with a doughnut. Don't hold them like a Frisbee.

   ✔ Don't leave the discs out in the sun or in the snow.

   ✔ Give them proud glances every so often.

The Buzzwords

Combine sound, data, computers, and music, and you find too many buzzwords to remember. Table 6-1 explains a few of the more common buzzwords clogging up the manuals.

Table 6-1	Weird CD-ROM Drive Terms
The Word	*What It Is*
3DO	A compact disc-based console created by a bunch of corporations hoping to create The Ultimate Home Game Machine. (Although it's not compatible with PCs, this console is described in Chapter 9.)
Access time	The number of milliseconds a drive takes to find and grab a piece of information.
Blue Book	CDs designed for laserdiscs use this format. (See Laserdisc players.)
Caddy	A little plastic case that holds a CD so it can be inserted into a CD-ROM drive.
CD-DA	Compact Disc Digital Audio. Also known as Red Book or CD-Audio, this is simply a music CD.
CD-i	Compact disc-interactive. Yet another game machine console, this one is by Philips. It can play music CDs, Kodak Photo CDs, and run special CD-i programs.

The Word	*What It Is*
CD+G	Compact Disc + Graphics. A standard for adding pictures to a regular music CD. (Very popular in Japan.)
CD-XA	Compact Disc Extended Architecture. An important new standard for packing different types of information onto a disc, such as computer data, sound, and pictures. Kodak Photo CD needs a CD-XA drive.
CD-ROM	Compact Disc Read Only Memory. A fancy name for a CD.
CDTV	Yet Another Home Game Machine, this one never took off. (See Chapter 9.)
Data buffer	A way to temporarily store information, leading to smoother transfers. Most drives come with a 64K buffer (or *cache*). Bigger buffers are better.
Data transfer rate (DTR)	The number of kilobytes of information a drive can squirt into your computer in a second. Normal speed is 150K per second; double-speed drives can move 300K per second; triple-speed drives can move 450K per second; and quadruple drives . . . well, you get the idea.
Double-speed	A drive that reads information twice as fast as original, music CD players.
External	A drive that lives in its own little box — not inside your PC.
Frequency response	The range of sound the CD can reproduce. If you listen to music on your CD-ROM drive, look for a frequency response close to 20 to 20,000 Hz.
Green Book	The format for CD-i (compact disc-interactive).
High Sierra	A format for placing files and directories on CD-ROM so that DOS can read it. Also known as *ISO 9660*.
Internal	A drive that fits inside your computer, like a floppy drive.
ISO-9660	A format for placing files and directories on CD-ROM so that DOS can read it. Also known as *High Sierra*.
Jaguar	Yet Another Game Machine, this one by Atari. It can play audio CDs, display Kodak's new Photo CDs, and blow up aliens in 3-D.
Jewel box	The cheap little plastic box that CDs come packaged in. See Fragile.
Juke box	Large CD-ROM drives that hold several CDs, thereby letting you switch between discs easily and expensively.
Kodak Photo CD	CD that stores photographs in a special format; requires a multi-session, Kodak Photo CD-compatible CD-ROM drive.

(continued)

Table 6-1 *(continued)*

The Word	What It Is
Laserdisc player	Similar to a VCR, this machine hooks up to a TV and plays back movies stored on discs. Some new specialized laserdisc players can play musical CDs, as well.
Multi-session	A CD-ROM drive that can read CDs after they've been changed, like a Kodak Photo CD that has had some more photos added to it.
MTBF	Mean Time Between Failures. The higher the number, the more durable the drive.
Optical storage unit	A fancy word for CD-ROM drive.
Orange Book	Standard for WORM format, also known as *Write Once Read Many* CDs. (Big companies use them to backup their boring computerized paperwork.)
Oversampling	A way to cut down noise and improve quality when reading a CD. The bigger the oversampling number, the better the quality.
Philips	A huge company that developed CD technology with Sony.
Quadruple-speed	A CD-ROM drive that reads information four times as fast as original music CD players.
Red Book	Nothing to do with the magazine, this term simply means a CD with music (like a Rolling Stones album) and no computer programs. Also means Compact Disc Digital Audio, or CD-DA.
SCSI	Small Computer System Interface. A way to link several computer gadgets together.
SCSI/2	Same as SCSI, but with a new and improved format.
Triple-speed	A CD-ROM drive that reads information three times as fast as original music CD players.
Yellow Book	A standard for compact discs that contains computer programs and data.

Chapter 7
Those Tempting Multimedia Bundles with *Everything*

In This Chapter

▶ How multimedia bundles differ

▶ What to look for in a multimedia kit

▶ How to load a multimedia bundle

▶ What kind of computer to use with a multimedia kit

*S*ome people like to live in places that are already furnished. They don't want to pick out a bunch of stuff at the furniture stores, arrange it in their living rooms, and then hear their friends guffaw if the modern couch conflicts with the fancy rose wallpaper. Other people buy fancy furniture at antique shops, arranging it until it looks just so.

The same thing applies to multimedia all-in-one upgrades. Instead of picking out a sound card, CD-ROM drive, and speakers — and hoping they work together — some people buy everything they need for multimedia into a single box.

Then it's easier to throw everything in the backseat, carry it in the front door, and transform your computer into a multimedia theater. Or does it? This chapter points out the good and the bad in the bundles.

What Is Included in a Multimedia Upgrade Package?

Like a furnished beach cottage, a multimedia upgrade package comes with *everything*. Plug it in, pop in the latest CD, and start questioning aliens about that 1963 UFO sighting in Houston. These upgrade packages are for consumers who want to *play*, not *putter* around inside their computers.

Some bundles are more comprehensive than others, however. Table 7-1 shows what items come packaged in a bundle — and what some companies often leave out.

Table 7-1	What to Look for in a Multimedia Bundle
Item	*Comments*
Sound card	Although sound cards come in all upgrade kits, music lovers usually prefer a 16-bit card over an 8-bit card.
CD-ROM drive	All kits include a CD-ROM drive, but make sure that it's a double-speed drive and not a single-speed drive.
Speakers	Some kits don't include speakers, which can cost anywhere from $10 to $100 extra. (Sometimes, you can simply hook up the whole computer to your stereo — see Chapter 13.)
Warranty	After shopping for price, check the package's warranty before making your final decision.
Joystick	No joystick? Add another $20 to $60 to the price.
Microphone	Plan to add voice notes to your documents? If there is no microphone, add another $10 to $20 to the price.
MIDI ports	Musicians (or potential musicians) should look for MIDI ports or a system that is MPU-401 compatible, which allows you to plug in a wide variety of keyboards and synthesizers.
Software	All kits come with software to control the gadgetry, but look for some freebies tossed in: free CDs with encyclopedias, games, or other fun stuff.

Will an upgrade kit make me open my computer?

Yes.

An upgrade kit is one of the easiest ways to dive into the multimedia swimming pool. Nevertheless, multimedia kits *still* have to be installed.

For the most part, you have to remove your computer's case, slide a card into a little slot, and put the case back on. Some kits make you plug two cards into two little slots. Does your computer have enough slots? (Chapter 2 covers the slot stuff.)

Finally, after sliding in the card and connecting a cable, you have to install software that makes the thing work.

- ✔ If your computer doesn't have many goodies on it — a scanner, modem, or network card — the installation shouldn't cause many problems.

- ✔ Chapter 10 describes how to add a card.

- ✔ Don't want to take your computer apart? Then ask the people at the store if they'll install it for you — for an extra fee, of course.

- ✔ Or avoid the whole upgrade hassle by simply buying a new multimedia-ready computer.

How do the multimedia upgrades differ?

Most multimedia upgrade packages come bundled in one of two ways, each described in the next two sections.

A bunch of separate boxes in a big upgrade box

Description: A company chooses a sound card and a CD-ROM drive that work well together, tosses 'em both into a cardboard box, and slaps a *Multimedia Upgrade* sticker on the side.

Pros: Because many sound cards and CD-ROM drives don't work well together, buying a matched set can be wise. The sound card can control the CD-ROM drive, so the kit usually requires only one slot; making it a bit easier to install. (Slots, cards, and Blackjack are covered in Chapter 2.)

Cons: Neither the sound card nor the CD-ROM drive will be top-of-the-line. And because the sound card and CD-ROM drive are still separate pieces of equipment, they're not all *that* much easier to install than buying your own, higher-quality sound card and CD-ROM drive.

One big plastic case with everything

Description: Somebody has picked out a sound card and a CD-ROM drive that work well together, wired them together, stuck them inside a plastic box, and called them an *Integrated Multimedia Component System*.

Pros: Because the card and CD-ROM drive are already connected and designed for simplicity, they're the easiest way to upgrade to multimedia. You probably have to install a card inside your computer, and a cable will run between the multimedia box and the card.

Cons: Although the sound card and CD-ROM drive aren't cutting-edge stuff, they'll be adequate for most needs. Because the card and drive are connected, you may have trouble upgrading one of them a few years down the road.

Read the multimedia bundles box carefully before buying it so that you know what you're getting. For example, a Sony Multimedia Bundle Starter Kit is just a CD-ROM drive with a few CDs tossed in. To get the sound card and speakers, you need the Sony Multimedia Bundle Complete Kit.

Watch Out for This Stuff

When shopping for multimedia upgrades, keep the following information in mind:

✔ Even the best upgrade kit can't revitalize an aging computer. For best results, add an upgrade kit to a 486 computer. Then make sure that you have a fast video card and a high-resolution monitor, both described in Chapter 4.

✔ Make sure that the upgrade you purchase is an MPC-2 rather than an MPC. MPC quality just isn't good enough anymore. (The MPC issue is covered in Chapter 1.)

✔ When buying a multimedia upgrade package, you pay a little extra for convenience. Buying everything separately and piecing it together yourself may save you some money — but it also may increase your aggravation level.

✔ There is a difference between a stand-alone multimedia platform and a PC multimedia upgrade. The first label refers to CD-i, 3DO, or a bunch of other game machines that run CDs. Make sure that you're getting an upgrade kit for your IBM-compatible computer — not a multimedia box that hooks up to your TV set.

✔ Although multimedia bundles rarely contain top-of-the-line stuff, this is usually a good feature — the company is sticking with time-tested technology that you don't have to kick as often.

✔ Some multimedia upgrade packages, such as Media Vision's Memphis, work as stand-alone CD players. Now you can entertain your neighbors by blasting a heavy metal CD — even while your computer is turned off!

✔ Be a little skeptical of the "$7,034 of free software" sticker on the box of many upgrades. Some of that software may be a boring demonstration version of a program, a copy of last year's CD that never went anywhere, or an old version of today's best-seller.

Should I Upgrade or Buy a New Multimedia Computer?

If your old computer is a 286, buy a new 486 computer with all the multimedia goodies already attached. If you're using a 386 with a low-resolution monitor, you may want to spring for a new multimedia computer, too. The new computer will probably cost less than an upgrade.

But if you're just trying to add sound and CD-ROM excitement to the 486 you bought last year, buy the multimedia upgrade kit — the easiest way to steer your computer into the drive-in movies along the Information Highway.

If you're planning to eventually add SCSI devices to your computer — a huge 600MB hard drive, for example — make sure that you can connect other SCSI devices to the sound card in the bundle.

Chapter 8

Your Plain Ol' TV Set (Computerized Channel Surfing)

● ●

In This Chapter

▶ Using a TV set as a monitor

▶ Using your monitor as a TV set

● ●

*B*ack in the 70s, when the first brave souls bought computers, they hooked 'em up to their TV sets. It seemed like the natural thing to do at the time. Then computer manufacturers began telling people to buy fake TVs called *computer monitors*. A mere television, they said, simply wasn't good enough.

Today, the urge to use a TV is even greater — especially for people with home theater systems, red plush seats, and popcorn makers. Why play multimedia games on a tiny 14-inch monitor when you can be exploring the Titan Colony on the big screen?

This chapter explains ways to connect your computer to a television set — and the reverse: embedding a TV screen in the corner of your monitor so that you can watch MTV while you work (and grab occasional screen shots for new wallpaper).

Using the TV as a Monitor

Hooking up a TV set to a computer is a lot rougher than it was ten years ago. The two may look similar, but a TV and a computer monitor are very different beasts. A monitor is designed for close-up work, where details matter. If you move your nose about four inches away from the screen, you still can read letters in a word processing program. A television, on the other hand, is designed to be viewed from the couch across the room — there is no need for detail. In fact, if you put your nose about four inches away from the TV screen, everything turns into big dots and lines.

The problem? To hook up a TV set to a computer, something has to chop a lot of detail out of your computer screen's images before they'll fit on the TV screen. That detail chopper is called, surprisingly enough, a *TV converter card.*

The TV converter card plugs into your computer like any other card. A cable runs from the back of the card to the cable or antenna connection on your TV set. (It can connect to a VCR, as well.) The converter card grabs the information heading for your monitor, chops out some of the detail, and sends the result to your TV.

- ✔ The circuitry for a converter card comes packaged in a little box for people who don't want to open up their converter. These converter boxes work great for laptops, too.

- ✔ Unfortunately, converter cards aren't a magical solution. They often add flickering lines or have trouble fitting the screen onto the TV set. The picture is either too small, with big black borders, or too big, with parts falling off the edges of the screen.

- ✔ If you're running Windows or doing any word processing, the picture on your TV looks terrible. Because most of the detail has been chopped out, the letters are hard to read.

- ✔ When the converters chop stuff out, they usually chop out every other line of information. The result? Most of the lines in a program — the borders of windows, for example — don't show up on the TV set.

- ✔ Finally, some good news: If you're running a multimedia program that doesn't have text or lines — Trip the Running Dinosaur games, for example — the image on your TV doesn't look half bad. If you just want to play games, take a look at the converters.

- ✔ You'll probably have to run your computer in *VGA mode;* most converter cards can't fit any other video modes onto your TV's screen.

- ✔ The United States and Japan use the NTSC system for broadcasting, so their converter cards are often called VGA to NTSC converters. Other countries broadcast using PAL, so they use a special VGA-to-PAL converter. And the French people, who have their own words for everything, use a VGA-to-SECAM converter.

- ✔ If you're looking for professional quality, don't bother with any VGA-to-TV converters priced less than $500. In fact, you may need the converters that cost around $1,300. (Just charge extra for your commercials.)

- ✔ Head for Chapter 15 for tips on installing a converter card.

Watching TV on a Computer

Chapter 5 discussed video capture cards — by plugging your camcorder into the card, you can play back videos on your computer's monitor. You can hook up your VCR to a video capture card, too. The VCR's tuner sends TV signals to the capture card, and you see the TV show on your monitor.

VCRs are pretty bulky to lug around, however, so some TV addicts came up with a TV card. A *TV card* combines the guts of a video capture card with a TV tuner. Now you can watch TV shows on your computer monitor — without pirating the VCR from the den.

- ✔ Most TV cards work under Windows, not DOS. Of course, everybody is using Windows by now.

- ✔ The best TV cards let you change the size of the TV picture while you're working in Windows. For example, you can keep the TV picture in a small corner of your screen during commercials and then blow it up to a larger size when *The Frugal Gourmet* comes back on.

- ✔ TV cards tend to be more cute than practical, however. First, a TV card almost always costs more than a plain old TV set. And your TV set's screen is probably a lot bigger than your monitor, too. Finally, everybody at the office will look at you suspiciously when the local cable guy starts hooking up your computer.

- ✔ Still, it's fun to go channel surfing while word processing.

Understanding This PAL, SECAM, and NTSC Stuff

In short, PAL, SECAM and NTSC are three different video standards. The United States uses the NTSC standard. Most of Europe uses PAL. And France and Eastern Europe hang tough with their own standard, SECAM. So what? Well, your TV set may not work if you carry it across the ocean, because the TV shows are being broadcast in two different formats (three formats, if you count France).

When buying TV stuff for your computer — capture cards and TV cards — make sure that you're buying the right format for your particular country, or the images may not line up right on-screen.

You'll find plenty more of this awkward stuff in Chapter 5.

TV Buzzwords

Table 8-1 What Those Weird Television Words Mean	
This Weird Word	*Means This*
Grainy	A popular term to describe pictures made of noticeably ragged squares.
NTSC	National Television Systems Committee, a U.S. group that decided back in 1953 how TV should be broadcast. The NTSC format is used in the U.S., Canada, Japan, Central America, and parts of South America and the Caribbean.
PAL	Phase Alteration Line, the video format used in most of Western Europe, Australia, and other countries.
SECAM	Séquentiel Couleur Avec Mémoire, the video format used in France and eastern Europe.
TV Converter	A plug-in card for your PC that lets you see stuff on the TV rather than the monitor. The cheap ones (under $500) don't work very well, and the expensive ones (over $1,000) work well but cost too much.

Chapter 9

Those *Other* Computers

● ●

In This Chapter

▶ Commodore's Amiga for desktop video

▶ Apple's Macintosh for desktop publishing

▶ Atari for desktop MIDI studios

▶ Silicon Graphics workstations for expensive graphics

▶ Philips CD-i console for home entertainment

● ●

*Y*our IBM-compatible PC isn't the only computer on the market that can handle multimedia programs. In fact, it might be one of the *worst* multimedia computers. At least that's what the owners of the competing machines say.

This chapter compares the competition with your trusty ol' PC.

Amiga

Commodore International, Ltd., a former typewriter repair business in Canada, made millions in 1969 by creating one of the first electronic hand-held calculators. Deciding that numbers sold better than letters, the company started pouring its money into personal computers.

The Commodore PET computer hit the shelves in 1977, followed by the VIC 20 in 1980, which became the industry leader. Two years later, the Commodore 64 hit the market and was snapped up by more than ten million users worldwide.

After releasing three computers with hot gaming action, Commodore decided to follow IBM's lead and create a Serious Business Computer. Commodore's business entry, the Amiga, not only ran spreadsheets and word processing programs, but it boasted the best sound and graphics on the market.

Game fans went wild, but business people blanched. Nobody took a *game machine* seriously.

Despite several remodels, the Amiga never took off — except with multimedia fans who recognized the value of a machine released five years before its time.

- ✔ Today, the Amiga remains one of the best machines for *desktop video* — editing movies on your computer. Don't be surprised when you see the description *Amiga Version* on a lot of video-editing software.

- ✔ The Amiga not only costs less than an IBM PC, it comes with built-in sound and high-resolution graphics.

- ✔ The Amiga comes with a built-in plug for routing pictures to a television, which is something a PC has trouble doing. (See Chapter 8.)

- ✔ The *Video Toaster,* released in 1990, gave the Amiga powerhouse video studio effects: a user could mix two films together or make one movie slide off the screen to reveal another movie beneath it. The Video Toaster sold so well that its creators earned enough money to release a PC version a few years later. (The PC version is pretty much an Amiga in a box that connects to the PC.)

- ✔ If you're interested in professional-level video — and you haven't already bought an IBM-compatible PC — take a good look at the latest Amiga and a Video Toaster before plopping down your money.

- ✔ The Commodore PET sells for about $50 as a collector's item, according to *The New York Times.*

Macintosh

The Macintosh — affectionately called the Mac — is the cheerful, easy-to-use computer that doesn't even *look* like a computer. In fact, the Macintosh screen, with its fancy fonts and cute graphics, looks more like a magazine page than a computer.

A game-based image nearly killed Commodore's Amiga, but the Macintosh's graphics image has made it a winner in the desktop publishing market. People use Macs to create professional posters and newsletters (and . . . *For Dummies* books, too, now that I think about it).

- ✔ The Mac's graphics-based image lives on. Most professional desktop publishers use a Mac to create catalogs, newspapers, and magazine layouts.

✔ In fact, the Macintosh's graphics abilities still outpace the PC's abilities. For example, when Kodak's Photo CD came out, the Mac could immediately grab the highest-resolution images from the disc. IBM-compatible PCs could not do that until six months later, when Kodak finally got around to writing the software.

✔ In addition, some of the best CD games are written first for the Macintosh. The Macintosh is attracting the MIDI audience as well. Oh, and the Mac is popular with animators, too.

If you're buying a computer primarily for graphics work — especially desktop publishing — take a good look at the Mac before buying a PC.

Atari

Business people have made it clear that they don't want a game machine on their mahogany desk. So even though Atari got a head start on computing with the first game machine (Pong), it lost millions when business people dismissed the company as a toy maker.

As described earlier, Commodore's Amiga had already grabbed the desktop video market and the Macintosh took over the desktop publishing and professional graphics market. So Atari lunged for the leftovers: the MIDI market. Described in Chapter 3, MIDI lets musicians record and edit music on the computer.

The Atari 520 ST came with built-in MIDI connections, and musicians snapped it up. It was cheap and ready to play.

But because the prices of PC sound cards keep dropping, Atari is losing its hold on the MIDI market. (In fact, this is why Atari is now retreating to the game market. Check out the hot new Atari Jaguar at a store near you.)

✔ Musicians who explored MIDI probably still have an Atari — either on their desk or in their garage.

✔ A few years ago, most MIDI programs only ran on an Atari. Today, the PC is catching up; plug in a $50 sound card, and the PC is ready for musicians.

✔ Don't count the Mac out for MIDI, either. It's becoming the standard in many Los Angeles recording studios.

Silicon Graphics Indy

Have you ever seen the weird TV commercials in which a toilet-bowl brush dances with a detergent box? The commercial looks like a slick cartoon, but with much smoother animation than Speed Racer or Scooby-Doo.

A wily desktop-video expert probably created these dancing cleansers with a Silicon Graphics workstation — a big chunky computer that laughs at DOS and Windows.

Workstations can cost $20,000 or more — way out of reach of the average PC owner. So Silicon Graphics created the *Indy*. A true multimedia powerhouse, the Indy computer comes with advanced video and sound editing (six channels), a color digital camera, a powerful processor, and a $5,000 price tag.

Simply put, it jams.

- ✔ That $5,000 price tag doesn't include a hard drive, unfortunately.
- ✔ If you're tired of the postage stamp-sized movies on your PC — and you have hit it big with Publisher's Clearinghouse — check out an Indy. (And get ready to check out a new operating system, too. You won't find DOS, Windows, or even OS/2 pulling the ropes.)

Phillips CD-i

When *paddle/ball* game machines like Mattel's Intellivision faded in the 1970s, everybody thought they were gone for good. Personal computers had pushed the game machines out of business.

But when Nintendo hit it big in the mid-1980s, other companies jumped back in. Philips, the company that invented CD technology with Sony, came out with its CD-i machine — a box that hooks up to your TV set or color monitor and plays a bunch of different types of CDs.

Short for *compact disc-interactive*, the CD-i loves CDs. It can play plain ol' music CDs, Kodak Photo CDs, CD+Graphics (CD+G) CDs, and with a few upgrades, Karaoke CDs and Video CD disks. (Hit Chapter 6 for more information on compact discs.)

The CD-i doesn't run DOS or Windows, however, so it won't run your favorite programs.

- Who's buying CD-i? People who don't like computers but still want to play with multimedia and CD technology.
- Some PC CD-ROM drives can read information stored on a CD-i compact disc. They cannot run any CD-i programs, however.
- Some compact disc programs come with a DOS and a CD-i version. These CDs work on either machine.
- For more information about Philips and its CD-i, call 800-845-7301.

Part II

Setting Everything Up
(or That Cable Plugs in Here)

The 5th Wave   **By Rich Tennant**

"WE FIGURE THE EQUIPMENT MUST HAVE SCARED HER AWAY. A FEW DAYS AFTER SETTING UP, LITTLE 'SNOWBALL' JUST DISAPPEARED."

In this part . . .

Computers aren't crafted from raw materials by skilled technicians with scientific backgrounds. They're simply *assembled* by somebody with a screwdriver, a rag dangling from his or her back pocket, and a box full of spare parts.

There's no mystery to adding or subtracting parts from your PC. Assemblers don't need to know anything about circuit boards, oscillators, or dB ratings. If you know how to use a screwdriver — and you unplug your PC first — you'll do fine.

This part of the book shows how to install a card, a CD-ROM drive, and a monitor. Then it shows how to connect a few non-computer parts: your home stereo, a camcorder, and your TV set.

And when you're done, the last chapter explains where to poke if the darn thing *still* doesn't work.

Chapter 10

Installing a Card

● ●

In This Chapter

▶ What multimedia cards will I need?

▶ Installing new cards

▶ This card doesn't fit!

● ●

*U*nless your multimedia computer came already set up, you'll probably end up installing a card or two during its lifetime.

Adding a card to your computer is a lot easier than it sounds. It's as easy as pushing a plate into the dishwasher and tightening one screw so that the plate doesn't fall out during the rinse cycle.

This chapter explains where to stick the card and which screw to tighten.

What Multimedia Cards Do I Need?

Computers never used to come with fancy swirling colors, built-in CD players, or any other *fun* options. Even today, all the fun stuff is an add-on accessory just like leather seats or four-wheel drive.

In the computer world, most accessories come on *cards*, which are described in Chapter 2. For multimedia computers, the following cards are considered standard equipment:

Video cards: *Every* computer needs a video card. There are no exceptions. If your video card is a few years old, you might think about replacing it with something a little peppier. (The peppier *accelerated* video cards get their due in Chapter 4.)

My computer doesn't have a video card!

Some faddish computers in the early 90s built their video card circuitry right into the motherboard itself, bypassing the card.

So how do you upgrade the video on these computers? Try just plugging in a newer, faster video card in the same slot that the other card lives in. Most computers are smart enough to sense the intruder; they shut off the built-in video and pass the chore over to your new, upgraded card.

If your computer doesn't recognize the newcomer, however, grab the manual and look in the index under the words *video, changing,* or *disabling.* Depending on the mood of the computer's designer, you might have to use some of the boring utility disks that came with your computer or flip a switch somewhere inside the computer before the new video card can take over.

Video capture cards: Described in Chapter 5, these cards aren't found in all multimedia computers — just the really fun ones. A capture card grabs incoming video from camcorders and VCRs and stores the movies as computer files. Don't throw away your regular video card, though. The two cards must work together. And if you want to grab sound tracks from camcorders or VCRs, you need a *third* card — a sound card. (See the following description.)

Sound cards: Sound cards can brighten up a dull computing day — once they're finally installed. Unfortunately, sound cards tend to be complainers, whining about things like IRQ addresses and DMA ports. (This ugliness is tackled in Chapter 16.) Better dig up a set of speakers, too, or you won't be able to hear your new sound tracks. Also, Chapter 13 shows how to connect the card to your stereo, so that lobsters will make more realistic sounds when dropped into boiling water during a CD-ROM cooking program.

Interface/controller cards: Some multimedia accessories don't have anywhere to plug in — until you plug in their *interface* or *controller* card. Bus mice, most CD-ROM drives, and a few fancy MIDI synthesizers plug into their own separate interface/controller card. These cards put a new jack on the back of your computer.

✔ The biggest problem you'll probably have with cards is finding room for them. Most computers come with eight slots or less. Multimedia computers need a lot of accessories, so the slots can fill up pretty quickly.

✔ The second biggest problem is finding the right type of slot for the right type of card. Chapter 2 has a handy ID chart to help figure out what fits where.

  ✔ The third biggest problem is that your newly installed card probably won't work.

  ✔ When it doesn't work, you can probably fix it by flipping a tiny switch hidden on the card — a task tackled in Chapter 16. Or sometimes the card's installation software can make the thing start working right.

Which Card Goes in Which Slot?

Sometimes too many choices can be confusing. For example, your computer might have four empty ISA slots and you've got one ISA card in your hands. Question: Which one of the four slots does the card belong in?

Answer: It usually doesn't matter. (And if you want to know what *ISA* means, head to Chapter 2.)

There are a few rules to follow when choosing among empty slots:

  ✔ Space the cards out. Try to leave an empty slot between cards so that each card has breathing room. The space helps keep cards from heating up and complaining.

  ✔ Avoid putting your sound card in a slot next to your video card. Some video cards give off an electronic-frequency, garbage-disposal noise that makes sound cards hum.

  ✔ Try to keep your video capture cards away from your power supply (the silver box in the computer's back-right corner). Some power supplies add visual static to your video recordings.

  ✔ Don't have *any* available slots? Chapter 2 offers a few tips for scrounging up extra room.

  ✔ The row of slots is called an *expansion bus* or *expansion slots*.

  ✔ Make sure the tabs on the bottom of the cards line up with the slots inside your computer. Figures 10-1 shows different types of cards and the slots they fit into.

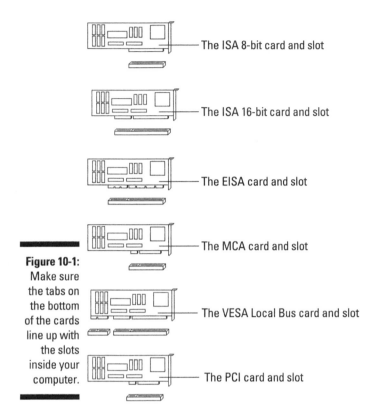

The ISA 8-bit card and slot

The ISA 16-bit card and slot

The EISA card and slot

The MCA card and slot

The VESA Local Bus card and slot

The PCI card and slot

Figure 10-1:
Make sure
the tabs on
the bottom
of the cards
line up with
the slots
inside your
computer.

How Do I Install a New Card?

Tools you need: Two hands, screwdriver

Cost: Anywhere from $30 to a few thousand bucks

Stuff to watch out for:

Cards are susceptible to static electricity. If the card came with a *3M Disposable Wrist Strap,* wear it just like the picture on the package shows. No picture? Then wear the collar around your wrist and stick the other end of the strap to some bare metal on your computer.

Didn't get a disposable wrist strap? Then take the cheap way out: before touching a card, tap your computer's case to release any of your body's static electricity. (You usually won't feel a static zap, but it's still a good precaution.) And don't pet the cat until you're through.

Don't let the cards bend while you're installing them. Doing so can damage their circuitry.

Computers expect only *one* video card. You drive it bonkers if you don't pull the old video card before adding the new one.

Handle cards by their edges only. The grease on your fingers can start eating away their electrical coating stuff.

Those harmless-looking little silver dots on the back of the card are really sharp metal pokers that can leave ugly scratches on your hands and blue language in the air.

Be sure to check Chapter 2 to make sure you're placing the right type of card into the right type of slot. Also, cards come in different lengths and thicknesses; you may need to rearrange your cards' positions to accommodate the different sizes.

If you're feeling particularly confident, just read the numbered steps and carry out each task. If any of the steps raise perspiration along your brow, read the paragraphs below each step for more information. (Then wipe your brow — you don't want any moisture on your computer's parts.)

To install a new card, follow these steps:

1. **Turn off your computer, unplug it, and remove the cover.**

   Please turn off your computer first and unplug it. You don't want to see sparks.

   Either four or five screws hold the cover onto your computer. The first four screws live in each of the four corners, as seen in Figure 10-2. Sometimes a fifth screw lives along the top edge, right in the middle; it might have to be removed, as well.

   Don't remove the screws closest to that round opening where the fan lives. Those screws hold the fan in place, not the cover.

   After removing the screws, slide the case toward the front of the computer. Give it a good tug and it should slide off.

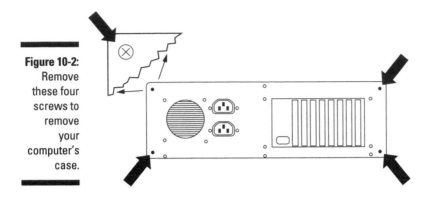

Figure 10-2:
Remove
these four
screws to
remove
your
computer's
case.

2. Find the correct slot for your card.

See the row of slots extending from the back wall of your computer, as in Figure 10-3? Your new card plugs into one of those slots. Don't confuse your computer's *expansion slots* — the slots where the cards plug in — with your computer's *memory slots* — the small slots where little three-inch memory-chip gizmos plug in.

The expansion slots butt up against the little vertical windows on the back of your computer; the memory slots don't.

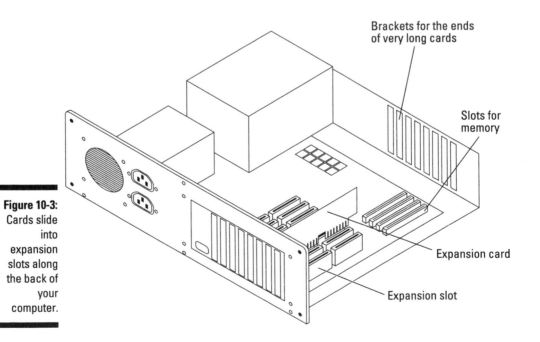

Brackets for the ends
of very long cards

Slots for
memory

Expansion card

Expansion slot

Figure 10-3:
Cards slide
into
expansion
slots along
the back of
your
computer.

Find the slot that has openings to match the tabs protruding from the bottom of your card. (See Figure 10-1.)

You might have to shuffle your old cards around until there's room for the new one to slide on in.

3. Remove the slot's cover.

To keep dust from flying in through the back of your computer, a flat little silver thing blocks the opening next to each unused slots. With a small screwdriver, remove the screw holding the cover in place. Keep the screw handy; you'll need it later to hold the card in place.

Dropped the screw inside your computer? Oh, no! Head for the end of this chapter for tips on fishing it back out.

Keep the flat little silver thing; it goes in your new spare computer parts drawer.

4. Push the card into its slot.

If you've read the card's manual, find the right switches and jumpers on the card and move them to the right places. Didn't read the manual? Don't worry — most cards don't make you fiddle with switches and jumpers until *after* you've installed them and they aren't working right.

Holding the card by its edges, position it over the slot, as in Figure 10-4. (The card in this figure happens to be a 16-bit expansion card.) The edge with the shiny metal bracket should face toward the back of your computer.

Slowly push the card down into the slot. You might need to rock the card back and forth gently to get it lined up right. Then give the card a good, steady push. You feel a satisfying "poomph" vibration when it pops in and comes to rest. Don't force the card if it doesn't feel right, though.

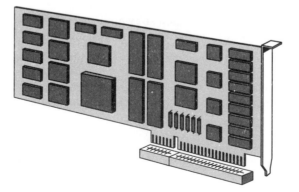

Figure 10-4:
Hold the card gently over the slot to make sure the tabs and slots line up exactly.

When the card is resting in its socket, make sure it's not touching any adjacent cards. Cards that touch can kill each other.

5. **Secure the card in the slot with the screw.**

Whether your card cost $30 or $3,000, it's held in place by a single screw — the same screw that held on that small slot cover back in Step 3.

Don't blow off this step; that little screw serves as an electrical connection between the card and your computer's chassis.

6. **Plug the computer back in, turn it on, and run the card's installation software.**

Don't touch anything inside your computer when the case is off and it's plugged in. Bad things can happen.

If the card works, great! Put the cover back on and start playing. If it doesn't work, try these things:

✔ Check the card's manual to make sure the card's switches and jumpers are set right. ("Hit Chapter 16 for switch-flipping tips," he said three times quickly.)

✔ After running the card's installation software, you probably have to reboot your computer before the card comes to life. Most card software puts a driver in one of your computer's special files. Your computer only reads these files when it's first turned on or when it's rebooted. (Press the Ctrl, Alt, and Delete keys simultaneously to reboot.)

✔ It can take some fiddling before a card starts behaving. Nine times out of ten, however, the problem lies with the software. The card may be sitting in the slot just perfectly, but the software is arguing with some other software or is trying to talk to the card on the wrong channel. (That's what all that switch-flipping is for.)

✔ If your video card's installation software lists weird things like *vertical scanning frequencies,* troop ahead to the end of Chapter 12 for moral support.

✔ Many cards simply provide connectors for cables. Look for little screws to fasten the cable down tight once it's connected. If these cables aren't fastened down tight, a simple jostle can jar them loose — leading to a half-hour of hair-pulling when the software suddenly stops working.

Uh, I Dropped a Screw Inside There Somewhere

Unless you're adding a card to an orbiting space shuttle, gravity works against you. One fumble sends a screw plunging deep into your computer's mechanical viscera.

Don't leave it there; the screw can roll against sensitive internal parts, causing your computer great pain. Instead, try these screw-retrieval tricks:

1. **If you can see the screw, try to grab it with tweezers.**

   Tweezers not long enough? Try wrapping tape, sticky side out, around the end of a pencil. If you can press the tape firmly against the screw, the screw may stick long enough to be pulled out.

2. **Can't see the screw? Tilt your computer gently.**

   The screw may roll to a visible location.

3. **Still stuck? Pick up the computer's case with both hands, turn it upside down slowly, and tilt it from side to side.**

   Watch closely so that you spot the screw when it falls out.

4. **No sign of it? Maybe the screw didn't land inside the computer after all.**

   Check the table area, carpet, and adjacent trash cans.

If the screw is still nowhere to be found, repeat Step 3 enough times until you're *sure* it's no longer inside your computer. The screw must have found a new karmic plateau and left this world. (Most computers stores sell replacement screws.)

Chapter 11

Installing CD-ROM Drives

● ●

In This Chapter

▶ Controlling CD-ROM drives through sound cards

▶ Installing an external CD-ROM drive

▶ Installing an internal CD-ROM drive

● ●

*S*o you finally took the plunge and bought a CD-ROM drive, eh? You won't regret it. *After* you've successfully installed it, that is. This chapter covers the nitty-gritty of installation. (See Chapter 6 for any other information about CD-ROM drives.)

Should I Hook Up My CD-ROM Drive to My Sound Card?

Computers don't normally come with places to plug in CD-ROM drives. So some sound card manufacturers graciously stepped in to solve the problem.

Many sound cards come with a special place — a CD-ROM *controller* — to plug in your CD-ROM drive's cable. The bad news: that CD-ROM controller doesn't always work.

The only way to know is to check your sound card's manual. Some sound cards only work with Sony and Mitsumi brand CD-ROM drives. Other cards, like some of the early Sound Blasters, only work with Panasonic drives. And still other cards only work with weird brands nobody has ever heard of.

✔ If you already have a sound card, check to see what CD-ROM drives the card can support. If you like one of those drives, buy it, take it home, and connect it to your sound card.

✔ If you already have a sound card but you don't like any of the drives the card supports, no need to fret. Just buy a controller card for the CD-ROM drive you want. You don't *have* to control CD-ROM drives through sound cards. But controller cards are pretty cheap, and they rarely argue with sound cards.

- If you already have a CD-ROM drive that's working well, buy any sound card you want. New sound cards won't affect working CD-ROM drives.

- Sound cards and CD-ROM drives that say SCSI somewhere on the box work with a wider variety of drives than those that *don't* say SCSI.

- If you want your sound card to support a SCSI CD-ROM drive and a bunch of other SCSI devices in a chain, blow off the sound card's connector altogether. Instead, use a higher-quality SCSI-2 card from Adaptec.

- More of this SCSI stuff is nailed down in Chapter 2.

How Do I Install a CD-ROM Drive?

Tools you need: Two hands, a screwdriver, and a controller card — either built-in to a sound card or on a card by its own

Cost: Anywhere from $200-$600

Stuff to watch out for:

Two types of CD-ROM drives are available: internal and external. Check out Chapter 6 if you don't believe me.

External CD-ROM drives come in little boxes that take up room on your desktop. The box sprouts two cords. One goes to the back of your computer, and the other, a power cord, plugs into a wall socket.

Internal CD-ROM drives slide into the front of your computer, right next to a floppy drive. Because the CD-ROM drive lives inside, it grabs its power from inside your computer: no need for a power cord.

No matter which drive you choose, you still have to open your computer's case. Don't think an external drive lets you off *that* easily.

Installing an external CD-ROM drive

External CD-ROM drives simply plug into your computer like a printer — there isn't much to go wrong.

To install an external CD-ROM drive, follow these steps:

1. **Turn off your computer, unplug it, and remove its case.**

   Turn off your computer and unplug it. Please.

   Four or five screws hold the cover onto your computer. The first four screws are in each of the corners, as seen in Figure 11-1. (Sometimes a fifth screw lives along the top edge, right in the middle. It might have to be removed, as well.)

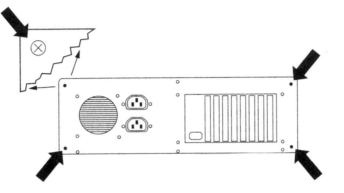

Figure **11-1:** Remove these four screws to remove your computer's case.

   After removing the screws, slide the case toward the front of the computer. Give the case a good tug and it should slide off.

   Don't remove the screws closest to the round opening where the fan lives. These screws are for your computer's internal *power supply*, not its case.

2. **Plug the CD-ROM drive's card into one of your available slots and screw it down.**

   Never installed a card before? Troop to Chapter 10 for the details.

3. **Replace your computer's cover and plug in your PC.**

   Don't touch anything inside your computer while it's plugged in. Keep any curious cats away, as well.

4. **Connect the CD-ROM drive's cable between the drive and the newly installed connector.**

   You should find a thick cord in the drive's box. One side of the cord plugs into the new connector you've just added to the back of your PC; the other end fits into the back of the CD-ROM drive's case.

   Some CD-ROM drive boxes have *two* places to plug in the cable. Flip a coin; either place usually works, and plugging it into the wrong one can't hurt anything.

   If you saved money and bought a *bare* drive through the mail, you won't have a card or a cable. You'll have to buy them at a computer store.

5. Plug in the CD-ROM drive and turn it on.

Keep rummaging in the drive's box for its power cord — it usually looks just like the black one that your computer uses. No spare wall outlets? Head for the computer store and buy a power strip. These marvelous gadgets turn one outlet into six.

6. Turn on your computer.

7. When the computer boots up, install the CD-ROM's software.

This usually entails sliding the CD-ROM drive's floppy disk in Drive A (or Drive B) and typing **INSTALL** or **SETUP**, depending on what your manual says, and pressing Enter.

Some programs ask you a bunch of questions; others do everything automatically. But the end result is the same: the program sticks a *device driver* into your computer's CONFIG.SYS file and reboots your computer. (That driver stuff is hammered down in Chapter 16; if you spot the word MSCDEX on a menu somewhere, head for the end of this chapter for an explanation.)

✔ When your computer is first turned on, it looks for the attached CD-ROM drive. If the drive is turned off, the computer won't be able to find it — and the computer won't bother looking for it again.

✔ The solution? Turn the drive on — and reboot your computer. This time, the computer should be able to find it. (You have to reboot your computer, or it won't notice that you've turned the drive on this time.)

For a few extra tips and tricks, head to the end of the "Installing an internal CD-ROM drive" section in this chapter.

Installing an internal CD-ROM drive

Internal drives can give you twice as much grief as external drives. First, internal drives plug into a card — either your sound card or their own controller card. Second, internal drives are wedged into a *drive bay* — the chunk of space already partially taken up by your floppy drives.

To install an internal CD-ROM drive, follow these steps:

1. Turn off your computer, unplug it, and remove its case.

If you're connecting the drive to a sound card, skip ahead to Step 3. Otherwise, go to Step 2.

If you're not sure how the case comes off, check out Step 1 of the "Installing an external CD-ROM drive," a few pages back.

2. **Plug the CD-ROM drive's card into one of your available slots and screw it down.**

   Never added a card before? Chapter 10 covers card installation, preparation, and shuffling.

3. **Slide the CD-ROM drive into the front of your computer.**

   This instructional step often inspires comments such as, "This guy's *nuts*," "Slide it in *there*?" "*Where?*" Hang tight, though.

   You need a vacant *drive bay,* which is an opening where disk drives normally live. Desktop computers come with two or three drive bays; tower computers — the tall, skinny computers — often come with twice as many.

   You push drives into bays from the front side of the computer. Figure 11-2 shows two floppy drives taking up two bays; the installer is pushing in the second drive. Your CD-ROM drive slides in the empty bay below it. So set the back end of the drive into your vacant bay and start pushing it in from the front. The CD-ROM drive should slide in easily.

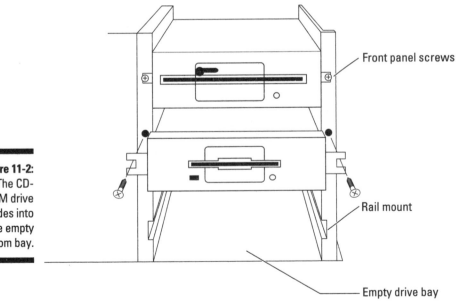

Figure 11-2:
The CD-ROM drive slides into the empty bottom bay.

Front panel screws

Rail mount

Empty drive bay

Don't have a drive bay for your CD-ROM drive? Buy a *Combo Drive* from Teac. It squeezes a 3½-inch floppy drive and a 5¼-inch floppy drive into a small unit that fits in one drive bay. Doing this immediately frees up enough room for an internal CD-ROM drive.

If the CD-ROM drive is not wide enough to fill the drive bay, you need *rails*, which are available at your local computer store. Screw the rails onto the drive and slide the rails into the grooves on the sides of the drive bay. You might have to push some cables out of the way first, but try not to disconnect anything.

Some CD-ROM drives can be mounted sideways, if your computer only has a sideways bay available. (If your computer has a sideways bay, the bay is next to the power supply or just to the left of the floppy drives.) Check the drive's manual before mounting it sideways, though; some don't work on their sides, especially the ones that don't use caddies.

Got the drive sitting in the bay? Don't screw it down yet! You still need to attach the cables, coming up in the next step.

4. **Connect the cables.**

   You need to fiddle with three cables.

   First, connect the cable between the CD-ROM drive and either its controller card or your sound card. This flat *ribbon* cable should fit onto the plugs only one way. (This cable lets your drive send information to your computer.) The connectors on both the card and the drive should look like Figure 11-3.

Figure 11-3:
A connector found on your CD-ROM drive and it's controller card or your sound card.

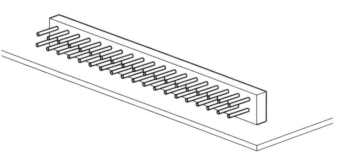

Second, rummage around the tentacles of wires leading from your power supply (that big silver thing in the back right corner). One of those cables (use any cable that fits) connects to a connector on the CD-ROM drive to give it power. The cable and connector look like the ones in Figure 11-4.

Last, plug a small three-, four-, or five-wire sound cable from the CD-ROM drive to your sound card. Your sound card can now pick up music coming from the CD-ROM drive. The cable and connector look like the small ones in Figure 11-4.

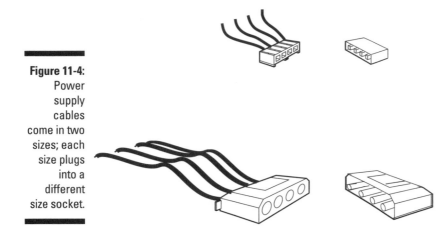

Figure 11-4:
Power supply cables come in two sizes; each size plugs into a different size socket.

You might have to slide the drive in and out of its bay in order to fasten all the connectors in the right place.

5. Screw the drive in place.

When you're sure that the cables are connected correctly and the drive is in the right spot, screw the sucker down.

Some drives screw in from the sides, but most fasten with two screws along the front, just like the floppy drive in Figure 11-2.

6. Replace your computer's cover, plug the computer in, and turn it on.

7. When the computer boots up, install the CD-ROM's software.

This usually requires sliding the CD-ROM drive's floppy disk in Drive A (or Drive B) and typing **INSTALL** or **SETUP**, depending on what your manual says, and pressing Enter.

Some programs ask you a bunch of questions; others do everything automatically. But the end result is the same: the program sticks a *device driver* into your computer's CONFIG.SYS file and reboots your computer. (That driver stuff is hammered down in Chapter 16.)

The software should take over the rest of the installation chores. If it tosses bits of weirdness like *interrupts* or *drivers,* page on ahead to Chapter 16.

If Windows doesn't recognize your new drive, hit Chapter 17 for tips on how to introduce them to each other.

Sending an External CD-ROM Drive's Sound to the Sound Card

Most CD-ROM drives have headphone jacks, but this isn't the best way to listen to CDs. Send your CD-ROM drive's sound to your *sound card* so that the sound can fill the room.

If you're using an *internal* CD-ROM drive — and you followed Step 4 in the installation instructions — the CD-ROM drive should be sending its sound to the sound card through the four tiny wires.

If you're using an *external* CD-ROM drive, look for a *Y-cable* that came with the drive. Shown in Figure 11-5, the cable has a stereo ⅛-inch plug on one end and two RCA connectors on the other.

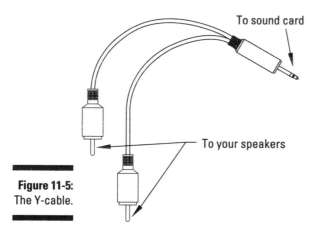

To sound card

To your speakers

Figure 11-5:
The Y-cable.

Found the cable? Then push the two RCA-connector-hat-things onto the two jack-head-things on the back of the drive. (Match the colors, if possible, by pushing the white plug onto the white jack, and red into red.) Then push the ⅛-inch plug into the sound card's input jack.

That's it.

If you plug your compact disc player's output into the sound card's Microphone jack, it's like screaming into your sound card's ear. It could damage the sound card, and it probably won't sound very good.

MSCDEX.EXE and Other Pesticides

This stuff is pretty technical, so don't read this section unless MSCDEX.EXE is giving you problems.

When CD-ROM drives first came out a few years back, Microsoft was stumped. How could they make DOS talk to these newfangled CD-ROM drives? So Microsoft came up with a translator program called MSCDEX.EXE. After running MSCDEX, your computer treats your CD-ROM drive just like any other drive. Most CD-ROM installation programs list MSCDEX in your AUTOEXEC.BAT file so that your computer loads MSCDEX automatically whenever it's turned on.

But there's more. Like any piece of new hardware attached to a computer, CD-ROM drives come with a *driver* — a piece of software that lets programs talk to the CD-ROM drive.

The CD-ROM installation program lists the driver in your computer's CONFIG.SYS file, where all the other drivers live. Your computer automatically loads those drivers every time it's turned on, as well.

Here's the line Toshiba's 3401 external drive put in my AUTOEXEC.BAT file:

```
C:\DOS\MSCDEX.EXE /D:MSCD000
```

Then the CD-ROM drive installation program put this line in my CONFIG.SYS file:

```
C:\UTIL\CD\DEV\MDSCD_FD.SYS /D:MSCD000 /N:1
```

See how the word /D:MSCD000 appears in each line? Technically known as a *D switch,* this little code word/number lets MSCDEX know which CD-ROM drive it's talking to. (Some energetic computer users have more than one.)

For example, one drive can use MSCD001 and the second drive can use MSCD002; in this way, DOS can tell which device driver controls which drive.

- MSCDEX has been bundled with DOS since version 6. It lives in your DOS directory.

- Even so, some CD-ROM drives come with a version of MSCDEX, and they use this version during the installation program.

- The result? You might get stuck using a version of MSCDEX that some part of your computer doesn't like, and things won't work right.

- The solution? Edit your AUTOEXEC.BAT file to try different versions of MSCDEX. If the one that came with DOS doesn't work, try the one that came with the drive.

✔ Don't run the MSCDEX command while you're using Windows; the command won't work right. Keep it in your AUTOEXEC.BAT file so that it loads automatically and you don't have to worry about it.

✔ If you're using MS-DOS 5.0 and MSCDEX Version 2.20 — the version of MSCDEX that comes with DOS 6.0 — you need C:\DOS\SETVER.EXE in your AUTOEXEC.BAT file. Otherwise your computer will mumble something about an incorrect DOS version. (MSCDEX 2.21, the one that comes with DOS 6.2, works with MS-DOS 5.0 *without* needing that SETVER nonsense.)

✔ Don't know what version of MSCDEX you're using? Type **MSCDEX** at a bare DOS prompt — that C:\> thing. Your computer should throw the version number at you.

✔ When inspecting your AUTOEXEC.BAT file on a rainy day, make sure that the MSCDEX command appears *before* the SMARTDRV command. This way, SMARTDRV knows you have a CD-ROM drive, and it uses a *cache* to speed up the starting process

A Friend Sold Me His Old CD-ROM Drive, But There's No Driver!

Like a child that won't sleep without the right teddy bear, a CD-ROM drive won't work until you have its *driver* — the special piece of software that lets software talk to it.

If you have a modem and you know how to download software from a computer bulletin board, you might be able to scrounge up a driver from the company's BBS. Here are a few numbers to call with your modem:

NEC BBS	508-635-4706
Philips BBS	310-532-6436
Sony BBS	408-955-5107

Or if you're a member of CompuServe, head for the CD-ROM Forum (**GO CDFORUM**). You'll find a motley assortment of drivers in the file libraries, ready for grabbing.

Blatant spousal plug: if modems sound murky, pick up my wife's book, *Modems For Dummies.* It runs you through the whole procedure, step by step.

Chapter 12

Installing a New Monitor

. . . .

In This Chapter

▶ Hooking up a new monitor

▶ Introducing the monitor to the video card

. . . .

*I*f you're looking for translations for all that technical gobbledygook surrounding video cards and monitors or you just need some general information, head for Chapter 4. This chapter sticks with something not so technical: where to plug in that new monitor and how to introduce it to your video card.

Installing a New Monitor

Tools you need: Screwdriver (optional), two hands (mandatory)

Cost: Anywhere from $150 to $3,000

Stuff to watch out for:

If you're installing a new video card as well as a new monitor, head to Chapter 10 for card-installation tips. In fact, if you don't upgrade your video card, your expensive new monitor will probably look the same as your old, ugly monitor. After all, a monitor displays only what the video card tells it to. After the video card is nestled snugly in place, head back here.

To install a new monitor, follow these steps:

1. **Turn off your computer, unplug your old monitor, and then unplug the monitor's cord from your computer.**

   The monitor plugs in to a little connection on the back of your computer (that connection is the butt-end of your video card, by the way). You may need a tiny screwdriver to loosen the tiny screws; other cords have bigger thumbscrews for people with big thumbs.

Sometimes the cord is easy to unplug: it simply falls off the back of your computer, just like it does whenever you rearrange the monitor on your desk. (That's why you should fasten down the tiny screws.)

Remember which little port the monitor's cable is plugged in to; that's where your new monitor's cable needs to go as well.

2. Remove the old monitor from your desktop.

But where do you put it? Probably in the garage, next to the old toaster oven. After a few months, feel free to call the Salvation Army or a similar group; the best charities drop by to pick up the stuff personally. Feel free to give them the toaster oven as well.

3. Remove the new monitor from the box.

Monitors always come in huge boxes with *lots* of packaging. The Styrofoam corner protectors and colored plastic wrap make nice modern sculptures.

If you're merely throwing away the packaging, however, scrutinize it carefully to make sure that you're not throwing away any cables. Cables sometimes come separately, wrapped up in hard-to-see little plastic bags.

4. Place the new monitor on your desk and plug it in the video port, as shown in Figure 12-1.

The port has 15 little holes in it, if you like to count things.

15-hole female
(fatter)

Figure 12-1:
Most monitors plug into a port like this.

If the monitor cable doesn't come attached to the monitor, plug it in — it only fits one way. Make sure that the cable is fastened securely to both the monitor and the computer.

If you have a tiny screwdriver, replace any of the screws you removed in Step 1. Cable not fitting? Then you're probably trying to plug it in the wrong place.

Swiveling monitors turn from side to side so that they're easy to see. Leave a little slack on the their cables so that a quick adjustment doesn't pull the cables off their connectors.

Most cables end in an oblong plug that is wider along one edge than the other. The wide edge of the plug almost always faces the side of your computer with the fan hole. Remember that, and you'll always know which end is right-side up.

Plug the monitor's power cord into the wall or a power strip, if you've finally given up and bought one of those, too.

5. **Turn on your monitor and then turn on your computer.**

   Your computer should start spewing words on-screen as it comes to life. Congratulations! You're almost through.

6. **Run your video card's configuration software.**

   Just like you need to tell magazines when you change your address, you need to tell your video card that you've changed monitors. Some video cards come with a program called CONFIG or something similar; others make you rerun their installation program.

   Either way, run the program that lets you tell the video card about your new monitor's special quirks. If you're lucky, the card's installation program lists your new monitor by name. Choose it from the list, and the card automatically knows how to squirt information properly for that monitor.

   If you're not lucky, you get to end the chapter the hard way — by going through the boring technical sidebar.

Quirky sync stuff

If your monitor says *multi* or *scan* somewhere in its name — multifrequency, multisync, ultrascan, ultra-multi, or something similar — it's probably a multiscan monitor. These versatile monitors can switch automatically from several different video modes, depending on what the software asks for.

However, your video card needs to know the monitor's *scan rates* so that it knows the proper way to squirt video information onto its screen.

Monitors fill the screen with pretty pictures by using line-by-line strokes, from top to bottom. The number of times per second that a monitor fills the entire screen is its *vertical scanning frequency*. A frequency of about 70 Hz is good — you don't notice much flicker on-screen. The bigger the number, the better.

Because different video modes pack different amounts of information on-screen, monitors use different vertical scan rates — also known as *refresh rates* — for each video mode.

The point? If your monitor isn't listed on your card's master list, you have to tell the card what refresh rate or frequency to use for each mode. So pull out your monitor's manual and start looking up *scan rates* or *scan frequencies*.

For example, the manual for my Dell UltraScan monitor lists the following scan rates:

640x480 at 60 Hz vertical refresh rate

800x600 at 56 Hz vertical refresh rate

1024x768 at 70 Hz vertical refresh rate

My ATI Graphics Ultra Pro video card's installation program didn't list the Dell monitor by its name, unfortunately, so I chose the software's Custom option. That menu listed several video modes and frequencies, so I picked the ones that matched the rates listed in the monitor's manual — stuff like 640x480 at 60 Hz vertical refresh rate. Don't choose any modes that are interlaced — they just make the screen flicker.

The program saved the new settings and automatically rebooted the computer when I pressed "Any Key" (the spacebar). When the computer came back to life, everything worked fine.

If your experience isn't as sweet, try choosing different software settings until you come up with some that work. You may have to fiddle with your monitor's screen-positioning switches until the screen is centered just right.

Finally, when paging through your monitor's manual for its frequencies, look for the numbers that have *Hz* after them, like 70 Hz. The numbers listed before *kHz* are *horizontal* scanning frequencies and are not the ones you need.

Chapter 13

Hooking Up Everything to Your Stereo

In This Chapter

▶ Playing your computer's sound through your home stereo

▶ Recording records and tapes onto your computer

*M*ost sound cards do not come with speakers. And the ones that do? They usually sound like squawking menus at drive-up fast-food joints. When you get tired of those french-fry-sized speakers — or if their cheap plastic casings break when little Jeffy tosses them on the floor — this chapter shows you how to hook up your sound card to your home stereo for some *real* sound.

Playing Your Sound Card through Your Home Stereo

Chapter 3 explains the advantages of hearing your computer programs played back through your stereo. But the hardest part of connecting your sound card to your home stereo involves the cord: how do you hide the darn thing so nobody trips on it?

If you have carpet, push the cord into the crack between the carpet and the edge of the wall. Use the right tool for the job — a spoon handle can push the cord deep into the crack along the base of the wall. No carpet? Buy a rug. But don't leave the cord lying out in the open. Somebody not only will trip over it, but also will pull your sound card out in the process.

Tools you need: A Y-cable (a ⅛-inch stereo plug with two RCA phono plugs, usually red and green; see Figure 13-1); one hand

Cost: About $5 to $10, if the sound card didn't already come with the correct cable

Stuff to watch out for:

Remember to keep the volume turned down on the stereo and the sound card while connecting the cables — you don't want to pop anything.

To play your sound card through your stereo, follow these steps:

1. **Turn down the volume on your stereo and sound card.**

   Turn down the stereo's volume knob, usually pretty easy to find.

   If you can't find your sound card's volume knob — which is either some-where on the back of the card or through its software program — simply turn off your computer (after saving your work, of course).

2. **Find the correct cable.**

   Chances are, you'll need a shielded Y-adapter cable, shown in Figure 13-1. This cable has a stereo ⅛-inch plug on one end and two RCA phono plugs on the other end. You can find the cable at Radio Shack. (The six-foot cord is part number 42-2481; the three-footer is number 42-2475.)

   The best sound card manufacturers throw the cord in for free; others make you head to Radio Shack (which is *charging* for its catalogs now!). If your computer and stereo aren't very close together, pick up a 12-foot stereo cable (part number 42-2356).

3. **Plug the ⅛-inch stereo plug into your sound card's speaker jack.**

   Hopefully your sound card has all its little jacks labeled so that you know which little hole does what. If it doesn't, you have to open the card's manual. (After you figure out which jack is which, head for the Cheat Sheet at the book's front so that you can write down which jack does what.)

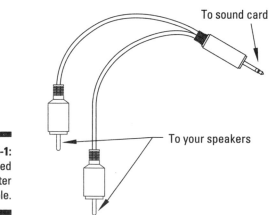

To sound card

To your speakers

Figure 13-1:
A shielded
Y-adapter
cable.

4. **Plug the two RCA phono plugs into the stereo's Aux Input or Tape Input jacks.**

Check the back of your stereo for some free input jacks; you should see several pairs of stubby little metal heads. Use the Aux Input or the Tape Input jacks — whichever is not being used.

One jack of the pair is probably red — push the cord's red plug into that jack. The other jack is probably black, white, or green — this jack is for your other plug, no matter what color it is.

Don't plug your sound card into the Phono jack, though. Your stereo doesn't expect such a strong signal from that jack. (If you throw caution to the wind and plug the cord in there anyway, keep the card's volume *very* low.)

5. **Turn on the stereo and switch it to Tape Input or Aux Input.**

Turn the stereo's input select switch to the jack you've used, either Tape or Aux.

6. **Play something on the sound card and adjust the volume.**

Run any program that has a lot of sound and start gradually turning up the volume on your stereo and sound card. If everything is hooked up right, the sound should start filling the room.

- If the sound doesn't start filling the room, make sure that the stereo is turned to Aux Input or Tape Input — or whatever input jack you plugged the sound card into. If the stereo is not turned to the correct input switch, your sound card won't come through. (Oh, is the stereo plugged in and turned on?)

- Keep checking your connections, as well. Make sure that the ⅛-inch stereo plug is sitting in the sound card's Speaker or Headphone jack — none of the card's other jacks will work. (Some cards label the Speaker or Headphone jack with the word *Out.*)

If somebody is walking from left to right in a computer game but the sound goes from right to left, your speaker plugs are reversed. Reversing the plugs on your stereo should fix it. For programs without stereo sound tracks, the positioning doesn't matter.

Some sound cards, such as Creative Labs Sound Blaster 16 SCSI-2, let you move a jumper on the card to disable the card's *internal amplifier*. Disabling the amplifier makes the sound come through your stereo a little bit cleaner. (Never fiddled with a jumper? Jump ahead to Chapter 16.)

Playing Your Home Stereo through Your Sound Card

How many years have you been telling yourself, "I've got to record that Beatles album and play it backwards"? When you're ready to see if Paul really *is* dead, try recording your tapes, records, or CDs to your hard disk — Windows' Sound Recorder can play any of your recordings backwards.

Even if you're not into the Beatles, you'll still be able to record snippets of songs to your hard drive and assign the snippets to events in Windows (a task tackled in Chapter 18). If you're not in-the-know about sound cards, head for Chapter 3 for the full scoop.

Tools you need: Two hands and a Y-cable (⅛-inch stereo plug with two RCA plugs, usually red and green)

Cost: About $5 to $10, if the sound card doesn't come with the correct cable

Stuff to watch out for:

The hardest part of playing your home stereo through your sound card is figuring out which jacks to plug everything into. If the jacks on the back of your stereo or sound card aren't marked, unfortunately you'll have to pull out their manuals.

Follow these steps to connect a cable from your stereo's output jacks to your stereo's input jacks:

1. **Turn down the volume on everything and find the correct cable.**

   This stuff is all covered in Steps 1 and 2 of the preceding procedure. (See Figure 13-1.)

2. **Plug the ⅛-inch stereo plug into your sound card's Input or In jack.**

   Hopefully, your sound card has all its little jacks labeled so that you know which little hole does what. If it doesn't, you have to open the manual. (Then head to the Cheat Sheet in the front of this book so that you can write down which jack does what.)

3. **Push the RCA phono plugs in to the stereo's Tape Output or Aux Output jacks.**

   Check the back of your stereo for its Output jacks; you should see pairs of stubby little metal heads. Some are red — for the red plug; others are black or white — for the other plug.

No Output jacks? You may have to unplug your stereo's tape recorder from your stereo so that you can use its jacks. After all, your computer is serving as a makeshift tape recorder.

4. **Play some music on your stereo and listen in through your sound card's speakers.**

Sound should start coming through your sound card's speakers. You may have to fiddle with the stereo's buttons to make sure that they're sending information out the Tape Output or Aux Output jacks.

◆ If you don't hear anything, check out the sound card's mixer software. Look for the Line In or Line spot and slide up the little controller.

◆ Keep checking your cable connections, as well. Make sure that the cord is plugged into the sound card's speakers, headphone, or Out jack — none of the others will work.

◆ Sound takes up *lots* of space on your hard drive. If you're pressed for space, cut back on the quality a bit to keep the files small: record the files in 8-bit mode, mono, and at 11Hz. (You can usually choose these options from the menu on your sound card's recording program.)

◆ If your computer has a CD-ROM drive — and you've hooked it up as described in Chapter 11 — you can record your Beatles songs straight from your Beatles CDs. You don't need to use your stereo's output jacks.

Chapter 14

Hooking Up a Camcorder or VCR to Your Computer

....

In This Chapter
▶ Choosing the correct cables
▶ Connecting a camcorder or VCR to a video capture card
▶ Connecting a camcorder or VCR to a sound card

....

Connecting a camcorder or a VCR to your computer is easy if you have the correct cables, sound cards, and capture cards. What surprises a lot of people (including me) is that video capture cards grab movies off your camcorder or VCR but don't grab the sound at the same time. If you want to hear a wailing baby during your spoon-feeding movie, you need a sound card, too. This chapter goes into detail about the correct cards and cables to use so that your camcorder and VCR work well with your computer. (If you're wondering why everyone is fussing over video capture cards, go back to Chapter 5.)

Choosing the Correct Cables

Some video capture cards come with their own cables; other manufacturers figure that your camcorder already comes with cables, so they don't include any with the video capture cards. But all the video capture cards I've seen can grab video by using either S-video or composite cables.

S-video cable: Super-VHS and Hi-8 camcorders and VCRs shoot video through something called an *S-video cable*. It's almost always black, with a plug on each end that looks like the one in Figure 14-1. If your camera has S-video, use it because it makes better-quality movies. (The jack is sometimes called a 4-pin DIN jack by the geekish.)

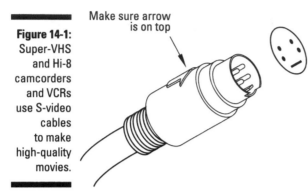

Make sure arrow is on top

Figure 14-1:
Super-VHS
and Hi-8
camcorders
and VCRs
use S-video
cables
to make
high-quality
movies.

Composite cable: If your equipment doesn't have an S-video jack, you are shooting your video through the alternative cable, called either *composite*, *RCA phono*, or just plain *video cable*. Shown in Figure 14-2, a composite cable is usually yellow and looks just like the cables collecting spider webs on the back of your home stereo.

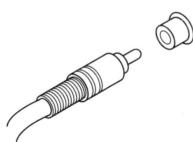

Figure 14-2:
The less-
expensive
VCRs and
camcorders
use
composite
cables to
send video
back and
forth.

Don't forget that you need a cable for your sound card, too, or you'll be recording silent films. Sound cards need a shielded Y-cable, with a ⅛-inch stereo plug on one end and two RCA phono plugs on the other, as shown in Figure 14-3. If your sound card didn't come with this cable, you can find one at Radio Shack. (The six-foot cord is part number 42-2481; the three-foot cord is part number 42-2475.)

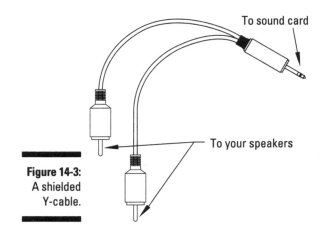

To sound card

To your speakers

Figure 14-3:
A shielded
Y-cable.

If your computer and VCR aren't very close together, you'd better pick up a
phono jack extension cable (see Figure 14-4). This cable has an RCA phono plug
on one end and a RCA phono jack on the other, with up to 12 feet of cable
between them. The cable comes in handy when your computer and VCR are on
opposite sides of the room.

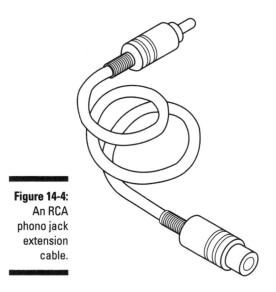

Figure 14-4:
An RCA
phono jack
extension
cable.

- Do you have a mono camcorder or VCR that uses composite jacks? You can get by with an inexpensive *A/V cable*. The cable consists of two wires (usually yellow and white); each wire ends with an RCA phono jack.

- You usually don't have to worry about cables. Your camcorder or VCR should have been packaged with the correct type.

- If you've lost your cables, you can find replacements at Radio Shack that cost between $5 and $17. (S-video cables are the expensive ones.)

- S-video cables plug in only one way — the right way. If the plug is not sliding smoothly into the jack, don't force it.

- Composite cables plug in any old way. Just push 'em on in.

- Finally, try not to use cables that are longer than 12 feet because you can lose some of your sound quality. (Gold-plated connectors help, too, if you want the *best*.)

Connecting a Camcorder or a VCR to Your Computer

Tools you need: Two hands, a sound card, a Y-cable for your sound card, and either an S-video or composite cable (both described in the preceding section).

Cost: $5 to $15 for cables, $400 to $700 for video capture cards (or a few thousand dollars for the *good* ones)

Stuff to watch out for:

Camcorders like to plunge toward the floor unannounced. Make sure yours is positioned securely on the desk or, better yet, on a tripod. To keep people from tripping over the wires, keep the cables strung along your desk, not draped along the floor.

Also, try to keep your video cables away from any power cords; power cords can introduce static.

To connect a camcorder or a VCR to your computer, do the following:

1. **Turn down the sound on your sound card.**

   You are connecting cables to your sound card, and you don't want to hear ugly pops.

2. **Find the correct cables for your video capture card and sound card.**

   Described in this chapter's first section, you need a Y-cable for the sound card and either an S-video or a composite cable for the video capture card.

3. **Connect the video cable between the Output jack on your camcorder/ VCR and the video capture card.**

   The S-video cable fits only one way; don't force it. Use either the S-video or the composite cable, but not *both*. Some cards don't like it when you use two different cables, and the movies don't look as good.

   Make sure that you're plugging the cable into your camcorder's/VCR's *Output* jacks. You want to grab information *from* them, not put information in them.

   If you haven't installed your video capture card yet, head for Chapter 10 (same goes for the sound card).

4. **Push the ⅛-inch stereo plug into your sound card's Input or In jack.**

   Don't know which sound card hole does what? You'd better check the card's manual. Then write the information down on the Cheat Sheet in the front of this book so that you never have to hunt through the manual again.

5. **Plug the RCA phono plugs into the camcorder's/VCR's Audio Output jacks.**

   Check the back of your camcorder or VCR for its Audio Output jacks. Do you see the pair of stubby little metal heads? One is probably red — for the red plug; the others are black or white — for the other plug.

   If your camcorder/VCR isn't stereo, you see only one jack — that makes it easy to find the right one.

6. **Play back a recorded tape on the camcorder/or VCR.**

7. **Look for the movie in Video for Windows.**

   If everything is hooked up correctly, you should see and hear the movie playing back in the Windows VidCap program.

   ✔ If the Windows VidCap video capture program is giving you problems, head for Chapter 20.

   ✔ If you don't hear anything, check out your sound card's mixing program. Chances are the mixer's Input or Line In volumes need to be turned up.

   ✔ Still not working? Head for Chapter 16 if things are looking serious.

Chapter 15

Hooking Up Stuff to a TV

• •

In This Chapter

▶ Choosing the correct cables

▶ Watching PC programs on a TV set

• •

*B*y now, just about everyone has heard the corporate types rubbing their palms together in anticipation over the upcoming merger of technology: your TV, telephone, computer, and microwave will soon turn into one big box so that people can download movies onto their TVs through the phone lines, keep track of the transactions on their computers, and reach into the monitors to grab a sandwich when the nights run long.

Chapter 8 explained the problems in linking your computer to a TV set. This chapter explains how to link them in case you want to hook them up anyway.

Choosing the Correct Cables

To see your PC programs on your TV, you need a converter, such as the ones described in Chapter 8. But you also need a cable to connect the TV and the converter. And where do you plug the cable in to your TV set? Most TVs offer one of the following four choices of jacks: S-video jack, composite jack, cable/antenna jack, and VCR jack.

S-video: Used by Super-VHS and Hi-8 camcorders and VCRs, *S-video connections* provide the highest-quality video. If your TV has an S-video jack, you see a small, round, flat spot with four holes, as shown in Figure 15-1.

If your converter also has an S-video jack, use an S-video cable to connect the two. The S-video cable is almost always black, with such plugs as the one in Figure 15-1. (Some technical manuals refer to an S-video jack as a *4-pin DIN* jack. Sigh.)

Composite: No S-video jack on your TV? Then look for a *Video In* jack, also called a *composite* or *RCA phono jack* by the confused. Shown in Figure 15-2, a composite jack is usually yellow and looks just like those stubby jacks poking through the dust on the back of your home stereo.

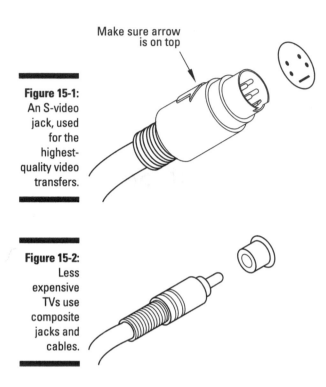

Make sure arrow
is on top

Figure 15-1:
An S-video
jack, used
for the
highest-
quality video
transfers.

Figure 15-2:
Less
expensive
TVs use
composite
jacks and
cables.

Cable/Antenna: Some of the older TVs don't have *S-video* or *composite* jacks. They only suck in their video through a cable from the wall (that cable TV stuff) or a rabbit-ears antenna (which dumps video into the TV through two screws).

In either case, you need something called an *RF converter*, found at Radio Shack or other electronics parts shops. Show the clerk the cable that came with your converter and then say whether you need to plug that cable into a TV with two screws (a 300-ohm input) or a TV with a cable-TV jack (a 75-ohm coax input.) Neither one should cost more than $10.

VCR: If your TV is already hooked up to a VCR, you probably don't need to go shopping. All but the most antique VCRs come with a Video In jack (a composite jack). Chances are, the cable that comes with your converter will plug into that jack. Your VCR subsequently shoots the picture into the TV.

If you're lucky, your converter has the cables you need. Some of them don't hook up to older TVs, though. So if your TV doesn't have S-video or Video In jacks, you probably have to shop for the RF converter.

> ✔ If your computer and TV aren't very close together, you'd better pick up some longer cords. Radio Shack carries 12-foot S-video and regular video cables for less than $20. (The S-video ones are the expensive ones.)
>
> ✔ S-video cables plug in only one way — the right way. If the plug is not sliding smoothly into the jack, don't force it.
>
> ✔ Composite cables plug in any old way. Just push 'em on in.

Watching PC Programs on a TV Set

Before you can watch PC programs on your TV, you need to buy a converter gadget — Chapter 8 provides background information on what the gadgets do, which one you need, and where to plug in the darn thing. Make sure that you're buying the correct converter for your country; you need either NTSC (for the United States and Japan), SECAM (for France and Eastern Europe), or PAL (for most other countries). Table 5-2 in Chapter 5 has a more detailed list of countries and their TV formats.

Don't have high expectations for quality unless you're just running graphics (movies or animation). Text and menu boxes (meaning almost anything in Microsoft Windows) will probably look terrible.

If you don't know what cable to use, check out the first section of this chapter.

Tools you need: Two hands, a converter card or box, converter software, video cable

Cost: From $300 to several thousand dollars

Stuff to watch out for:

Don't expect to see a very clean picture if you're running Windows. TV sets are meant to display animation and video, not text and lines. And expect to spend a few minutes tweaking the converter's knobs and software before the picture will look good.

To watch PC programs on a TV, follow these steps:

1. **Turn off your PC and monitor.**

2. **Install the converter.**

   If your converter comes on a card, see Chapter 10 for installation tips.

   If your converter comes in its own little box, just plug its AC adapter into the wall.

3. **Unplug your monitor from the wall and the computer; plug its cord into the converter's VGA Out port.**

   Your monitor still displays your programs, just as before. As your PC sends pictures to the monitor, however, the converter listens in and tosses the images on the TV screen.

4. **Plug a cord from your computer's VGA port into the converter's VGA In port.**

   The converter should come with a cord. Plug one end into your VGA card's port and plug the other end into the converter's VGA In port.

5. **Connect the TV to the converter.**

   Go back to the first section of this chapter if you're not sure which kind of cable you need: S-video, composite (video/phono), or a special RF adapter for those *really* old TVs.

   If you're using S-video or composite cable, tell the TV to listen to its Video jack, not its antenna. How? Some TVs make you push, flip, or twist a mechanical switch; others make you run through an on-screen menu by using their remote control. (Still others make you tune in channel 91 or 93.)

   Or, if you've plugged the cable into the VCR, make sure that you tell the VCR which Video jack it should be listening to so that it sends the correct signal to the TV.

6. **Run the software.**

   Most converters come with special software to reduce flicker from the TV. This software is usually a *memory resident* program, which needs to be loaded when your computer starts.

Now it's fiddling time. Unless you're blessed by the television-transmission gods, the picture probably looks terrible.

- Because of the differences between computer video and broadcast-quality video, the color on the TV probably doesn't look as good as the color on your monitor.

- Tweak some knobs on the TV and converter to adjust the picture. You can usually make the picture look too big, where part of the program hangs off the edges, or too small, where big black borders surround its edges.

- Don't try to run in a video mode higher than 640x480. Most cards can't handle a higher mode, and the ones that can have to chop out so much detail to squeeze it on the TV that everything looks weird. (Chapter 4 covers video modes.)

- Don't forget to connect your sound card to the home stereo, too, for the complete "home computer/theater" effect.

TIP

Keeping your TV screen from looking just awful

It's a shame, but televisions just can't keep up with your computer monitor for clarity and color in their pictures. For best results, though, try these tips:

◆ Stick with *graphics* programs — either games, animation/movies, or presentation programs. Avoid anything with text or lines (which means avoiding Windows, if at all possible).

◆ If you are using Windows, make all the fonts *big*. Windows normally keeps its fonts at about 12 points; move them up to at least 20 points. For example, to make File Manager's fonts bigger, choose Font from its Options menu. Then choose 20-point Helvetica.

◆ Don't use wallpaper; stick with the basic gray background so the flicker doesn't show up so badly.

◆ Keep Program Manager in a relatively small window in the center of your screen. Move any other windows toward the center of the screen, too — otherwise, they'll probably be hanging off the edge of your TV screen.

◆ Finally, if you're going to be giving a presentation, set up Windows a few hours beforehand and save your changes. This way, you don't have to enlarge your fonts, change your wallpaper, and change Program Manager's size while everybody in the boardroom yawns.

Chapter 16
It Doesn't Work!

· ·

In This Chapter

▶ Irritating IRQ conflicts

▶ Avoiding DMA and address conflicts

▶ Yanking jumpers

▶ Flipping DIP switches

▶ Fixing older cards

· ·

I'm sorry you're reading this chapter. If you're here, that means your computer is not working right. All that pending multimedia excitement has turned into pounding multimedia frustration. Chances are, the dumb part's stupid manual doesn't help. It probably says something about changing IRQs or DMAs or something even harder to remember.

This chapter explains what that dumb stuff means so that you know which parts to poke in order to get the show back on the road.

Irritating IRQ and Interrupt Conflicts

During a harried day, people respond to interruptions all day long. If the phone rings, they stop reading the paper and answer it. If the UPS man knocks on the door, it's time to set down the phone and open the door. If a speeding sports car crashes through the bay window, it's time to sign the UPS form and quickly move out of the way.

Harried multimedia computers also spend their lives responding to interruptions. In fact, an *interrupt*, often dubbed an *IRQ*, is a doorbell of sorts for gadgets to get your computer's attention. Push your mouse across your desk, for example, and the mouse rings your computer's doorbell — its interrupt — to tell the computer it has been moved. The computer takes note and updates the mouse-arrow's position on-screen.

A door has only one doorbell, but computers have 15 interrupts, each connected to a different gadget. If two gadgets — a sound card and a video capture card, for example — start ringing the same doorbell, the harried computer doesn't know which one needs attention. So it usually ignores both of them and keeps on reading the paper.

Unfortunately, new multimedia cards sometimes can't tell which interrupts have already been grabbed by other parts of your computer. And even if you install the card perfectly, it may not work. There is usually no physical harm done to the card; it just doesn't have an interrupt to get the computer's attention.

✔ If you're having an IRQ problem, you may be experiencing one or more of the following symptoms: the computer freezes up; there is no sound or a small snippet of sound constantly repeats; the installation program can't find what you've installed; or the thing just doesn't work.

✔ Not surprisingly, computers refer to their interrupts with a number, anywhere from 0 through 15.

✔ Disk drives, keyboards, hard drives, and other parts have already grabbed some of the available interrupts, which sometimes leaves only slim pickin's for all the incoming multimedia parts. Table 16-1 shows which part uses what interrupt.

✔ When you're installing a sound card or other new multimedia part and it wants an interrupt, start by telling the part to use IRQ 5 or IRQ 7. These interrupts are the two most popular.

✔ How do you tell gadgets to use different IRQs? For the most part, you move a jumper on the card or flip one of its DIP switches — techniques described later in this chapter. Other gadgets let you choose interrupts from their installation software.

✔ If you inadvertently choose an interrupt that another part is already holding on to, nothing explodes. Your new gadget just won't work. Keep trying different interrupts until one finally works. Then you're done. You don't need to bother with it again.

✔ If you don't feel like using trial and error to find an unused interrupt, write down which interrupts are already used up by your computer's gadgets. Then when a new IRQ-hungry part comes along, you know which ones are used up. The table on the Cheat Sheet at the front of this book is a handy spot to write down your IRQs. Write down parts like sound card and internal fax/modem in the first column and, in the second column, record the IRQs they've grabbed.

You don't like tables? Then just write down the IRQ number on the front of the gadget's manual. You'll need it later. Trust me.

Table 16-1	A List of Likely Interrupts to Grab	
Interrupt	*Owner*	*Comments*
IRQ 0	Timer	Used up
IRQ 1	Keyboard	Used up
IRQ 2	Motherboard	Usually used up
IRQ 3	COM 2, COM 4	Used up
IRQ 4	COM 1, COM 3	Used up
IRQ 5	Second printer port	*Try this one!*
IRQ 6	Floppy-disk controller	Used up
IRQ 7	First printer port	*For best results, give this one to your Sound Blaster-compatible sound card*
IRQ 8	Your computer's clock	Used up
IRQ 9	Network stuff	This one *may* be free (and if it is, the computer will call it IRQ 2; go figure)
IRQ 10	Nothing	*Try this one!*
IRQ 11	Nothing	*Try this one!* (SCSI cards like this one)
IRQ 12	Nothing	*Try this one!*
IRQ 13	Coprocessor	Usually used up
IRQ 14	Hard drive	Used up
IRQ 15	Nothing	*Try this one!*

Addresses and DMA Stuff

Some gadgets get greedy. They not only ask for things like an IRQ, described in the preceding section, but they also ask for more arcane bits of weirdness, such as an *address* or *DMA*. Some want a number for an address, some want a number for a DMA channel, and some want both.

Address: Your computer assigns an *address* to some of its parts so that it can find the parts later. Not all gadgets want or need their own address. But some newly installed gadgets ask for their own address, and expect you to know the road map off the top of your head.

Because your computer usually has plenty of addresses to spare, most gadgets simply choose an address at random, hoping that nothing else has grabbed it. But if the address is already claimed, the two parts start arguing and stop working.

DMA channel: The same thing happens when a newly installed gadget grabs a *DMA channel* that another gadget has already snagged. The gadgets simply don't work. The solution? Make your incoming part grab a different address or DMA. You usually need to fiddle with the card's jumpers or DIP switches. Other gadgets let you change them through their installation software, which is a lot easier than taking off the computer's case.

But which address or DMA should you choose? Sometimes a card's installation program offers a suggestion. If it doesn't, simply go by trial and error. Eventually, you'll stumble across an address that nobody has staked out.

✔ There is no harm done by choosing the wrong address or DMA. You won't break anything. The gadget just doesn't work until you've handed it an address or DMA that nobody is using. And some friendly cards even share DMAs.

✔ After you've chosen a DMA, address, or IRQ, write it down. (See the handy Cheat Sheet at the front of this book.) Some programs quiz you — for example, the program may ask you what IRQ your sound card uses. Unless you know, you are stuck.

✔ DMA stands for Direct Memory Address. Yawn. Some cards work best if you choose *16-bit* DMAs; others get by with an *8-bit* DMA. Try the 16-bit setting first, and if it freezes your computer, change it to the 8-bit option.

I/O addresses for *memory* and I/O addresses for *hardware* are different. Software — such as spreadsheets and word processors — looks for addresses in memory; hardware — such as sound cards and scanners — looks for hardware addresses. The two kinds of addresses, memory and hardware, are on completely different computer streets.

Jumper Bumping and DIP Switch Flipping

Did your software or manual tell you something like "Shunt Jumpers 5 and 6" or "Flip DIP switches 3, 5, and 8 to ON"? If so, then this is the section you need. You'd better grab some reading glasses or a magnifying glass. I'm talking *tiny* here.

Why is this stuff all so stupid?

The folks who made the first IBM computer didn't expect it to be a roaring success. They didn't expect people to hook them up to their camcorders ten years down the road. So the creators didn't make computers very easy to expand. And that's why adding new pieces to a computer is so complicated—you're trying to put a third story on a one-room fishing shanty.

The manufacturers understand this problem and try to help. Most new cards make a concerted effort to find out what IRQs are available. Some cards come with an installation program that scans your computer for free IRQs even before you install the card. Based on the results, it tells you what switches to flip. Other installation programs wait until after you've installed their cards, and then they scan the computer and choose the settings through a software menu.

Unfortunately, it's not easy to tell which cards are using what. Interrupts are used to get a computer's attention. If a card is not trying to get the computer's attention, then the installation program may not notice the card lurking in the background.

The solution? Patience. Eventually, you'll find a solution that works.

One last thing: if you're using DOS 6 or Windows 3.1, type **MSD** at the command line to load Microsoft Diagnostics. Click on the IRQ Status button to see a list of the IRQs and what gadgets are using them. If you see a blank space in the Detected column, that IRQ may be free for the taking.

Moving jumpers around

A *jumper* is a tiny plastic box that slides on or off of little pins to turn something (a part) on or off. Most cards contain jumpers and pins. The part's manual tells you what pins to fiddle with. The pins themselves have little labels next to them, giving you a fighting chance at finding the correct ones.

For example, do you see the little numbers and letters next to the little pins in Figure 16-1? The jumper box is sitting across the two pins marked J1, which means the jumper is set for J1.

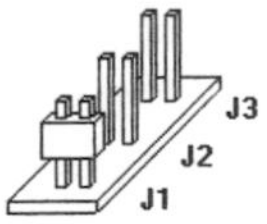

Figure 16-1:
This jumper is set for J1.

If the manual says to set the jumper for J2, then slide that little box up and off the J1 pins and slide it onto the pins marked J2. The pins then look like the illustration in Figure 16-2.

Figure 16-2:
This jumper
is set for J2.

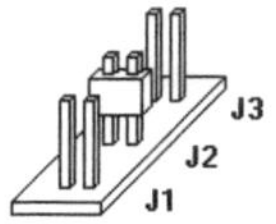

Quick and easy. In fact, it was too easy a concept for computer designers, so they complicated matters. Now some jumpers don't use pairs of pins; instead, the pins are in a straight line, such as in the illustration in Figure 16-3.

Figure 16-3:
This jumper
is set
between
pins 1 and 2.

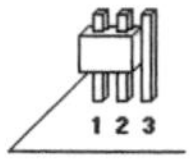

In Figure 16-3, the jumper is set between pins 1 and 2. If the manual says to move the jumper to pins 2 and 3, slide the jumper up and off the pins and then slide it back down over pins 2 and 3, as shown in Figure 16-4.

Figure 16-4:
This jumper
is set
between
pins 2 and 3.

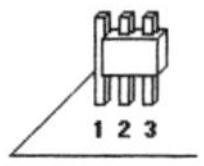

By moving the jumper from pin to pin, you can make the gadget use different settings. The jumper is sort of a "gear-shift knob" for computer circuitry.

✔ If a manual says to *shunt* a pair of pins, it's telling you to connect the two pins. For example, pins 2 and 3 are shunted in Figure 16-4.

✔ The hard part is grabbing that tiny box thing so that you can slide it on or off. A pair of tweezers or needle-nose pliers can help. Did you drop the little box inside your computer? The last section of Chapter 10 offers tips on fishing out dropped obstacles.

TIP

✔ If the manual says to remove a jumper, don't remove it! If you slide the little box off the pins, it can easily camouflage itself among the paper clips in your desk drawer, and you'll never find it again. Instead, leave the little box thing hanging on one prong, as shown in Figure 16-5. The computer still thinks the jumper has been removed. But because it's still attached to a pin, it's handy if you ever need to slide it back on.

Figure 16-5:
Don't
remove a
jumper; let it
dangle.

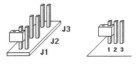

✔ When the little box is over a pair of pins, that jumper is considered *closed* or shunted. If the box is removed, that jumper is called *open.*

✔ If you don't have a manual, how do you know what the jumpers are supposed to do? You don't. You have three options: call the gadget's manufacturer and ask for a new manual; see if the store has a manual lying around; keep moving the jumpers around until you stumble across the combination that works.

✔ Some cards are nice enough to label their IRQ and address jumpers clearly. You'll see tiny labels next to the pins.

Flipping a DIP switch

The first personal computer didn't have a keyboard. Its owners bossed it around by flipping dozens of tiny switches across the front of its case. It made computer games a challenge, but, hey, these people were pioneers.

Today's computer owners still have to flip little switches, but not nearly as often. And thank goodness! The few remaining switches have shrunken to microscopic sizes. In fact, they're too small to flip with your finger. You need a little paper clip or a ballpoint pen to switch them back and forth.

These little switches are called *DIP switches.* Figure 16-6 shows two different varieties: one with sliding controls and one with rocker switches.

Figure 16-6:
Sliding DIP
switches
(left) and
rocker DIP
switches
(right).

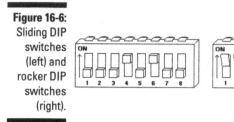

Do you see the little numbers next to each switch? And do you see how one side of the switch says ON? When you push or flip a switch toward the ON side, you're turning on that numbered switch.

In Figure 16-6, for example, both DIP switches show switch numbers 4 and 6 as being turned on. All the other switches are turned off.

- DIP switches and jumpers are pretty much on their way out. Some of the latest cards and motherboards let you control all the settings through their software. The process is just as aggravating, but at least you don't need such tiny fingers.

- Before flipping any DIP switches, draw a little picture of the way they are currently set. Then if something dreadful happens, you can flip them back to normal.

- The sliding DIP switches pictured in Figure 16-6 have sliding controls. You slide the little box toward ON to turn *on* that numbered switch. You slide it away from ON to turn it *off*.

- The rocker DIP switches in Figure 16-6 have rocker controls. You depress the switch toward ON to turn on that numbered switch. You depress the switch away from the ON side to turn it off.

- Feel free to flip a DIP switch with the tip of a ballpoint pen, but don't use a pencil. The tip of a pencil can break off and jam the switch, making life seem a little more weary.

- Some manufacturers feel that labeled switches are too easy for consumers to figure out, so they leave out the word ON. Instead, a little arrow sits on one edge of the switch. Just remember that the arrow points in the ON direction.

- To further confuse things, some manufacturers use the words OPEN instead of OFF and CLOSED instead of ON.

- Some really offbeat manufacturers label their DIP switch with a 1 for ON and a 0 for OFF.

- DIP stands for Dual In-line Package, as well as being a convenient epithet and a messy sauce.

My Card Doesn't Work!

If your "defective" card doesn't work, chances are the computer just doesn't know it's there. The card sits unnoticed, like a sprig of broccoli lodged between your date's front teeth. If your card seems a little absentminded, try these tricks.

- ✔ Push the card into its slot more firmly. Sometimes the cards try to escape with age.

- ✔ If the card is getting old, try cleaning it. Turn off your computer, remove the card, and use a pencil eraser to clean its contacts — the metallic things on the tab that fit into the slot. When the contacts are shiny, blow off all the eraser crumbs and push the card back into its slot.

- ✔ Make sure that you've secured the card in place with its screw. Some cards make an electrical connection through that screw. Also, without that screw, some cards fall out of their slots when you plug a cable into the computer.

- ✔ Still doesn't work? Round up the usual gang of suspects: conflicts between IRQs, DMAs, or addresses.

Part III
Doing Stuff! (or How to Start Playing)

The 5th Wave   By Rich Tennant

©RICHTENNANT

"Frankly, I'm not sure this is the way to enhance the colors on the Kodak CD photo."

In this part . . .

Putting together a multimedia computer is like stringing the lights around the Christmas tree. The *expensive* Christmas tree. (And expensive lights, too, for that matter.) It's a lot of work, making sure everything's plugged in and that the cat can't bring it all down with one well-placed tug.

But when you're done, it's time to forget all that bothersome stuff — ignore those boring cables, cards, codecs, and screwdrivers. That's where this part of the book comes in. It explains how to turn on all the blinking lights and let the multimedia show begin.

Chapter 17

Making Windows Scream and Flash!

In This Chapter

▶ Working with Media Player

▶ Adding a Windows driver

▶ Making Windows play CDs

▶ Playing movies in Media Player

▶ Switching between Windows video modes

▶ Understanding MIDI

▶ Making multimedia objects

▶ Making a multimedia postcard

*M*icrosoft grabbed the stage for the multimedia market several years ago. If you're going to run multimedia programs, you'll probably be running them through Microsoft Windows. Do you want to capture video clips? You'll probably be using Microsoft's Video for Windows, the program packaged with most video capture cards. (It gets its own discussion in Chapter 20.) Do you want to listen to sound files or watch movies or animation? Windows' built-in Media Player program can do the job.

Windows tries its best to do things automatically, but you have to take it by the hand in a few areas and show it what equipment you've installed and how Windows should use it. This chapter tackles some of the parts in Windows that you have to adjust before all the multimedia equipment feels welcome.

Working with Media Player

Windows Media Player gets a real workout by the multimedia crowd because it lets you watch movies, listen to CDs, listen to sound files, and do stuff that people probably haven't *thought* about doing yet.

By itself, Media Player is nothing more than the front panel of a VCR, as shown in Figure 17-1. But that same VCR-like batch of buttons — play, fast-forward, rewind, and a few others — controls anything you're trying to play in Windows, whether it's a movie, a sound, or an animation of a steaming artichoke.

Drag bar to move different parts of video

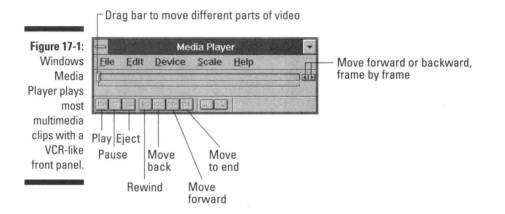

Figure 17-1:
Windows
Media
Player plays
most
multimedia
clips with a
VCR-like
front panel.

Move forward or backward, frame by frame

Play Eject
Pause   Move
          back
          Rewind   Move
                     forward
                         Move
                         to end

To see what your version of Media Player can handle, click on the Device option from the Media Player menu. Another menu drops down, as shown in Figure 17-2, that lists the kinds of things your version of Media Player is currently set up to play.

Figure 17-2:
Media
Player lists
the types of
files it is
able to play.

The Media Player displayed in Figure 17-2 can play music CDs (CD Audio), movies, animations, videos, MIDI songs, and recorded sounds. How come? Because a bunch of multimedia software packages added their Windows *drivers* to the pot and let Media Player know how to play their particular offerings. Drivers get their own section later in this chapter, if you're curious (or desperate and frustrated, for that matter).

✔ When you install a new Windows multimedia program — Video for Windows, for example — the new program usually adds a new line to Media Player's Device menu so that you can play its files.

✔ Some multimedia programs come with their *own* programs to play back their sounds or movies. Nevertheless, Media Player most likely can play these files, too, so you don't have to learn a new program.

✔ Sometimes Device doesn't show up on the Media Player menu because Media Player's window is too small. Stretch out the window an inch or so along one edge, and Device should pop up between the Edit and Scale.

✔ Blatant book plug department: If concepts such as "stretching windows along one edge" seem a little foreign to you, check out the book *Windows For Dummies*. It shows how to stretch, open, close, and clean up Windows' windows.

Playing a file in Media Player

Whether you're playing back a movie, sound, or bizarre dream sequence, Media Player treats them all the same. Click on the Device option on Media Player's menu and then click on the type of file you want to play, such as those listed in Figure 17-2.

Media Player displays a familiar-looking box — the same box you've been using to open a file in any Windows program. If you click on the Video for Windows option, for example, a box appears that shows any Video for Windows files living in the current directory. If you don't spot any Video for Windows files — they end in the letters AVI — use the boxes to the right to switch directories. Double-click on one of the AVI files, and Media Player brings it on-screen, as shown in Figure 17-3.

Figure 17-3:
Double-click on the name of a file in the dialog box, and Media Player brings it on-screen.

Are you ready to start watching the video? Then click on Media Player's Play button — the black triangle on the left — and the file should start playing. In fact, the word *playing* appears at the top of Media Player's window, as shown in Figure 17-4.

Figure 17-4:
Media
Player
indicates
on-screen
that it is
playing the
video.

✔ Instead of opening Video for Windows files (AVI files) by clicking on Media Player's Device menu, you can choose Open from Media Player's File menu. But then Media Player shows you *all* the files in the current directory, not just the AVI files. The Device menu handily filters out all but the types of files you're looking for.

✔ Your Media Player may look a bit different than the one pictured in this section. This difference is probably because your Media Player hasn't been upgraded to play videos, a job described later in this section.

✔ The fastest way to play a file is to find it listed in File Manager. After you double-click on its filename, Media Player leaps to life and begins playing the file immediately.

✔ OK, there is an even *faster* way to play files. Load Media Player and minimize it to an icon at the bottom of the screen, right below your open File Manager window. Then point at the file's name in File Manager, hold down the mouse button, point at the Media Player icon, and let go of the mouse button. Media Player instantly starts playing your file. (This process is called *dragging* the filename, by the way.)

✔ Windows lets you run two or more copies of Media Player at the same time. But don't get too fancy — if you try to play two movies simultaneously, you're asking for a *very* slow balloon ride.

Playing videos in Media Player

For the most part, Media Player is as easy to figure out as a VCR. Easier, in fact — there's no blinking clock to curse at. But if a weird Media Player option leaves you confused, check out Table 17-1. (Anything in Media Player's OLE Object dialog box doesn't appear in this table — OLE stuff gets its own section later in this chapter.)

Table 17-1	Media Player Reference
This Setting	*Does This*
Auto Repeat	Found under Options from the Edit menu; click here to see the video repeat, repeat, repeat.
Auto Rewind	Found under Options from the Edit menu; click here to make the video automatically rewind after being shown.
Configure	The last choice in the Device menu, this lets you change playback settings. You can play back a video in full screen, for example.
Copy Object	Found in the Edit menu, this works like any other copy command: it sends Media Player's contents to the Clipboard for pasting into other programs. To change how things look when pasted, click on the OLE Object boxes under the Options menu. (Then head to the Object section later in this chapter; Objects are kinda weird.)
Full Screen	Found in the Configure setting from the Device menu, check this setting to make Windows disappear while playing the video; the video then hogs the screen. (And it looks pretty awful, too, especially if you click on Zoom by 2 — that *really* makes the video hog the screen.)
Selection	Do you just want a small part of your movie to head for the Clipboard when copied? Then choose the frames you like with this command. Choose Selection from the Edit menu; then click on the From option and enter the numbers of the frame's beginning and end.
Skip Frames if Behind	Does your video keep going after the sound track stops? Click on this option, found in the Configure setting in the Device menu, and Media Maker skips some video to keep up with the sound track.
Window	Found in the Configure setting from the Device menu, this setting plays the video back in a window. (See Full Screen.)
Zoom by 2	Found in the Configure setting from the Device menu, this setting doubles the size of your video — and often slows it down, too.

Scale, Time, Tracks, and Stuff

Media Player always displays a thick bar, as shown in Figure 17-4. This line represents the media clip you're playing. (*Media clip* is computerese for plain ol' sound, music, or movies.)

Two options, Time and Tracks, appear in Media Player's Scale menu. Although these options look important, they don't affect the quality of what is playing on-screen. They just change the little numbers that hover above that lone bar in Media Player.

Choosing Time makes Media Player display how much *time* the media clip takes up. With this information, you know how long your video, sound, or song will last. Choosing Tracks, however, tells Media Player to display which song it's playing out of a series of songs. If you're playing a CD, for example, you can tell you're playing the third song from a series of ten; the numbers appear right above the bar.

If you've upgraded Media Player to play movies, you see a new option: Frames. This option makes Media Player display the number of frames — individual pictures—that makes up your particular movie.

Upgrading Media Player to play movies

Back in the old days, when Microsoft released Windows 3.1, nobody figured that computers would be playing movies. So the Media Player in Windows 3.1 played only songs and sounds. As videos became more profitable . . . er . . . popular, Microsoft wrote a piece of software called Video for Windows. When you install it, it overhauls Media Player and adds new buttons, new options, and fresh popcorn between the seats.

The only problem is finding it — the latest version of Video for Windows isn't sold in the stores. Instead, many companies give it away. Most video capture cards come with a copy, for example, so people can edit the videos they've captured from their hard drive.

If you're looking to *play* videos — not make them — pick up something called a *runtime* version of Video for Windows. It can't do any film editing or capturing; it just lets you watch videos. But it's free, so most people aren't complaining — if they can find it, that is. If you haven't found a runtime copy included with any of your Windows software or equipment, grab a modem (or a friend with a modem) and download the software from Microsoft's BBS — all for the price of a phone call.

To download the software, follow these steps:

1. **If you have a modem, you can use Terminal to grab the runtime version of Video for Windows off Microsoft's BBS on CompuServe.**

   The program comes packaged in a file called VFWRUN.EXE.

2. **Use File Manager to create a directory on your hard drive called TRASH; move VFWRUN.EXE into the TRASH directory and double-click on its filename.**

    TRASH is just there for temporary use; you can delete it later. VFWRUN breaks itself into bunches of smaller files when you double-click on its filename. (Press F5 from within File Manager to see those files; sometimes File Manager is too lazy to update your screen automatically.)

3. **Double-click on the SETUP.EXE program in your TRASH directory.**

    This step tells Video for Windows to install itself. As it settles in, the program usually sends out a dialog box telling you to look for a newer video driver. (Driver hassles are covered later in this chapter.)

4. **Finally, when the Video for Windows program finishes installing itself, delete the TRASH directory and everything in it.**

    The program has already copied all its important files to the right place, so you can get rid of the packaging.

✔ Media Player plays movies in a postage stamp-sized window, a bit of normalcy discussed in Chapter 5. You can enlarge the picture up to four times, though, with this trick: hold down Ctrl as the video plays back and press the numbers 1, 2, 3, or 4. Depending on the number, Media Player makes the picture grow from small-and-quick to huge-and-slow. Press Ctrl+1 to move back to normal.

✔ To make your movie always start up in a certain size, check out the Configure option from Media Player's Device menu. Click on Full Screen, for example, to make your movies take up the whole screen. Zoom by 2 makes the movies play back at twice the size as normal.

✔ For some microscopic excitement, start playing your movie and minimize its window, turning it into an icon at the bottom of your screen. The movie still plays, but from within the icon.

Adding Windows Drivers

Have you ever stepped into a strange taxi in a foreign city and tried to get to the airport in a hurry? It's not easy — unless you have a friendly driver who knows the car, the city, and the airport. Tell the driver to head for the airport, and the taxi starts to zoom in the right direction.

Windows doesn't know anything about all the strange new multimedia equipment people are stuffing inside their computers, either. So Windows also needs a *driver,* a piece of software that helps Windows control different brands of sound cards and video capture cards.

Most manufacturers include a Windows driver with their products. For example, the installation programs for some sound cards often slip a driver into Windows without your noticing it. Then when you open Windows, the sound card is already making noise.

But if the program doesn't automatically add the driver, you have to do it yourself, and that's where this section comes in. You also need this section if you're adding a new driver — one that the company has finally purchased — to replace an older one that has been giving you problems.

Making Media Player play CDs

Windows doesn't automatically assume you want to hear Willie Nelson songs on your CD-ROM drive. Before Media Player lets you listen to CDs, you need to add something called a *CD Audio driver*. Adding this driver is an easy process that starts by opening the Control Panel and double-clicking on the Drivers icon. A Drivers dialog box pops up, as shown in Figure 17-5.

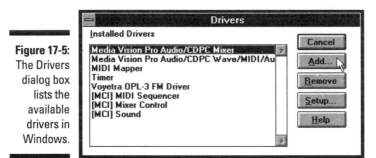

Figure 17-5:
The Drivers
dialog box
lists the
available
drivers in
Windows.

If you see the line [MCI] CD Audio on the list, you're already set up, and Media Player can already play audio CDs. Head for the first bulleted item at the end of this section for instructions.

If the line isn't listed, click on Add. You'll see the [MCI] CD Audio line on that list, so double-click on it. If Windows finds a driver already living on your hard drive, click on the Current button. If Windows doesn't find a driver, it asks you to insert one of its original disks (usually Disk 4).

You do have those Windows 3.1 disks lying around, don't you? Windows installs the drive and asks to reboot your computer. Save your work and let Windows shut itself down and re-emerge on-screen — this time with a Media Player that can play Willie Nelson CDs.

✔ To play your CDs, choose CD Audio from Media Player's Device menu. (See Figure 17-2.) Windows looks for a music CD in your CD-ROM drive and starts playing its first song.

✔ Do you want to skip a song? Click on Media Player's big black arrow pointing to the right.

✔ To hear music CDs, you need to hook up your CD-ROM's sound output to your sound card. Chapter 11 covers this procedure.

✔ Sometimes Windows works better if you leave a CD sitting in the drive — even when you're not using it. (Barb, this book's copy editor, swears that she's heard Windows searching both forward and backward through her Beatles collection.)

Adding other drivers to Windows

Either manufacturers are becoming nicer or they're tired of hearing phone calls from frustrated users. Either way, they're starting to automate the process of installing Windows drivers. For example, the installation program for Creative Labs' Sound Blaster not only puts Sound Blaster's DOS programs onto your hard drive, but it also adds the proper Windows drivers, too. When you load Windows, Sound Blaster is waiting for you, ready to go.

The more spiteful manufacturers force you to install Windows drivers yourself. The chore goes like this: double-click on the Drivers icon in Windows' Control Panel. When the dialog box pops up, click on Add. Is your new piece of equipment listed? Simply double-click on its name, and you're home free.

If the equipment is not listed, click on the line that says Other or Unlisted or Updated Driver. Stick the disk that came with the equipment into your floppy drive and click on OK. The gears churn, and Windows lists the drivers on that disk. Double-click on the one you want, and you're through. *After* you let Windows shut down and start back up, that is.

Switching to Different Video Modes

Multimedia programs can be pretty picky about how Windows treats them. Some insist that Windows run in 256-color mode. Others ask for 64,000 colors or even 16 million. Windows can accommodate their demands, but *you* have to specifically tell Windows to start wearing different colors.

You need to tell Windows to run in a different *video mode*, a concept banged around in Chapter 4. Although some programs ask for video modes that Windows — and your video card — aren't powerful enough to handle, the following two sections explain how to find out what video modes your version of Windows can run.

Using Windows Setup to change video modes

To save some time, save your work before changing video modes. Windows always wants to shut down and restart itself before displaying a different batch of colors.

Here's how to find out what video modes your version of Windows *can* handle, as well as how to switch to a new video mode, if it's offered:

1. **Double-click on the Windows Setup icon in Program Manager's Main window.**

   The Main group window should be holding the icon — a little picture of an open box of floppy disks sitting next to a dead-looking computer. Double-click on the icon, and the Windows Setup program hops on-screen.

2. **Choose Options from the Windows Setup window.**

   The Options menu drops down, as shown in Figure 17-6.

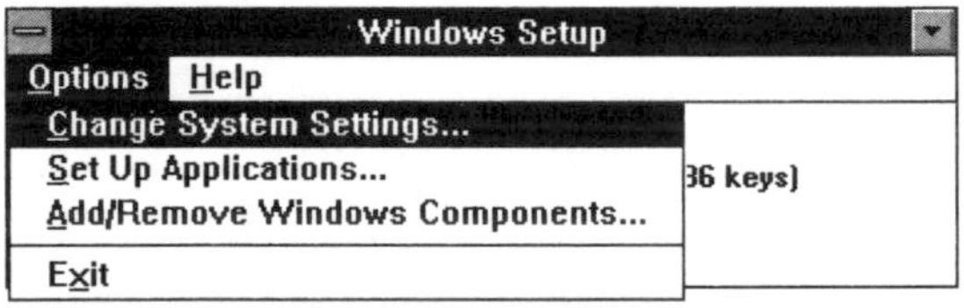

Figure 17-6:
The Options
menu.

```
┌──────────────────────────────────────────────┐
│ ─            Windows Setup                  ▼ │
├──────────────────────────────────────────────┤
│ Options  Help                                 │
│ ┌──────────────────────────────┐             │
│ │ Change System Settings...    │             │
│ │ Set Up Applications...       │  36 keys)   │
│ │ Add/Remove Windows Components...│           │
│ ├──────────────────────────────┤             │
│ │ Exit                         │             │
│ └──────────────────────────────┘             │
└──────────────────────────────────────────────┘
```

3. **Click on the Change System Settings option.**

   The Change System Settings dialog box appears (as shown in Figure 17-7), where you can change the appearance of Windows.

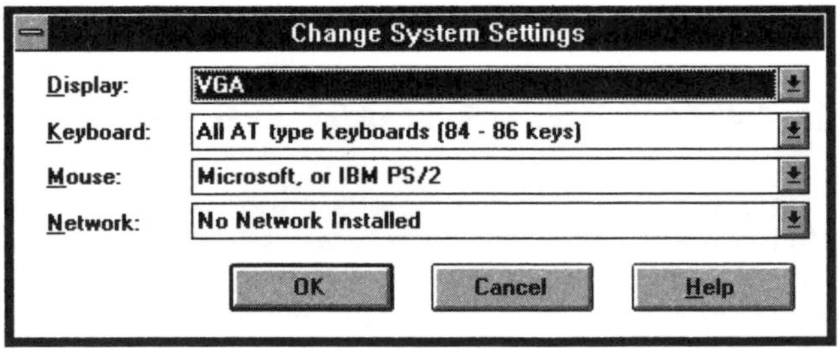

Figure 17-7:
In the
Change
System
Settings
dialog box,
you can
make
changes to
Windows'
Setup.

```
┌──────────────────────────────────────────────────────┐
│ ─              Change System Settings                  │
├──────────────────────────────────────────────────────┤
│  Display:    │ VGA                               │ ▼ │
│  Keyboard:   │ All AT type keyboards (84 - 86 keys)│ ▼ │
│  Mouse:      │ Microsoft, or IBM PS/2            │ ▼ │
│  Network:    │ No Network Installed              │ ▼ │
│                                                        │
│      ┌────OK────┐   ┌──Cancel──┐   ┌───Help───┐        │
│      └──────────┘   └──────────┘   └──────────┘        │
└──────────────────────────────────────────────────────┘
```

4. **Click on the Display option.**

   A list of video modes pops up.

5. **Click on the video mode that the program requests and then click on OK.**

   Windows asks permission to shut itself down and load back up. When it comes back, Windows should appear dressed in the colors that your multimedia program asked for.

   ✔ Sometimes programs ask for video modes that your computer simply can't handle. This means you have to buy a new video card or monitor — or a whole new computer, if you're serious about all these expensive multimedia colors.

   ✔ Depending on what mode you ask for, Windows may ask you to insert a disk. Keep your original Windows disks handy, just in case; the disks that came with your video card may be needed, as well.

   ✔ Most of today's multimedia programs require at least 256 colors displayed at 640x480 resolution.

   ✔ Windows refers to your monitor and video card combination as a *display* mode, not a video mode — but they're actually the same thing.

Now Windows won't work!

Have you ever changed a small detail in Windows only to find that Windows no longer works? If you accidentally choose a video mode that Windows can't handle, Windows refuses to load. Even worse, it doesn't give you any hint as to what is wrong.

If you choose a new video driver — or any other driver, for that matter — and Windows suddenly stops working, you can change it back to normal. Type the following two lines at the DOS prompt, one after the other, pressing Enter after each one:

```
C:\> CD \WINDOWS
C:\WINDOWS> SETUP
```

These two lines put you in your Windows directory and load the DOS version of the Windows Setup program. Using the DOS version of Setup, change the video driver back to the old one — the one that worked. This technique should bring Windows back to normal. If you can't find a driver that looks familiar, choose the plain old VGA mode driver, which should get Windows back on-screen.

Switching video modes through a card's software

Some manufacturers decided that Windows makes too much of a fuss about changing video modes, so they wrote their own programs to replace Windows Setup. For example, ATI's Graphics Ultra Pro series of cards comes with a Windows program (called FlexDesk) for switching between video modes, as shown in Figure 17-8.

Figure 17-8:
Some video cards come with a program to easily change video modes.

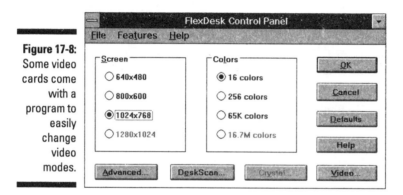

First, click on one of the resolutions listed in the Screen box; then choose one of the color amounts listed under the Colors box. Click on OK, and Windows shuts itself down and restarts in the new video mode. Your video card might offer a similar program.

Objecting to Object Embedding and Linking

Leave it to the computer industry to take the most entertaining computer technology in years and give it a boring name like Object Linking and Embedding. At least it has a fun abbreviation: OLE!

OLE works like this: for years, Windows could only paste boring things like words and charts. And after these objects were pasted into a report or letter, they just sat there. But with OLE, objects now can move and shake after they've been pasted. Double-click on a picture of a hot-air balloon, for example, and a video starts, showing the balloon taking off. Or double-click on a picture of Mr. B.B. King and hear a fat-thumbed guitar lick.

An object can be anything that fits in a file — a video of a hatching duckling, the sizzling sound of Kentucky Fried Chicken, or a typed treatise on vegetarianism. Windows lets you either embed or link objects, two subtly different ways of pasting information. Both are described in the next two sections. Beware, however, that this object stuff can get *mighty* complicated until you've done it a few times.

Embedding an object

Embedding an object is just like pasting it — but the object stays alive. Double-click on it and it plays.

For example, you can embed a sound in Write by following these steps:

1. **Load your sound into Sound Recorder.**

   Choose Open from Sound Recorder's File menu and double-click on the filename that you want to paste into Write.

2. **Choose Copy from Sound Recorder's Edit menu.**

   Absolutely nothing happens — nothing that you can see, anyway. But in the background, Sound Recorder sends a copy of the sound to the Clipboard.

3. **Load Write and choose Paste from its Edit menu.**

   Poof! The sound appears as a Sound Recorder icon in Write. Double-click on the icon, and the sound plays.

Whatever you are pasting into the document stays there, *embedded* in the file. In the preceding steps, you can save your Write file to a floppy disk and load it onto another computer. Because the sound is still embedded in Write, it plays back — as long as the other computer has a sound card (and a copy of Windows Sound Recorder).

✓ There is an exception (as always) to embedding objects in a file. Although sounds and pictures can be embedded easily, movies cannot. They're too big. If you try pasting a movie into Write, the first frame of the movie appears. Then if you double-click on the movie, it starts playing from within Write. However, it plays because Write hopped over to the movie's file on your hard drive, grabbed it, and started playing it. The file itself isn't embedded in Write, just its location.

✓ So? If you've embedded a movie into Write and saved the file as MYMOVIE.WRI, don't count on that movie being contained inside the Write file. If you open the Write file on another computer and try to play back the movie, Windows just looks confused and asks where it can find the movie.

✔ There is a sneaky way to embed movies, however. It's called the Object Packager, and it's described later in this chapter.

✔ Most of this Object Embedding and Linking stuff is complicated when you attempt it with the little programs that come with Windows. Most major Windows programs handle all the OLE nuances in the background so that you don't have to worry about understanding the grand scheme of it all.

Customizing your embedded clips

Media Player lets you customize how a media clip looks when it's played back from another document. Click on the Options choice from the Media Player's Edit menu. The dialog box shown in Figure 17-9 appears, where you can fine-tune how your object behaves when it lives in another document.

Figure 17-9:
Use Media
Player's
Options
dialog box to
change the
appearance
of pasted
objects.

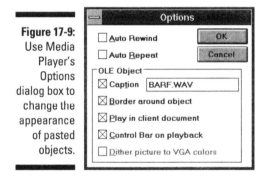

Caption: Do you want a caption to appear beneath your pasted clip? Then type it in here. If you don't type anything, Media Player substitutes the filename. (Boring.)

Border around object: For nitpickers *only*. An icon or movie that is pasted into a document like Write can show up either as the first picture in the movie or the first picture in the movie with a little black line around it. (Ho hum.)

Play in client document: After you've pasted a movie into a document, it sits there, showing its first image. When double-clicked, do you want the movie to leap from the document and start playing in its own window? Or do you simply want the movie to start playing from within the document? Check here, and the movie stays put in the document while playing back.

Control Bar on playback: Some people like the little bar that normally appears beneath Media Player's movies so that they can control how the movie plays back. Others think the bar is a distraction. This option lets you choose whether it appears.

D̲ither picture to VGA colors: Most little movies use at least 256 colors. Click here, and they stay in 256 colors — but their little picture in the document uses only 16 colors to keep down the file size. (Remember, movies don't get pasted — only their filenames and locations appear on your hard drive.)

Linking an object

Linking an object works a lot like pasting or embedding it. For example, you may have a favorite guitar riff stored as a WAV file. Copy the sound to the Clipboard from Sound Recorder and then choose Paste L̲ink while in Write. The Sound Recorder icon appears in Write, just as if you had embedded it.

But you didn't really paste the sound file into Write. You just pasted the filename. When you double-click on the Sound Recorder icon, Windows looks up the filename, grabs the file, and starts playing your favorite guitar riff.

What's the point to this witless complication? Because you're not pasting the actual sound file itself, you can edit the sound file later on down the road. Then the next time you double-click on the Sound Recorder in Write, you automatically hear the edited version.

Because Write doesn't hold the actual file — only a reference to the real file — Write always has the most up-to-date version, no matter how many times you update your favorite guitar riff. And it doesn't take as much space in your Write document.

- Are you tired of having to update four spreadsheets for the customized memos you distribute to your butler, maid, chef, and dumbwaiter operator? Then keep one main spreadsheet but use Paste L̲ink to put a copy of that spreadsheet in each memo. Then when you update your main spreadsheets, the spreadsheets in the other four are automatically updated, too, and are ready for distribution.

- *Embedding* an object puts a copy of its information into another file, where it can be edited or played back later. *Linking* an object puts a copy of the information's location in a file, where it is automatically updated if the original version changes.

- Not all programs support Object Embedding and Linking. Write, Media Player, Sound Recorder, Paintbrush, Cardfile, and Object Packager support OLE. Terminal, Notepad, and a few others are still afraid of it.

- If something goes haywire when you're playing back an embedded movie, double-click on the movie's title bar (the strip across its top). Media Player stops hiding in the background, leaps on-screen, and lets you fine-tune the playback with its batch of VCR-like buttons.

✔ Do you have a collection of sounds, pictures, and videos from your most recent vacation? Head for the last section of this chapter for tips on making a multimedia postcard. You can embed these sounds in Write and then copy them to a floppy disk that your friends can play back on their own computers.

✔ Windows' Object Packager can also create objects, but it's not as easy to use as pasting them with Media Player. (You'll find this out yourself if you read the Object Packager section a little later on in this chapter.)

✔ The Paste Special option lets you fine-tune your pasting with three options. The first option, Media Clip Object, works just like regular Paste: it pastes the complete object — sound, video, or art. The other options, Picture or Device Independent Bitmap, paste only the art contained in the object — the first frame of a movie, the object's icon, or other graphics representing the object.

Packing an object in Object Packager

Windows' Object Packager is a strange little program. The name doesn't give many clues as to what it does, and the icon looks even stranger. Shown in Figure 17-10, the icon shows a musical note, a piece of paper, and a moldy blue doughnut being dropped into a yellow take-out food box.

Figure 17-10:
The Object
Packager
icon.

Basically, Object Packager lets you subtly change objects before embedding or linking them. Yawn. Use Object Packager's Import command from the File menu to bring in the file you want to pretty up. Then choose among the following options:

Assign any icon to any data. You don't like using the Paintbrush icon for all your embedded pictures? Click on Object Packager's Insert Icon button to choose among any other icons on your hard drive.

Add a label to any object's icon. Normally, Windows lists an object's filename beneath its icon. Select Label from the Edit menu and type in something snappier for Windows to use.

Assign any icon to a command line (DOS or Windows). An object doesn't have to be a file. If you're a command-line veteran, choose Command Line from the Edit menu and type in your command. Then when you double-click on the pasted object, it runs that particular command.

✔ Nine out of ten Windows users don't bother using Object Packager. And
   nine out of ten Windows users who have tried it wonder why they did. You
   really haven't missed much.

 ✔ Besides, Windows is supposed to be getting people away from things like
   command lines.

Wading through MIDI

Described in Chapter 3, MIDI is a way for musicians to record synthesized songs
on a computer. But the first time you try to play a MIDI file in Media Player,
Windows may toss up a "you goofed" box, such as the one shown in Figure 17-11.

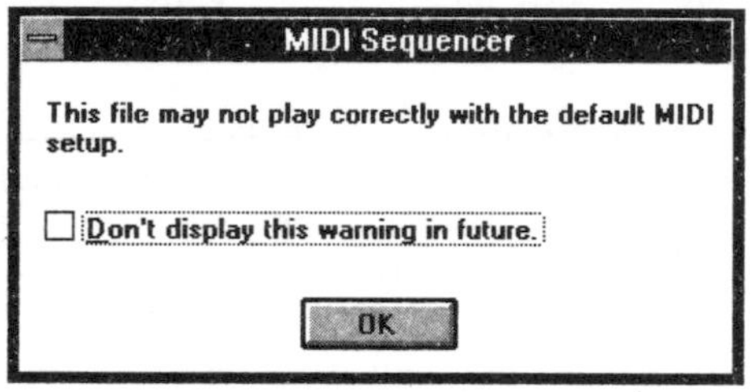

Figure 17-11:
Windows
doesn't like
some MIDI
files.

> **MIDI Sequencer**
>
> This file may not play correctly with the default MIDI
> setup.
>
> ☐ Don't display this warning in future.
>
> OK

You didn't goof, however. You merely stumbled into yet another computer
industry conflict over who is storing information the right way. It's an ugly
mess, so skip this section and listen to a CD in your CD-ROM drive. But if you're
curious — and don't mind wading through some history — stick around.

To contain a song, a MIDI file simply lists the order in which certain musical
notes are played and the instruments that the notes should sound like. MIDI
files contain 16 channels, enough to sound like 16 different musicians playing in a
band.

Computers can only digest numbers, so MIDI assigns a number to each instrument sound. A Fender Stratocaster can be number 38, for example. But here's
the problem: different companies assign different numbers to their instruments;
therefore, a MIDI file that sounds like a lovely piano concerto on one person's
software sounds like tubas on another's software.

Eventually, the industry released a *General MIDI standard*, where each instrument (128 of them, actually) got its own personal number. People with expensive synthesizers rejoiced; people with sound cards didn't. In those early days,
computer sound cards couldn't handle 16 channels. So when making Windows,
Microsoft decided to break up the MIDI standard into two parts, Basic and
Extended, described as follows:

Basic: To accommodate cheap sound cards, Basic uses MIDI channels 13 through 16, with channel 16 getting the drums. If you're using an early AdLib-compatible sound card, you should probably choose the Basic setting whenever it appears. Sure, Basic allows only four instruments, but these instruments are enough to keep the older sound cards busy.

Extended: To satisfy the more powerful cards and synthesizers, the Extended setting tells the card to listen to channels 1 through 10, with channel 10 getting the drums. Because Extended gets ten channels, songs sound better when played back.

Because Microsoft broke MIDI into two standards, it told companies to write *two* versions of their MIDI songs and stick all the information in the same file. The song file's first ten channels play back on Extended settings, and the leftover channels play back on Basic settings. In this way, Media Player automatically plays the right version of the song, whether it's on a cheap sound card or an expensive synthesizer. At least, this is how it's all *supposed* to work.

Very few songwriters listened to Microsoft's programmers, however, and kept writing their MIDI files the same way as before — using any channels they wanted. And that's why you keep seeing the warning message in Figure 17-10. The message simply means the song wasn't written to Microsoft's specifications.

- ✔ The solution to the warning message? Click in the box that says `Don't display this warning in future`. Now Windows simply plays your MIDI files automatically — whether the saxophones sound like clarinets or not.

- ✔ Sometimes the song sounds fine, even though it's not up to Microsoft's standards.

- ✔ If the song sounds weird, however, you can either enjoy it as alternative music or mess with Windows MIDI Mapper, described in the next section.

- ✔ Windows comes with a MIDI file called CANYON.MID. Because this is an official Microsoft-sanctioned MIDI file, CANYON.MID plays in Windows without causing any fuss. It's often the only MIDI file that does.

- ✔ One way to avoid these MIDI problems is to avoid Windows MIDI programs. But a better solution is to avoid Media Player when playing MIDI programs. Many Windows MIDI programs simply bypass Media Player and step over its limitations by providing their own MIDI players.

Making do with MIDI Mapper

When Windows turns your ragtime piano music into an accordion solo, it's obvious that Windows is using the wrong instrument. What is less obvious is how to make Windows put down the accordion and sit down at the piano bench. That less-obvious program is called MIDI Mapper, and it's Windows' method of making all the musicians stand up and move to different chairs.

To call up MIDI Mapper, double-click on its icon from the Control Panel. Do you see the name listed in MIDI Mapper's Name box? (See Figure 17-12.) This name is the gizmo that Windows thinks it's sending MIDI information to — in this case, Sound Blaster 16's External MIDI setting.

Figure 17-12:
The MIDI
Mapper lets
you choose
where
Windows
sends MIDI
information.

	MIDI Mapper	
Show		Close
⊙ Setups ○ Patch Maps ○ Key Maps		Delete
Name: SB16 Ext MIDI		Help
Description: Sound Blaster 16 MIDI Port		
Edit...	New...	

If your sound card is not listed, click on the Name box to see other listings. When you spot yours, click on it or click on the name of what your sound card emulates, usually AdLib or Sound Blaster. Then click on the Close button to finish the job.

✔ Don't be disappointed if things still sound strange. Because different MIDI songs use different MIDI formats, the songs may sound weird even when your sound card is hooked up perfectly.

✔ If the MIDI Mapper icon doesn't even show up in the Control Panel, your sound card's driver is probably not installed correctly. The "Adding Windows Drivers" section earlier in this chapter covers installation chores.

✔ Most cards automatically set up MIDI Mapper to match their own settings. For example, Sound Blaster 16 put its own name in the MIDI Mapper box when I installed it, and it worked fine. But when I installed Sound Blaster's Wave Blaster upgrade chip, I had to change the listing to SB16 Ext MIDI by myself.

✔ Some sound cards add three choices to MIDI Mapper: Basic, Extended, and All. Try choosing the Basic option first. Then if the songs still don't sound right, try the other options.

✔ You may find yourself constantly switching between different MIDI Mapper settings in order to hear different MIDI songs in Media Player.

If your MIDI file sounds *almost* right on your Ad Lib-compatible sound card, try this: open MIDI Mapper from the Control Panel, click on Setups, and click on the Edit button. Then, in the row for channel 10, click on the Active column until the X disappears. Click on OK to save your changes and click on Close to get rid of the window. This dance step sometimes fixes the sound problem.

Making a Multimedia Postcard in Write

The most fun in having a multimedia computer comes when you show it off to friends and family. This section shows you how to create a multimedia *digital postcard* on a floppy disk, ready for mailing.

While on your trip, collect snippets of travel memories, such as photos, movies, and sounds. (Smells can't be computerized, yet.) Then — unless you've got one heck of a laptop — create this postcard on your desktop computer at home. You'll find all the Windows instructions you need in this chapter.

When making the digital postcard, the challenge isn't making the right movies or finding the right sound. The challenge is trying to make everything fit on your floppy disk. A 3½-inch high-density disk holds only 1.44MB of space. Follow these steps to make your digital postcard:

1. **Create a POSTCARD directory on your hard drive.**

   Use File Manager's Create Directory command from its File menu. You need a place to store your files while working.

2. **Collect your multimedia mementos.**

   Start gathering your computerized remembrances of the trip and copying them to the POSTCARD directory:

   Kodak Photo CD: Described in Chapter 19, Kodak Photo CDs are an easy way to turn your regular 35mm camera photographs into computer files. Use Kodak Access software's Export command to save the pictures as 256-color BMP files at 256x384 pixels. These pictures average about 100K each.

   Camcorder stills: Chapter 20 shows how to extract still pictures from anything you've videotaped with your camcorder. Using Intel's Indeo codec, pictures with 240x180 resolution average around 50K.

   Movies: If you have a video capture card, described in Chapter 5, stick a short movie on your postcard. To keep the file size small, keep the movie short and snappy. With a small size (160x120), 8-bit sound, 15 frames per second, and high-compression, you'll probably have less than ten seconds to work with. (Movie capturing and editing gets its due in Chapter 20.)

   Sound: You can grab sounds off your camcorder's sound track or a tape recorder you took along with you. Or, while you're putting your postcard together, you can record yourself talking into a microphone connected to your sound card (covered in Chapter 18.) To keep the file small, record in mono 8-bit sound at 11 kHz.

   As you copy your files to the POSTCARD directory, keep an eye on their file sizes. You don't want the contents of all the files in the directory to be more than 1.44MB.

3. Open Write and start pasting clips into the file.

To paste a picture or BMP file, load the file into a graphics program, such as Paintbrush or BitEdit (it comes with Video for Windows). Select the image and use the program's Copy command to copy it to the Clipboard. Then choose Paste from Write's menu. The picture appears in Write, as shown in Figure 17-13.

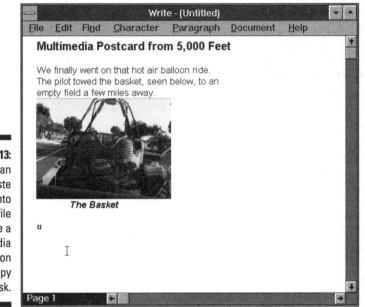

Figure 17-13:
You can paste pictures into a Write file to create a multimedia postcard on a floppy disk.

To paste a sound or WAV file, load your file into Sound Recorder and choose Copy from Sound Recorder's Edit menu. Then choose Paste from Write's menu. The Sound Recorder's icon appears in Write, as shown in Figure 17-14.

To paste a movie or AVI file is a little trickier, but here's a quick way: open File Manager, point at the filename of your movie, hold down the mouse button, point at a spot in your Write document, and let go of the mouse button. You've dragged the movie into the Write document, and it is represented by Media Player's icon, shown in Figure 17-15.

Be sure to add a little bit of text to the file, too. You don't want to send a blank postcard with only pictures.

Figure 17-14:
When
pasted,
sounds
appear as
icons.

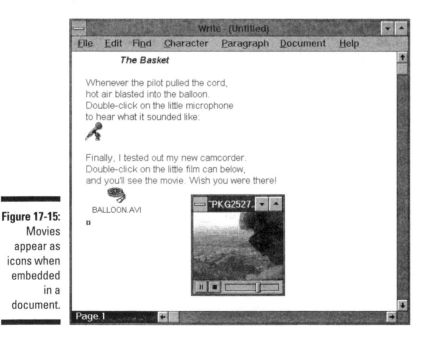

Figure 17-15:
Movies
appear as
icons when
embedded
in a
document.

4. **Save the file and copy it to a floppy disk.**

   Save the file in Write, copy it to a floppy disk, and you're done. You've created a multimedia floppy postcard and stored it in a single file that any Windows owner can easily play. If the Write file is bigger than 1.44MB, you have to start trimming — cut out a picture here and there or recompress your video.

   A few caveats: not all your friends have a multimedia computer with a sound card; and if their video cards can display only 16 colors, the pictures won't be very impressive.

   Finally, your friends need a copy of Video for Windows runtime version (described earlier in this chapter), or they can't watch the movie. You probably got a copy of the runtime version with your video capture card, so give your friends a copy of it along with your floppy postcard. (Microsoft wants you to give that file away — you're not breaking any laws.)

Chapter 18

Recording and Playing Sounds on Your PC

∙ ∙

In This Chapter

▶ Changing the volume

▶ Adjusting sound in games

▶ Setting up software to record sounds

▶ Recording a sound in Windows

▶ Playing back sounds in Windows

▶ Adding sound effects

▶ Assigning your own sounds to Windows events

∙ ∙

*T*his chapter is dedicated to Michael, a 12-year-old boy in New Hampshire, who wrote me a letter asking where he could find a good "barf" sound file. Michael, if your sound card can play a barf sound, it can record one, too, and this chapter is going to show you how.

If you're not a 12-year-old looking for barf sounds, stick around anyway; you'll find out how to record serious soundtracks for your business presentations. Or — if you're making presentations for Pepto Bismol — you can do both!

A sound card is your quickest ticket to multimedia: it's cheap; it lets you hear the sounds and music packed in most of today's multimedia software; and it's pretty easy to use. If you can talk into a microphone, you can start recording your own sounds.

Finding the Volume Knob

The first thing you need to do is find out how to adjust the volume on your sound card. Sounds are almost always either too loud or barely audible. Almost all cards have different ways to change the volume, but here are a few ways to start:

✔ Some cards, like Sound Blaster, have a tiny round wheel sticking out of the back of the card. Yes, it's difficult to reach, especially when the computer is pushed up against the wall, like most computers are. But remember that it's there. If the sound starts screeching, you may need to get to it in a hurry.

Or if your sound card is hooked up to your stereo, use your stereo knob.

✔ Some ProAudio Spectrum cards let you change the volume by pushing keys. Press Ctrl+Alt+U to raise the volume. Press Ctrl+Alt+D to lower the volume. Or turn off the volume by pressing Ctrl+Alt+M. This trick works best in DOS programs, however; don't count on it always working in Windows.

✔ Look for the sound card's mixer program. For example, the Sound Blaster's mixer program is SBSET.EXE or SB16SET. Type one of these two commands at your DOS prompt, and the mixer program pops up. If your mouse works, click on the little bars next to Master and slide them to the left. If your mouse doesn't work, tap the Tab key 11 times (sigh) and press your keyboard's left-arrow key. Substitute the right-arrow key to raise the volume.

✔ If you're in Windows, look for the sound card's Windows mixer program. Chances are you'll find the mixer program in the Program Manager window that your sound card created when you installed it.

✔ If the sound starts blasting and your guests wonder why you can't do a simple thing like adjust the volume on your $3,000 computer, take the simple way out: reach for the speaker cable that connects to the card and give it a good yank. Quick and easy.

✔ Finally, if you're setting up your sound card for games, check out Chapter 22 for some more tips and tricks and just plain sneaky things.

Setting Up Software to Record Sounds

Windows 3.1 comes with Sound Recorder software that can turn your words and noises into a computer file, ready for playback.

Most sound cards come with their own recording program, as well. But no matter what software you're using, it gives you a quiz before letting you record anything. The answers to the three most important questions are listed in the next three sections.

Should I record in mono or stereo?

A sound that is recorded in stereo is more realistic than one recorded in mono, but stereo causes a few problems in computers. First, a sound card can only record in stereo if it has two microphones — one for your left speaker and one for the right. Most sound cards come with only one microphone, so you're stuck with mono.

Second, even if you do round up two microphones — or if you're recording something off a stereo CD or tape — you need twice the file space to store a stereo sound than to store a mono sound. After all, stereo is really two separate recordings mixed together and played back at the same time.

If you're short on hard disk space, stick to mono.

Should I record in 8-bit or 16-bit?

Most recording programs ask whether they should record in 8-bit mode or 16-bit mode. If you don't have a 16-bit sound card, you're stuck with 8-bit — the decision is made automatically.

But if you have a 16-bit sound card (these cards usually have the number *16* in their names, such as ProAudio Spectrum 16), you can use either mode. Recording in 8-bit creates smaller sound files, but they don't sound as good as if they had been recorded in 16-bit mode. Again, the amount of room on your hard drive is the determining factor.

Should I record in 11, 22, or 44 kHz?

Here's yet another decision sound-recording programs make people agonize over. Should you record in 11, 22, or 44 kHz mode? (22 kHz is almost as good as 44 for most things.) Recording in 44 kHz makes for great sound — studio folks record musical CDs in this mode — but 44 kHz makes for huge sound files, too.

Recording at 11 or 22 kHz doesn't sound as good, but it keeps the file size down.

Get to the point already!

OK, here's the point: When deciding how to record sounds, simply try recording them at all the options your software offers: 8-bit and 16-bit; mono and stereo; and 11, 22, and 44 kHz. Then play back your recorded file and give it a good critical listen. If it sounds great, look at the sound file's size. If you can spare that much room on your hard disk, save it!

But if you can't devote 2MB of hard disk space to a cool barf sound, record by using one of the smaller numbers, switch to mono, or do both.

> ✔ If you want definitions of all the kHz numbers and stuff, head to Chapter 3.
>
> ✔ Windows' Sound Recorder takes a middle-of-the-road approach. It doesn't give you a quiz about recording options. Instead, it automatically records in mono at 22 kHz, using 16-bits for a 16-bit sound card and 8-bits for 8-bit cards. You can't change Sound Recorder's mind about sound quality or file size.

Recording in Windows Sound Recorder

Is your sound card installed? (Chapter 10 covers the installation.) Are the Windows drivers installed? (Chapter 17 has that story.) Then you're ready to record something by using the Windows Sound Recorder. In fact, even if your sound card came with its own recording software, Sound Recorder is a quick and easy way to get your sounds on disk. To use Sound Recorder, follow these steps:

1. Double-click on Sound Recorder icon from the Program Manager.

Usually lurking in the Accessories group, the Sound Recorder icon looks like a little microphone. A double-click brings Sound Recorder on-screen, as shown in Figure 18-1.

Figure 18-1:
Windows'
Sound
Recorder
can record
sounds and
add a few
special
effects.

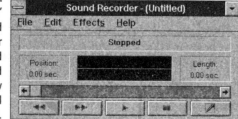

2. **Prepare to record your sound.**

   Check your sound card to see where the microphone plugs in. (After you've figured it out, write down the location on the Cheat Sheet in the front of the book so that you don't have to peek at the sound card with a flashlight anymore.)

   Or if you're recording from your computer's CD-ROM drive, make sure that your music CD is loaded and ready to be played back.

   Finally, if you're recording from your home stereo, make sure that the cables are hooked up correctly. (Chapter 13 covers this topic.)

3. **Adjust your sound card's mixer, if it has one.**

   Most sound cards come with a *mixer*, software that lets you choose what you're recording and fine-tune the recording level. For example, you can choose to record from the microphone, CD-ROM drive, home stereo, MIDI synthesizer, or even several sources at the same time. For example, Sound Blaster 16 comes with the mixer program shown in Figure 18-2.

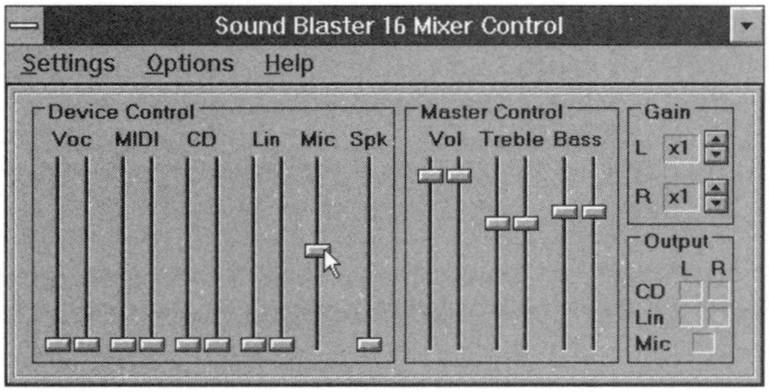

Figure 18-2:
Sound
Blaster's
mixer lets
you fine-
tune what
you're
recording.

4. **Click on the Sound Recorder button with the picture of the microphone.**

   Sound Recorder immediately starts recording any incoming sounds and temporarily stores them in your computer's memory.

5. **Start making the sound to be recorded.**

   It's time to start making noise: barf into the microphone, play your music CD, or start whatever else you want to record. If everything is hooked up correctly, the little green line inside Sound Recorder begins to quiver, reflecting the incoming sound, as shown in Figure 18-3. The bigger the quiver, the louder the sound.

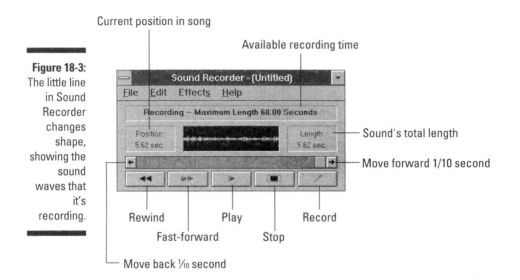

Current position in song

Available recording time

Figure 18-3:
The little line
in Sound
Recorder
changes
shape,
showing the
sound
waves that
it's
recording.

Sound's total length

Move forward 1/10 second

Rewind   Play   Record

Fast-forward   Stop

Move back ¹⁄₁₀ second

Do you see where Sound Recorder says `Maximum Length 60.0 Seconds` near the window's top in Figure 18-3? This message indicates the number of seconds of sound that Sound Recorder can capture before it turns off. The more memory your computer has, the more seconds of recording time a recording program can give you. (Sound Recorder can't handle more than 60 seconds, but other recording programs can.)

Don't record any sounds for too long — they consume an incredibly large amount of disk space. When your recording is done, jump to Step 6 as soon as possible.

If the little wavy green line starts bumping into the top or bottom edges of its little window, your sound is coming in too loud. To avoid distortion, turn down the volume by turning down your home stereo, using the mixer program to cut back on the volume, or telling Mick Jagger to keep his lips from flapping onto the microphone.

6. Click on the black square button to stop recording.

Sound Recorder stops recording new sounds.

7. Click on the Rewind button to rewind.

The Rewind button — the first button on the left — has two black triangles facing left.

8. Click on the single black triangle to hear your recording.

Does it sound OK? Great! But if it's not perfect on the first try, just erase it by selecting New from Sound Recorder's File menu. This step lets you start all over. Jump back to Step 3 to adjust any sound levels or cards and try again with a new recording.

When your recording sounds perfect — or just needs a little sound trimmed off the beginning or end — move on to Step 9. You can edit any extraneous sounds later.

9. **Choose Save from the File menu and save the sound to a file.**

   Type in a name for your file, just as if you were saving a file in a word processor or spreadsheet.

✔ Sound Recorder gets lazy when saving files. You need to type in the WAV extension yourself. Unlike most other Windows programs, Sound Recorder doesn't add an extension automatically.

✔ When not using your microphone, turn it off and keep its level low in your sound card's mixing program. Microphones can bring accidental noise into other recordings.

✔ If your sound card comes with a mixing program, use it. Keep all the volume levels low for everything but what you're recording.

Playing Sounds in Windows

Compared to recording sounds, playing sounds is a breeze. You don't need to wade through any complicated menus or decipher any numbers.

To play a sound in Windows, find that sound's filename in File Manager. (Sound files end with the letters WAV.) Then double-click on the filename. Sound Recorder hops on-screen, sound in hand. Click on the Sound Recorder's Play button — the middle of the five buttons — and Windows plays your sound.

✔ Actually, Windows *tries* to play the sound. For example, if the file was recorded by somebody at 44 kHz — and your sound card can only handle 22 kHz — Windows doesn't play it.

✔ To hear a lot of files in a hurry, load Sound Recorder and minimize it to an icon at the bottom of the screen. Then drag filenames from File Manager and drop them on the Sound Recorder icon. You instantly hear the sounds played back.

Editing Sounds and Adding Special Effects

After you've recorded a sound, you don't have to merely save it. You can edit it — just as if it were a letter. Most sound recording programs let you chop out portions of sound at the beginning or end; others let you alter the sound slightly.

✔ To delete extraneous sounds at the end of a recording, slide Sound Recorder's control bar to where you want the recording to end. Then choose Delete After Current Position from the Edit menu.

✔ To delete extraneous sounds from the beginning of a recording, slide Sound Recorder's control bar to where you want the recording to begin. Then choose Delete Before Current Position from the Edit menu.

✔ Do you want to hear two sound files played back at the same time? Load your first file in Sound Recorder and choose Mix with File from the Edit menu. Sound Recorder combines the two files. Save the mixture under a new name so that you don't overwrite your old file.

✔ To hear two sound files played back one after the other, use Sound Recorder's Insert file command from the Edit menu. Sound Recorder combines the two, playing one after another. Save the file under a new name, however, so that you don't overwrite your old file.

✔ If you hear a pop when a recording begins or ends, Sound Recorder's Delete features can easily erase that sound from the file.

✔ Windows' Sound Recorder works well for simple recording and editing, but the sound recording software that comes with your sound card can probably handle more detailed jobs.

Table 18-1 shows some of the sound effects you may see on a menu and what effects they have. Windows' Sound Recorder can perform the first five effects in the table.

Table 18-1	Sound Effects
This Effect	*Does This to the Sound*
Increase/decrease volume	Makes a sound louder or softer. If you make it too loud, however, it turns into pure distortion. Cool!
Increase/decrease speed	Turns voices into either chipmunk sounds or HAL sounds (at the end of *2001: A Space Odyssey*).
Add echo	Makes sound repeat subtly but can sound like "pings" if overused.
Reverse	Just like it sounds, this plays a sound backwards. (Try it on CHORD.WAV, a sound that comes with Windows.)
Mix	Combines two sound files so that they play back simultaneously.
Reverb	Makes something sound like it was recorded in an empty warehouse.

Making Windows Explode When It's Angry

After you have had a sound card for a while, you get used to Windows playing back certain sounds when certain things happen. You hear a happy "Ta-da" sound when you start Windows for the day. When you shut Windows down, you hear a little chime sound. If you do something wrong in a program, you hear an angry chord played by a frustrated piano player.

These sounds start getting old after a month or two — and the mind starts to ponder. Computers don't explode — but what if Windows made an explosion *sound* instead of that wimpy chord sound when something goes wrong?

Here's your chance to add explosions to Windows, by following these steps:

1. **Record your explosion and copy the file to your Windows directory.**

   Start by grabbing some dynamite from a nearby construction site and packing it loosely around the microphone.

   A slightly less messy method is simply to gurgle into the microphone while recording with Windows' Sound Recorder, a process described previously in this chapter.

   Or if you have any albums, CDs, or tapes with explosions on them, record those. Chapter 13 shows how to hook up your sound card to your home stereo.

   After the file is copied to your Windows directory, it's easier to find later.

2. **Double-click on the Control Panel's Sound icon.**

   The Sound dialog box comes on-screen, as shown in Figure 18-4. The dialog box contains *events* that produce certain sounds when the Sound Recorder encounters them while you're working. Don't be surprised if your dialog box looks a little different, because many programs add their own sounds and events. Table 18-2 explains what the events mean.

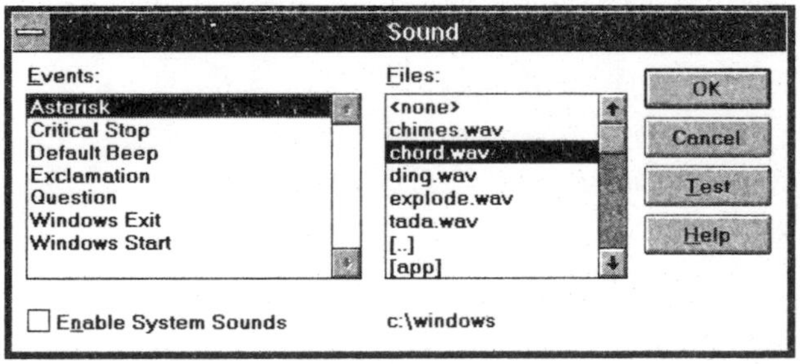

Figure 18-4:
The events with their corresponding sound files.

If you haven't installed or set up a sound card, Windows doesn't let you change any of these settings. The sounds are *grayed out* — dimmer than the rest of the text.

3. Click on the Exclamation event and then click on your explosion file.

If you don't see your explosion file listed by name, you probably didn't copy it to your Windows directory. So either click on the little boxes to move to the directory where the file is living or stop what you're doing and copy the file to your Windows directory. (Sometimes it's easier to find sound files if they're all living in the same directory.)

Do you see the Enable System Sounds box? If checked, Windows will play all the sound files you've connected to your events. If it's not checked, Windows will only play sounds when it loads and exits.

4. Click on the Test button.

Windows plays your explosion file and gives you a feel for what lies ahead.

5. Click on the OK button.

This step saves your choice. Now, whenever you make a mistake in Windows, you'd better stand back.

To hear the boom for the first time, make a mistake on purpose: open a Write file, move to the front of the first line, and press your PageUp key. Boom!

What are events, anyway?

When Windows flashes a message on your screen, it is creating an event. Usually you'll see an icon next to each message. The following table shows the icons you'll see for each event.

This Event and Picture	*Mean This*
Asterisk/Information	A box appears on-screen that offers more information about your current situation.
Critical Stop	An urgent box warns of dire consequences if you proceed, but it lets you click on the OK button to keep going anyway.
Default Beep	The most common event, this means you've clicked outside of a dialog box or done something equally harmless.
Exclamation	This box urges caution, but to a slightly less degree than the Critical Stop warning.
Question	A box is asking you to choose among a variety of choices.
Windows Exit	Plays when you shut down Windows.
Windows Start	Plays when you load Windows.

Chapter 19

Putting Photos on Your PC (That Kodak CD Stuff)

● ●

In This Chapter

▶ What's Kodak Photo CD?

▶ How much does Kodak Photo CD cost?

▶ What sort of CD-ROM drive and software do I need?

▶ What format are the pictures?

▶ How can I make a multimedia photo album?

● ●

*F*or years, Kodak has covered the fireplace mantel market. Nine out of ten family mantels boast a family photograph, usually a wedding picture or high-school prom photo.

Today, Kodak is heading for the computer market. People have been taping photos to the sides of their monitors for years, but Kodak wants something more. They want people to display their photos on the monitor itself — using Kodak's Photo CD technology.

This chapter covers Kodak's Photo CDs — what they are, what they can do, and whether it's time to move your pictures from paper to pixels.

What is Kodak Photo CD?

Kodak Photo CD isn't anything mysterious. You point and click your same old camera, just like normal. You drop your film off at the counter and pick up your negatives and prints the next day. (Or the next hour, if you live close enough to the right place.)

Kodak Photo CD doesn't change any of that. The person behind the counter simply hands you a *compact disc* along with your negatives and prints.

If you have the right type of CD-ROM drive — and the right kind of software — you can see your recently snapped photos on your monitor. And after the picture is on the screen, you can do just about anything: turn your spouse into wallpaper, toss a picture into a business report or desktop-published brochure or flyer, or simply keep your family's scrapbook on your computer. Your pictures won't turn gray, fall out, or get thumbprints when perused by friends at parties.

- A Kodak Photo CD looks like any other CD. It's a gold-colored disc with the words *Kodak Photo CD* stamped on the top in black letters.

- Your Photo CD comes with a *contact sheet.* A contact sheet is a five-inch square picture with an itty-bitty picture of each image stored on the CD. (It's easier to tell which pictures are on which disc that way.)

- You don't *need* to have all your pictures copied to a CD when they're developed (although it's often cheaper this way). If only two of the pictures look decent, take those negatives back to the developer. They'll stick those two pictures onto the CD, leaving the others off. (Some developers charge a minimum fee, though, so ask for the cost when you drop your negatives off.)

- Or if you prefer everything on CD, don't bother having prints made. Simply ask the developer to develop the negatives, store the images on the CD, and forget about making prints. You can have prints made from the CD later on down the road.

- Photo-fun department: copy a photo from the CD to your hard drive. Use graphics-editing software to copy a second nose onto Aunt Hannah. Copy the edited file to a floppy disk, take it to a photo lab, and get a couple of prints made. (Check in the Yellow Pages under Photo Finishing or Photo Lab.)

- Kodak Photo CD veterans call the discs *PCDs* (Pee-Sea-Deez), short for *Photo CDs.*

- Finally, Photo CD is for users of 35mm film; older film is truly history. Photo professionals who use weird film formats like 70mm or 120mm film can get special Photo CDs made to handle the extra images.

What's All This Kodak Stuff Going to Cost Me?

OK, here's the question everybody wants an answer to: How much does all this stuff cost? Just like film-developing costs, Photo CD costs vary. When you drop off a roll of film, some places charge 65 cents per picture, with a $15 minimum.

The cost goes up a buck or so for slides or if you want previously developed pictures transferred to disk. Add in the cost of prints, if you want to show pictures of Little Joey to people who don't have computers yet.

Some places also charge for the CD itself — often $10 or more. The good news? You can reuse the same CD to have up to 100 pictures stored on it. (This reuse trick only works for *multisession* CD-ROM drives, described in the next section.)

When you add everything up, you can count on spending about $25 to $35 for your 24-exposure roll of film to be developed, printed, and copied to a Photo CD.

- ✔ There's more. After you have the Photo CD, you need a CD-ROM drive to read it. The CD-ROM drives that can read 'em are described in the next section.

- ✔ You'll want a video card with at *least* 256 colors. With only 256 colors, your pictures will only look OK — nothing spectacular. For *wow*, you'd better have a 24-bit video card — these cards can display more than 16 million colors, making the photos look like, well, *real* photos.

- ✔ Finally, you'll need software; it's not included with the Photo CD. Kodak's cheapest picture viewer retails for $39.95. Called Kodak Photo CD Access, it lets you zoom in to certain areas and save the results as BMP, EPS, PCX, RIF, TIF, or WMF files. (It's available for DOS, Windows, and the Macintosh.)

- ✔ Although Kodak thought families would snap up Photo CDs to show on their TV sets, households have been slow to buy home entertainment consoles like CD-i and 3DO (covered in Chapter 9). So Kodak has grabbed the computer market, instead. Kodak Photo CDs are the least expensive — and most convenient — ways for computer owners to convert their photos into computer files.

Will My CD-ROM Drive Work with Kodak Photo CDs?

Kodak's CDs store their information a wee bit differently than most other computer CDs. This means that some CD-ROM drives can't read them — you won't be able to see the pictures on the monitor.

To make sure your CD-ROM drive can read Kodak Photo CDs, look for three things:

- ◆ If it says Kodak Photo CD compatible right on the box, you're home free. In fact, most CD-ROM drives sold today are Kodak Photo CD compatible.

- ◆ If the drive can handle the CD-XA disc format, it can view a Kodak Photo CD.

- ◆ And if the drive can handle CD-XA discs *and* says it's multisession, you're also home free. Multisession drives can read Kodak Photo CDs even after you've added a second or third batch of photos to them.

- ✔ Computers aren't the only things that can read Kodak Photo CDs. Kodak sells Photo CD players — little CD-ROM drives that you can hook up to your TV set — for about $250.

- ✔ Home entertainment centers like 3DO and CD-i can also read the discs, displaying the pictures on your television set.

- ✔ CD-ROM drives don't need to be particularly fast to read a Photo CD; they just need to be compatible with Kodak's disc format.

What Software Do I Need for Photo CDs?

If your CD-ROM drive can read the Photo CDs, you can view that hot-air balloon photo on your monitor — *if* you have the right software. Because the discs don't come with software, you need to scrounge it up on your own.

Most graphics software companies are now adding support for Photo CDs; eventually, you'll be able to call up Photo CD files (they end with the letters *PCD*) as easily as if they were BMP or PCX files.

If your CD-ROM is attached to a SCSI card, you might find that the SCSI card comes with the software. For instance, many Adaptec cards come with Lantern, a photo-CD viewer.

If you don't have graphics software like Adobe's PhotoStyler, Kodak will be happy to sell you its own viewing software. Kodak's $39.95 Photo CD Access software, seen in Figure 19-1, is probably the least expensive way to view your pictures and transfer them into more common graphics files.

Access brings up a *contact sheet*, which is a window containing thumbnail-sized pictures of all the photos on the CD. Double-click on the tiny picture you want to see, and Access brings it to the screen. Then, with the photo on the screen, you can cut out the yucky parts, rotate the pictures, or enlarge certain areas to see more detail. (Is that *really* a UFO just above that third haystack?)

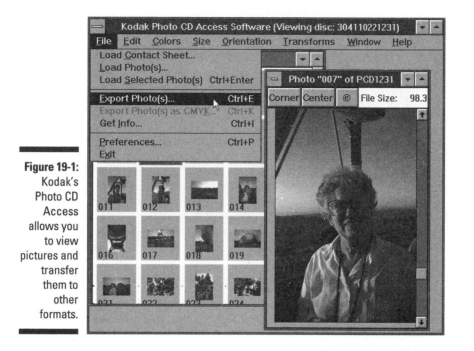

Figure 19-1:
Kodak's
Photo CD
Access
allows you
to view
pictures and
transfer
them to
other
formats.

Done? Push a button and Access lets you save your newly edited picture as a BMP, PCX, EPS, RIF, or other popular file format.

   ✔ If your pile of Photo CDs starts looking as packed as a shoe box full of negatives, check out Kodak's Shoebox software. It creates a file on your hard drive that contains a contact sheet for all your Photo CDs, making it easier to remember which photo is hiding on which CD.

   ✔ Kodak makes other software for setting up presentations, playing back CD-i Portfolio discs, and making slide shows.

   ✔ Software for opening Kodak's PCD images has been slow in coming, primarily because Kodak charges software makers fees for the right to open Photo CD files. You probably won't see free Photo CD viewing software for a long time.

Where Can I Get Photo CDs Made?

Because the Kodak Photo CD technology is still new, it's not always easy to find a place that will transfer your photos to disc.

Many photo shops (even the one-hour developers) can't make the CDs themselves but can ship your order to a place that does. You'll probably have to wait up to two weeks to get your CD, but it's convenient to drop off your film at a local shop. It's also expensive.

Some of the larger photo shops can transfer your pictures to CDs. Because Photo CD equipment is mega-expensive, these shops only thrive in large cities.

The final alternative is to go mail order. In fact, that's where your local one-hour photo developer sends its Photo CD requests. A mail-order service usually offers the lowest prices and fastest service — many offer overnight or 48-hour turnaround.

> ✔ Because Photo CD technology is still new, not all labs use people trained in this technology. If possible, shop by recommendation to find a place that's done a good job for somebody else.
>
> ✔ If your lab didn't do a good job, complain. Most labs will redo the job for free if the first didn't turn out.
>
> ✔ For a list of Photo CD developers in your area, call Kodak's Photo CD hotline at 800-235-6325. They'll tell you anything you want to know about Photo CDs, including the closest place to drop off your film.

What Format Does a Photo CD Use?

After developing your film, the Kodak Photo CD-making machine scans each negative in five different resolutions, from quick and dirty to incredibly detailed. The machine then puts a copy of each photo resolution onto the Photo CD — that's right, your disc contains *several* different copies of each photo, as seen in Table 19-1.

Table 19-1	Kodak Photo CD Resolution Types
Resolution	*How They Differ*
128x192	Allows you to see pictures quickly
256x384	Provides pictures for quick, low-resolution uses
512x768	Creates moderate-resolution pictures that look good on TV
1024x1536	Provides high-resolution images that look good on High Definition TV
2048x3172	Creates photograph-quality images for printing (when copied to your hard drive, these can eat more than ten megabytes of space)
4096x6144	Extra-high resolution that comes on Kodak's Pro Photo CD discs; designed for professionals

Different resolutions work best for different tasks. Smaller images work best where speed, not quality, is important. Or if you plan to touch up some pictures and print them out, go for the highest-quality image your computer can handle.

Kodak's discs come in three types:

Kodak Photo CD: The CD most people are talking about, this disc can hold 100 photos, each stored in the first five resolutions from Table 19-1 — more than enough for most people's needs. The CD serves as a "digital negative" of sorts; even if you've lost your original negatives, you can still get prints made from the CD.

Kodak Pro Photo CD: For professionals who use 35mm, 70mm, 120mm, and even 4x5-inch film, these discs are the best choice. They contain the same resolutions found on the regular Photo CDs but also contain a super-high 4096x6144 resolution. Because the extra resolution takes up extra space, the disc can't hold 100 pictures. Other than that, Pro Photo CDs are identical to regular Photo CDs, and they use the same software.

Kodak Photo CD Portfolio Disc: These multimedia discs contain sound *and* pictures and are aimed at the presentation, kiosk, and commercial markets. People with CD-i and 3DO units can pop in a "Marshall Field's Holiday Gift Guide" Portfolio disc and shop for Waterford crystal ($250). It's a multimedia computerized commercial!

- ✔ To pack all these photos onto a CD, Kodak uses a secret compression mechanism. If you peek at the Photo CD in Windows File Manager, you won't spot any BMP or PCX files. The files on Kodak CDs end with the letters *PCD*, and only Kodak-licensed software can open them.

- ✔ More and more graphics packages are starting to support the PCD file format, though, letting you open the files without buying Kodak's software.

- ✔ If your graphics program won't open the files, your cheapest alternative is Kodak's Photo CD Access software, described earlier in this chapter. For about $40, you can turn Kodak's PCD files into BMP files to pop into the family newsletter.

- ✔ Kodak includes a Photo CD player with its Access software, so computer owners can also shop for Waterford crystal on Portfolio discs.

Making a Multimedia Family Album on Your Hard Drive

If your photos are computerized, you might as well computerize your family album, too. Follow these steps to make a multimedia photo album using Windows Write and Kodak's Access software.

1. **Load Windows and put the Kodak Photo CD in the CD-ROM drive.**

   Nothing new here; just be sure to put the CD in a caddy if your CD-ROM drive expects one.

2. **Open Kodak's Access software.**

   Double-click on the Access icon from Program Manager, and Access hops to the screen, as seen in Figure 19-2.

3. **Load the contact sheet.**

   Choose Load Contact Sheet from the File menu. When Access asks which drive your CD-ROM drive lives on, click on the proper letter. (It usually guesses the right drive but it asks you to click, just to be sure.) Access brings up the contact sheet — a page of tiny pictures showing what's on the disc.

   Access slows down when displaying a lot of photos on its contact sheet. To speed things up, make your contact sheet a single row of pictures. Access only has to display a few contact sheet photos that way and won't slow down by constantly showing them all. To make the changes permanent, choose Preferences from the File menu and change the Contact Sheet Defaults to Single Row instead of Columns.

4. **Double-click on the desired photo.**

   When you double-click on the itty-bitty picture in the contact sheet, Access brings that little picture's *real* picture to the screen, as seen in Figure 19-3.

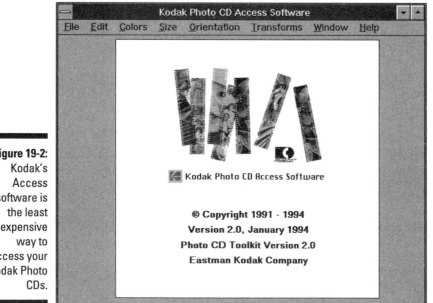

Figure 19-2:
Kodak's Access software is the least expensive way to access your Kodak Photo CDs.

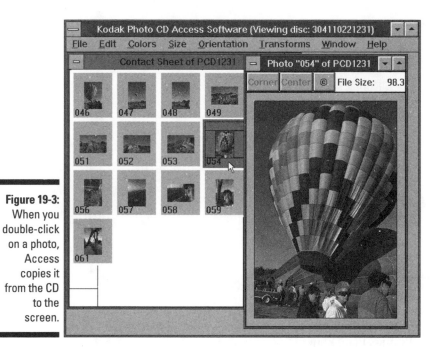

Figure 19-3:
When you
double-click
on a photo,
Access
copies it
from the CD
to the
screen.

5. Adjust the photo's size and color.

Does the photo look too big or too small on the page? Change its size by
clicking on Size from the top menu. A list of different resolutions will
drop down — the bigger the numbers, the bigger the picture will grow on
your screen.

Big pictures and lots of color take up a lot of hard disk space on your new
family album. If you want a more manageable photo album, stick with the
smaller pictures and lower colors. (Choose 256 Colors from the Colors
menu, and the picture will only include 256 colors of the original. All the
pictures in this chapter started out as 256-color images before transform-
ing into black-and-white book pictures, by the way.)

6. Click on Copy.

Does the picture look good? Then click on Copy from the Edit menu.
Nothing happens. At least, it *looks* like nothing happened. But under the
covers, Access quietly sends a copy of your photo to Windows Clipboard.

If you're doubtful, double-click on Windows Clipboard Viewer icon and
take a look. The picture should be sitting pretty.

7. Open Write and choose Paste Special.

Double-click on Write's icon from Program Manager and choose Paste
Special from the Edit menu, as seen in Figure 19-4.

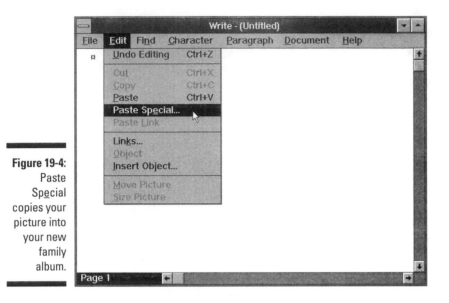

Figure 19-4:
Paste
Special
copies your
picture into
your new
family
album.

When the little box full of options comes up, double-click on the word Bitmap. Poof! Your picture pops into Write, as seen in Figure 19-5.

8. Add titles and captions in Write.

Now comes the fun part. Type in any comments or captions you'd like to save with the photo. Get as fancy as you want, perhaps adding the words *Family Album* to the top, like in Figure 19-6.

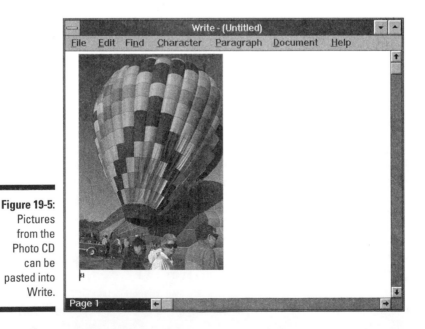

Figure 19-5:
Pictures
from the
Photo CD
can be
pasted into
Write.

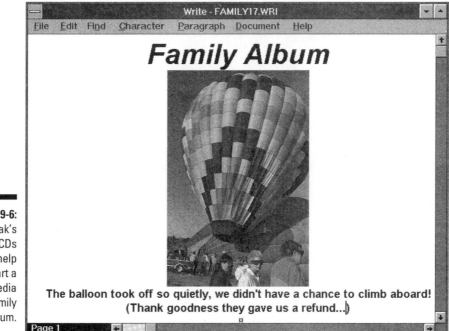

Family Album

The balloon took off so quietly, we didn't have a chance to climb aboard!
(Thank goodness they gave us a refund...)

Figure 19-6:
Kodak's
Photo CDs
can help
start a
multimedia
family
album.

If the picture suddenly looks weird with inverted colors, *stop*. You've accidentally told Write to edit your photo — and if you type anything into the keyboard, Write will delete your photo, replacing it with your incoming words! The fix? If Write highlights the photo, making it look weird, press your left-arrow key. Doing so moves the cursor to the space just before the picture. Hit Enter a few times to move the photo a little further down on the page and then you'll have more room to type. Whew.

From here, you're on your own. Feel free to add some sounds (described in Chapter 18). Load your sound into Sound Recorder and choose Copy from its Edit menu, just like you did with Kodak's Access software. Then choose Paste from Write's Edit menu. A little microphone appears in your Write file, ready to play back the sound when you double-click on it.

Or if you've been capturing your camcorder's videos onto your hard drive (Chapter 5), copy a video into the family album, as well.

You're only limited by your imagination (and your budget, and the patience level of your spouse when you start spending more time playing with the family album than your family. Be careful. . . .).

Chapter 20

Video for Windows, Camcorders, and Movies

• •

In This Chapter

▶ Understanding Video for Windows

▶ Recording in VidCap

▶ Optimizing your video recordings

▶ Changing videos in VidEdit

▶ Editing out the dopey stuff

• •

*I*n the prehistoric days of computing — about four years ago — a sound card was tops for multimedia. If your computer could record and play sounds (beeps didn't count), your computer was considered a first-class act.

Today, mere sound is not enough. Multimedia computers need to play movies — anything from old snippets of John Wayne movies to Florida travel videos. And to be truly on top, computers need video capture cards so that they can create movies as well as play them back.

Chapter 5 covers video capture cards, which are the devices that can computerize your home videos. This chapter covers Video for Windows, the software included with most of the capture cards. By peeking at Video for Windows now, you're also getting a preview — because Video for Windows will be standard equipment on the next version of Windows.

And don't throw away your sound card. Video capture cards capture only video. You still need your sound card to capture the sound track.

What Is Video for Windows?

Video for Windows isn't a single program that comes in a box. No, when people say Video for Windows, they could be talking about several different things.

First, the Video for Windows *runtime version* is a way to watch movies, not record them. Described in Chapter 17, the runtime version can't capture movies or control any video capture cards. It simply upgrades the Windows Media Player so that it can play back movies.

The other Video for Windows software comes packaged with most video capture cards. It's a two-program set. The first part, VidCap, grabs the incoming video off your VCR or camcorder and stuffs it into a file on your hard drive. Then the second part, VidEdit, kicks in so that you can open your newly captured video file, chop out the boring parts, and compress the video file so that it's not so laughingly large.

- ✔ How big is laughingly large? Well, a postage-stamp-sized movie lasting one minute with medium quality can consume about 20MB of your hard drive. VidEdit compresses the file — but until it's compressed, a video file can eat up that much space when VidCap first pulls it in. (Unless you have an Intel Super Video Recorder, described a little later.)

- ✔ Microsoft used to sell Video for Windows in the stores for about $200. Nobody bought it because it came free with most video capture cards. So Microsoft isn't selling the latest version, Video for Windows 1.1, either. It's just packaging the version with most new video capture cards.

- ✔ Are you stuck with the old version? Call the maker of your video capture card or whomever sold the software to you. You may get a discount on the upgrade to version 1.1.

- ✔ Because Video for Windows can control different brands of video capture equipment, its menus look slightly different on different computers. Some menus may be changed, or some options may not work with a particular card. (You haven't done anything wrong.)

- ✔ If you only want to watch movies, not play them, Chapter 17 shows how to install the runtime version; the rest of this chapter shows how to create and edit movies.

Recording Your Videos with VidCap

Are you ready to record your own movies? First, make sure that your video capture card is hooked up to your camcorder or VCR. (This step is covered in Chapter 14.)

The next step is to *defragment* your hard drive. Without getting into specifics, defragmenting a hard drive is like making a clean spot on your desk by swiping everything into a corner with your elbow, leaving a nice fresh spot to put things. With a defragmented hard drive, Windows can store the video as quickly as possible. Have you ever defragged? Chapter 29 gets you started. It's an important step if you want the best video quality possible.

Next, double-click on the VidCap icon. (Don't confuse it with the Windows Recorder icon, which belongs to one of the programs that comes with Windows 3.1. Recorder captures only macros — keystrokes — and you're after something more exciting than that.) When VidCap rises on-screen, it looks like a dark little movie screen, as shown in Figure 20-1.

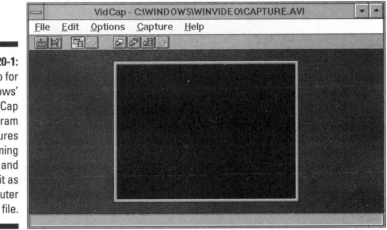

Figure 20-1:
Video for Windows' VidCap program captures incoming video and stores it as a computer file.

Finally, before starting to record, you probably want to tweak the various settings in VidCap to fine-tune your computer's performance. VidCap has just as many buttons as your camcorder.

If you're not a tweaker, never will be, and don't care about any of the boring menu options, just head for the end of this chapter, where you'll find a fast tutorial for getting that movie on the hard drive as quickly as possible. (And editing out any embarrassing parts, as well.)

Setting the capture file

Your computer takes a little bit of time when creating a file on a hard drive — not much time, but a little disk-housekeeping is involved. In order to pack incoming video onto your hard drive as quickly as possible, VidCap wants you to create a file in advance. This advance file, called a *capture file*, is a temporary holding tank for your incoming video.

Choose Save Captured Video As from VidCap's File menu, shown in Figure 20-2, and type in a filename and size. Optimally, you want a capture file of the maximum size — 60MB — which is large enough to record almost two minutes of high-quality video or four minutes of video with slightly less quality.

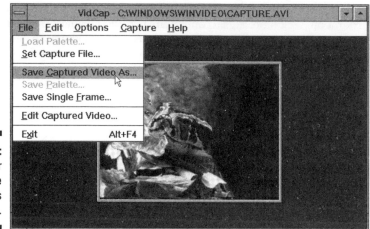

Figure 20-2:
Make your
capture file
as large as
possible.

If 60MB is too big, try recording smaller videos. If you limit the video to less than 30 seconds, you can probably get by with 20MB or so. Welcome to the huge-hard-drive world of video editing!

✔ Your captured video won't *always* be as large as your capture file. The file just serves as a storage spot. After you've captured the video, you can compress it into a smaller file by using VidEdit, Video for Windows' partner.

✔ If you're going to be recording a lot of video, however, you need a *big* hard drive.

✔ Unlike other video capture cards, Intel's Smart Video Recorder compresses video at the same time it grabs it. This technique has two advantages: The program doesn't need a huge capture file; and you don't need to compress the video in VidEdit, a process that can take several minutes to an hour or so, depending on the quality.

✔ If your incoming video gets too big to fit in the capture file, nothing explodes. Video for Windows simply makes the file bigger. But that last minute scrounging for hard disk space can slow down your movie capture, leaving some jerky spots.

Adjusting the audio format

Video capture cards capture only video — they don't record any sound with the movies. This can be a big letdown when you're shooting music videos. However, VidCap is polite enough to send the video's sound track to your computer's sound card. The *sound card* grabs the incoming sound and quickly passes the information to Video for Windows, which stores it with your video file.

This process is pretty automatic and behind the scenes, actually. However, to change your sound recording quality, click on Audio Format from VidCap's Options menu. The Audio Format dialog box, shown in Figure 20-3, pops on-screen.

Figure 20-3:
For the smallest recordings, choose these audio settings in the Audio Format dialog box.

Audio Format

Sample Size
- ◉ 8 bit   ○ 16 bit

Channels
- ◉ Mono   ○ Stereo

Frequency
- ◉ 11 kHz   ○ 22 kHz   ○ 44 kHz

OK
Cancel
Level...

For the smallest video file, stick with the audio settings in Figure 20-3. Choosing any of the other settings immediately doubles the amount of space the sound track uses in your video file.

Click on the Level button and then play the video you want to record. A little audio meter pops up, letting you know whether you should adjust your sound card's mixer to record at a higher or lower rate.

Adjusting the video format

VidCap can record big movies that plod along slowly like a slide show. Or it can record thumbnail-sized pictures that look zippy and lifelike. Only you and your computer can find a happy medium.

To adjust the video's look and feel, choose Video Format from VidCap's Options menu. Although different menus look different for different cards, most menus let you change the video's size, quality, frame rate, and number of colors.

Size: Try recording at the tiniest size, usually 160x120, and then play back the video and see how it looks. OK? Then try the next highest size, usually 240x180, and see if your computer can keep up. When the video starts looking a little jerky, go back to the preceding size: you've found your computer's limit.

Quality: Some cards let you choose your video's quality by sliding a little bar to such options as High Quality and Low Quality, Worse and Better, or Sucks Exponentially and Yowza. You'll have to experiment to find a compromise between file size and quality.

Frame Rate: Start by setting the rate at 15 frames per second, which is half the frame rate you see on TV. The thrill of seeing video on a computer makes up for the slightly jerky quality of the video.

Colors: Finally, if you have an 8-bit video card — which can handle only 256 colors — you have to fiddle with *palettes*, or you'll wind up with a black-and-white movie. If your card can handle more than 256 colors, you don't have to worry about palettes — or the technical sidebar that follows.

When recording video through VidCap, make it as high quality as your equipment can manage. The resulting file is huge, but the VidEdit program gives you more control over how to cut down its size.

If you don't create a palette, you'll get a black-and-white movie!

Although 8-bit, 256-color video cards are getting old, they can still display a pretty lifelike picture — if you squint a little. But here's the catch: although these cards can really display 256,144 colors, they can show only 256 of these colors at the same time.

For example, a picture of an orange origami crane can contain only 256 colors. To look its best, the picture probably contains close to 256 shades of orange alone. With 256,144 colors to choose from, the picture can contain some pretty realistic detail. The particular colors making up the crane picture are known as a *palette*. Each 256-color picture uses a palette that looks best for its contents.

Now, here's the problem: your video card switches to different palettes when you're looking at different pictures. After all, the palette used for your orange crane would look terrible on a picture of a bluebird. The video card needs to switch to a different palette. (In fact, this palette switching is why the screen looks weird when you switch between 256-color pictures. As Windows displays the current picture's palette, it's forced to use that palette for all the pictures in the background, too.)

So? Well, a video consists of hundreds of 256-color pictures, slapped on-screen, one after the other. How can Windows find a mere 256 colors to depict all these pictures? It can't, so VidCap doesn't bother. It merely records the video in black and white.

How can you get color? By creating the palette yourself. Choose Palette from the Capture menu. Then tell VidCap to create a palette from a single picture and use that palette for the rest of the movie. Or you can tell VidCap to watch what you're recording and create an average palette based on the colors used most often. When VidCap starts using your new palette, your movie will be in color — but it won't look spectacular.

Your best bet? Trash the card and buy one that can handle more than 256 colors. Your second best bet? Keep your clips short and don't film things with a lot of colors. If you're going to be filming people, make sure that VidCap creates your palette based on frames with a lot of skin color, or everybody will look washed out.

One last thing: when you're choosing a palette, VidCap wisely suggests that you use only 236 colors, not the full 256. What gives? Windows uses 20 colors for its little bars and windows, so it prefers you not snatch these 20 colors away. (Windows runs a little faster in this way, too.)

Adjusting the video source

VidCap needs to know where your video is coming from. If you're recording live from a beach cottage in France, you need to push different buttons than if you're recording from a VCR in an Australian time-share. When you choose Video Source from VidCap's Options menu, you probably have to choose between the following options:

Composite or S-Video: Covered in Chapter 14, these options describe your camcorder or VCR's format. (S-Video is the fancier option that the salesperson tried to talk you into purchasing at the consumer electronics store.)

Input Type: What broadcast format does your country use? France uses SECAM; Australia likes PAL; and the United States prefers NTSC. Head to Chapter 5 for instructions if you're vacationing in Peru or Singapore and then click on the appropriate format here.

VCR: Are you recording something that is coming from videotape? Then choose the VCR or VCR Input option; otherwise, the screen looks tilted at the top. If you're recording something "live" with your camcorder, don't check the VCR box.

Picture: Most cards let you fiddle with the contrast, brightness, tint, and other levels. Unless your video is looking really weird, leave the controls alone.

✔ What happens if you choose PAL when you need NTSC? Nothing horrendous. The picture just looks tilted at the top. Switch to NTSC, and the picture evens out. (United States users probably want 60 Hz NTSC, if the menu lets you choose between 50 and 60.)

✔ You probably don't have to fiddle with that NTSC or SECAM/PAL stuff more than once. Most cards let you save the settings the first time you change them.

Previewing the video and other options

Sometimes VidCap doesn't put your incoming video on-screen; the window stays blank. To turn on the video, click on Preview Video from the Options menu so that you can see what you're doing. If you can already watch your video through your camcorder or TV set, try leaving the option turned off. Sometimes, everything works a little faster in this way. (In fact, some cards turn off the preview while they're recording.)

Also, some fancy video grabber cards do fancy things with *overlay*, a way of mingling your video with your computer graphics for special effects. Not all cards come with overlay. If they support it, however, check out the Video Display and Overlay Video choices under the Options menu to see what it can do.

Capturing options

VidCap can capture video in three ways: one picture at a time, a few pictures here and there, or the "grab all the pictures and toss 'em in the trough" mode. You'll find a little more detail on each in the paragraphs that follow:

Single Frame: If you see a good-looking picture in your video, choose Single Frame from the Capture menu. If you have quick-enough fingers, you can tell Video for Windows to grab the picture before it passes. Why bother? Well, most capture cards can grab a single frame at 640x480, but they max out at 320x240 when grabbing an entire movie. If you're looking to capture *big* wallpaper files, try Single Frame.

Frames: This mode works just like single-frame: you click when you want to grab an individual picture. However, this option puts a handy button on-screen, as shown in Figure 20-4. Just keep clicking as the movie goes by, and VidCap grabs the pictures you've chosen.

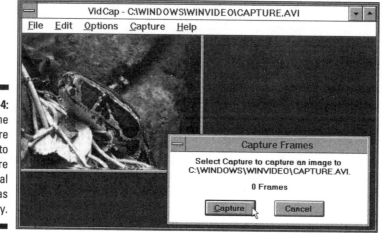

Figure 20-4: Click on the Capture button to capture individual pictures as they go by.

Video: By far the most useful, this mode lets you capture complete movies, not just a few stray pictures. However, you can still pull a few favorite pictures out of the movie while you're editing it. (The pictures will be only as large as the size of the movie, though.)

When you choose Video, a new dialog box pops up, as shown in Figure 20-5, with a whole bunch of other options. I have listed them in order of importance, in case you start yawning and don't finish.

Figure 20-5:
The most
often-used
menu in
VidCap, this
lets you
change the
video's
frame rate.

Capture Video Sequence

Frame Rate: 15.000

☒ Enable Capture Time Limit

Seconds: 15

☒ Capture Audio

Capture Method
⦿ Directly to Disk
○ Capture to Memory

☐ MCI control of source video

OK
Cancel
Audio...
Video...
Compress...
MCI...

Frame Rate: This option controls how lifelike your movies appear. The stuff on TV is flashed by at 30 frames per second (FPS). Computers are usually stuck with 15 FPS, or they can't keep up. Curse and then try out 15 FPS; it's not all that bad, actually.

Capture Audio: If there's an X in this box, VidCap records the sound track. You don't want sound? Then click in the box until the X goes away.

Enable Capture Time Limit: Do you want to record just ten seconds of video and then stop? Click here and enter **10** in the Seconds box. Otherwise, VidCap keeps recording video until you beg it to stop. (Clicking the mouse works just as well as begging.)

Capture Method: Capturing video to memory makes for better quality videos than capturing to your hard drive, especially on older 386 computers. But unless your computer has more than 8MB of RAM, it can't capture more than a few seconds of video. Stick with the Directly to Disk option.

✔ For last-minute tweaks to audio or video levels, click on the Audio or Video buttons shown in Figure 20-5. These buttons bring up the same boxes found under the Audio Format and Video Format choices from VidCap's Format menu, but in a more convenient way.

✔ People with fancy laserdisc players and other equipment can choose the MCI control of source video option. If you have the correct Windows drivers, VidCap talks directly to the equipment, making it easier to capture individual frames.

✔ After you've captured your video, you're still not through. You've only grabbed the *raw* material. Now you have to use VidEdit to compress your video into something usable.

✔ Although VidCap lets you jump right to VidEdit by choosing Edit Capture Video from the File menu, your computer may not have enough memory to run both programs at the same time. If Windows sends you an error message, run the two programs separately.

> ✔ You can edit your capture file directly in VidEdit, but to be on the safe side, choose the Save Captured Video As option from VidCap's File menu. With this option, you have a master copy in case anything bad happens.

Editing Out the Bad Stuff in VidEdit

Recording videos on a PC is like setting everything up for a ski jump: lacing the boots up tight, standing at the top of the hill, and then . . . waiting 10 or 15 minutes before you get to move. VidEdit can take from several minutes to several hours before your newly captured video is compressed and ready for final viewing.

Although VidCap pours your video onto your hard drive, VidEdit, shown in Figure 20-6, adjusts your footage before making the final movie.

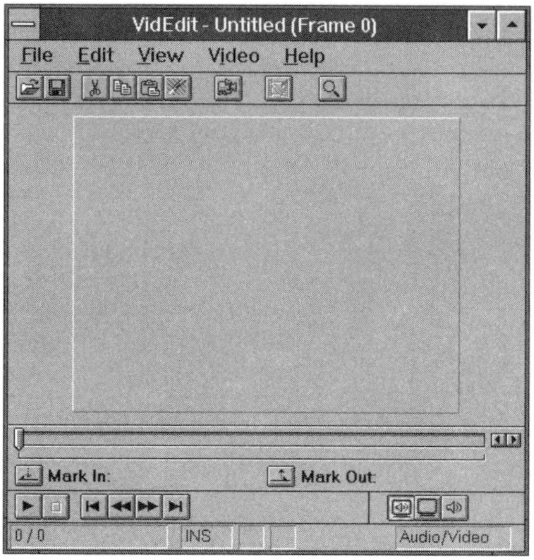

Figure 20-6:
VidEdit
helps you
edit your
captured file
into a
finished
video.

Although VidEdit can play back your movie, the movie doesn't run at full speed until it has been *compressed*. Compression, also covered in Chapter 5, cuts out some of the extraneous detail so that your computer can play back everything as smoothly as possible. But as I mentioned before, compression can take anywhere from a few minutes to a few hours.

While in VidEdit, you can examine your captured video, picture by picture; slice out the bad parts; splice in some better parts; and save the whole thing in a compressed file that not only runs more smoothly but also takes up less space than the original captured video. The next few sections explain what it takes to make VidEdit do everything as painlessly as possible.

Changing videos in VidEdit

VidEdit opens files the same way as other Windows programs. Choose Open from the File menu and double-click on the file you want to edit. VidEdit brings the file to the forefront, as illustrated in Figure 20-7.

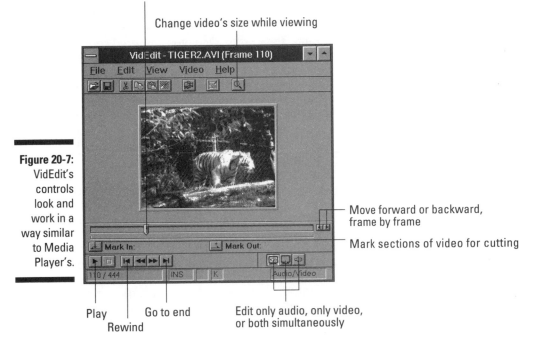

Slide this to move around in the video

Change video's size while viewing

Move forward or backward, frame by frame

Mark sections of video for cutting

Play

Rewind

Go to end

Edit only audio, only video, or both simultaneously

Figure 20-7: VidEdit's controls look and work in a way similar to Media Player's.

Do you see the buttons along the bottom of the screen that look like a VCR's controls? They work just like the buttons in Media Player (and the ones on your VCR, too). To watch the movie, click on the little black arrow on the left, and the movie starts playing back. Figure 20-7 shows some of the buttons you'll be using most often.

Your raw, unedited video looks a little rough when you play it back — but that's why you're in VidEdit. VidEdit lets you do three main things: cut out any dopey parts (and add in anything better), make sure that the sounds coincide with the video, and compress the final video into a smaller file. These choices are all covered in the following sections.

As discussed in Chapter 5, videos are a bunch of pictures strung together; however, they're often a bunch of half-pictures. Each frame in the movie isn't always a complete image — sometimes one image relies on information in earlier frames. If you freeze an image in VidEdit and it looks weird, press F5. VidEdit redraws the screen, which creates the full frame.

Editing the bad parts and putting in the good parts

Just as a word processor lets you cut and paste words, VidEdit lets you cut and paste video clips. For example, if you shot only four 3-second snippets of video on your last field trip, you can cut out everything in between the four snippets. VidEdit also lets you rearrange their order. Or, if you captured some video in another file, you can paste it in the field trip file, as well.

Cutting out bad parts: To cut out some video you don't want, you need to tell VidEdit what to get rid of. The end of the chapter offers a full tutorial, but here's the gist of it: move to the start of the video's bad part and press the Mark In button, shown in Figure 20-7. Move to the end of the video's bad spot and press the Mark Out button. Then choose Delete from the Edit menu, and VidEdit snips out the part of the video you've marked.

Pasting in new parts: Pasting a different video into your current video is just as easy. Move to the spot where you want the new video to appear and choose Insert from VidEdit's File menu. When the dialog box comes up, double-click on the incoming filename.

Synchronizing: When playing back the video, does the building fall down before you hear the sound of the explosion? Then *synchronize* the two by choosing Synchronize from the Video menu. Click on the little arrows next to Audio Offset to make the sound of the explosion start a little earlier or later in the video. Then click on the Play button to see if you've nailed it down correctly.

✔ Most word processors offer an Overwrite mode: when you type new letters, they *overwrite* the old ones. VidEdit offers the same option. So before pasting video into your current video, look for the letters INS at the bottom of VidEdit's screen to make sure that you're in Insert mode. If you see the letters OVR, press the Insert key; otherwise, VidEdit overwrites your preexisting video with anything you paste.

✔ Sometimes, the postage-stamp-sized movie is hard to see. To make it bigger (or smaller), choose Zoom from the View menu. (Clicking on the little magnifying-glass icon cycles the video through its different sizes.)

Deciding how to save the video

When processing words, you're finished after you have arranged the words in the proper order, and the paragraphs flow from point to point. Unfortunately, this process is not true with video. After you've perfectly arranged all your video sequences — cutting out the bad parts and adding in some good stuff — your work is just starting: you need to tell the computer how to save the video, which is often the most complicated part of VidEdit.

If PCs could handle videos as well as they do words, you wouldn't have to mess with all this stuff. But because PCs can barely handle video, you need to baby them when saving the video file. VidEdit offers dozens of file-saving options through a plethora of menus, but the easiest way to access them all is to choose Save As from the File menu. When the dialog box pops up, click on the Compression Options button. Rest your clicking finger and then click on the Details button. Finally, click on the Preview button, and you see the dialog box in Figure 20-8.

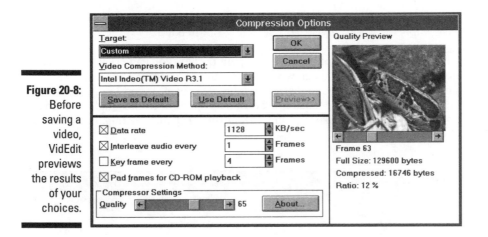

Figure 20-8:
Before saving a video, VidEdit previews the results of your choices.

The compression options perform the following tasks:

Target: Will your video be played back from a hard drive, a slow 100KB/sec CD-ROM drive, or a fast, 300KB/sec CD-ROM drive? Choose your target in this box, and VidEdit fills out the rest of this form, automatically estimating the best options for saving your video.

Video Compression Method: Click in this box to choose your *codec*, the mathematical formula VidEdit uses to squeeze your video into a small file. After choosing a codec, look at your previewed image to the screen's right. Figure 20-8 shows how the codec affects your video.

Save as default: Are you finished filling out the form? Click here, and VidEdit remembers to bring up this already-filled-out form the next time you're ready to save a video.

Use Default: Have you changed some options but want to return to what you started with? Click here.

Data rate: Usually set automatically by the Target option, this tells VidEdit how much information it can pack into the file — and *still* make the file playable by the Target, be it a slow hard disk or CD-ROM drive.

Interleave audio every: Leave this at 1.

Key frame every: Keep this number below 15. If your video contains lots of changes — a moving car, for example — keep the number low, even down to 1. If your video doesn't change much — a sunset, perhaps — raise the number. You have to experiment to find the best setting.

Pad frames for CD-ROM playback: Click here if your video is destined to live on a compact disc; otherwise, this setting is not needed.

Compressor Settings Quality: By leaving out details, you can create a faster, smoother video, but the image won't be as sharp. Figure 20-9, for example, compares two different quality settings using Microsoft Video 1 compression. The image on the left side takes up 38K of disk space at the 75 Quality setting. The image on the right takes up only 11K at the 50 Quality setting, but it starts to lose some focus.

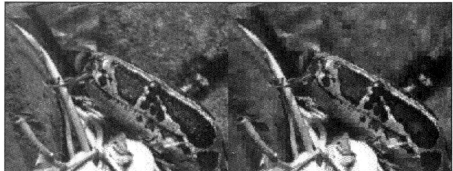

Figure 20-9:
The image on the right takes up less disk space than the one on the left, but it is not as clear.

✔ When you change any of the options, keep an eye on the preview image displayed in the upper-right corner. It shows the effect that your choice has on the image's quality.

✔ If you have an Intel Smart Video Recorder, you don't have to mess with this part of VidEdit's menus. Intel's card compresses the images as they come down the wire, and they're ready to play, as is. Just use VidEdit to chop out the bad parts, not to compress the video.

✔ After you choose all your options, click on the OK button, and VidEdit starts compressing your video. Depending on the video's length, quality, and compression options, the process can take several minutes (Microsoft Video 1) or several hours (Cinepak Codec by SuperMatch).

Making a Video (and Editing Out the Bad Parts)

If you don't want to bother reading this whole chapter, then jump right in here and start following the numbered steps. If any of the steps sound a little off-kilter, check out the deeper explanations earlier in this chapter.

Some companies customize the Video for Windows menus so that they pertain to their own brands of cards, but the basic steps for editing a video are the same. The following steps show you how to move a video from your camcorder to your hard drive, edit it, and save it as a file:

1. **Defragment your hard drive.**

   This is always a first step. Described in Chapter 29, defragmenting keeps your hard drive running at its fastest.

2. **Set up a capture file.**

   You haven't used VidCap before? Then choose Set Capture File from the File menu and type in a filename. VidCap temporarily stores your incoming video in that file.

3. **Hook up your VCR or camcorder to your capture card.**

   Chapter 14 has step-by-step instructions and pictures of the cables.

4. **Load VidCap and push the play button on your camcorder or VCR.**

   If you don't see the video on-screen, such as in Figure 20-10, click on Options and choose Preview Video; otherwise, VidCap doesn't bother displaying the incoming footage.

Figure 20-10:
Choose
Preview
Video from
the Options
menu to
see your
incoming
video.

5. **Choose Video from the Capture menu.**

   A dialog box pops up with several options, discussed in the "Adjusting the video format" section of this chapter. Because Video for Windows automatically estimates your best choices, you probably don't need to fiddle much with the options, if at all.

6. **After choosing your options, click on the OK button.**

   Your hard drive rumbles for a few moments as Video for Windows gets ready for the incoming video. When it's ready, it flashes a button on-screen, as shown in Figure 20-11.

7. **Click on the OK button to start capturing the incoming video; click the mouse or press Esc to stop.**

   Choose Video from the Capture menu five or six seconds before you want to start recording; it often takes VidCap several seconds to prepare itself, and you don't want any important video to flow by when VidCap isn't recording.

8. **Save your recording.**

   When VidCap stops recording video, choose the Save Captured Video As option from the File menu and type in a filename. Now it's time to edit out the bad parts.

9. **Load your recording into VidEdit.**

Figure 20-11:
Click on the
OK button
to start
recording
video.

If you have lots of memory, feel free to keep VidCap and VidEdit running at the same time: just choose Edit Captured Video from VidCap's File menu, and VidEdit comes on-screen, video in hand, ready for editing.

If Windows sends messages muttering about a lack of memory, shut down VidCap and load your saved video into VidEdit. This procedure takes up a lot less memory.

Either way, VidEdit looks like Figure 20-12.

Figure 20-12:
VidEdit can
slice out
bad parts of
your video.

10. **Find the section you want to delete.**

    In this case, the view of the couple walking down the street is nice, but the video ends with a boring shot of the street. So I simply fast-forward to the boring part of the video by using VidEdit's scroll bar.

11. **Click on the Mark In button.**

    Now I select the part to delete by clicking on the Mark In button, which puts a marker at the spot where I'm ready to start deleting.

12. **Move to the end of the section that you want to delete and click on the Mark Out button.**

    Again, I use the VidEdit's scroll bar, but this time to move to where the boring spot stops. When I click on the Mark Out button, VidEdit highlights the section of video I don't want, as shown in Figure 20-13.

Figure 20-13:
VidEdit
highlights
the section
to be
deleted.

13. **Choose Delete from the Edit menu.**

    VidEdit dutifully snips out the offensive section of video.

14. **Save the completed video.**

    Choose Save As from the File menu and click on Compression Options to bring up a list of compression options. For quick and dirty results, stick with the Microsoft Video 1 option. The others take longer but give better quality.

That's it. Your video plays back more smoothly after it has been compressed. Compression can take a long time, however, so take some time away from your computer. Clean the lens on your camcorder, start planning the next shoot, or spend some quality time with the family.

Part IV
Making Custom Setups (or Doing Some *Serious* Work)

The 5th Wave — By Rich Tennant

"The system came bundled with a CD-ROM drive, a sound card, and the developer's out of work nephew."

In this part . . .

With a multimedia computer, you can play games, amuse and educate the kids, record some rock and roll, or create stunning presentations to impress the boss.

But each setup requires its own special tweaks. This part of the book shows how to create a MIDI music studio, the ultimate game machine, and a way to turn daydreams into moneymaking presentations and animations.

Chapter 21
Setting Up a MIDI Music Studio

● ●

In This Chapter
▶ Hardware you need
▶ Software you need
▶ Money you need
▶ Stuff to watch out for

● ●

Hardware You Need

You're lucky — setting up a computer for music is one of the least expensive ways to put a multimedia computer to work. Computers can record sounds in two distinctly different ways: digitally and through MIDI. Each requires different setups.

Digital recording. Using digital recording, your computer acts as a tape recorder, listening to sound waves and stuffing them onto the hard drive. Actually, musical compact discs are digital recordings: A computer converts the incoming sounds to numbers; the numbers are packed onto a disc; and your CD player turns the numbers back into music.

In fact, Neil Young hates CD technology *because* it turns his music into numbers. Digitized sound loses the *passion* of the music, for cryin' out loud; gimme analog any ol' day. Anyway, to reproduce sound clearly, computers need lots of numbers. A typical CD holds about 650MB's worth.

Recording MIDI information. With MIDI, your computer works more like a note taker than a tape recorder. The computer watches what musical notes you play and stores the information in a file. Because the computer is not recording the actual sounds — just information about them — MIDI files require a lot less space on your hard drive.

Chapter 3 goes into more detail about the differences between recording MIDI or actual sound (digital recording); the rest of this chapter explains the different computer setups you need for each type of recording.

The computer

To record sound, you need slightly different computer setups, depending on whether you're recording MIDI or digital sound.

MIDI: Because the computer is merely writing down what notes you're playing, you can get along fine with an old 386 — perhaps even an AT with a 40MB hard drive (unless you want to run Windows programs).

Digital Recording: If you are recording actual sounds, however, you need a 486 for consistent, top-quality stereo sound. And count on a whoppingly large hard drive — remember, each song can easily take up 60MB of space. Start with a fast 500MB hard drive and don't record too many songs at the same time.

The sound card, microphone, and speakers

You also have to start referring to your computer and instruments as *gear* if you're a serious musician. This section covers the gear you need for a desktop music studio.

Sound card

Musicians are immediately faced with two options. First, they can opt for an expensive synthesizer controlled by a cheap sound card. The expensive synthesizer creates the actual sounds; the cheap sound card only serves as a *MIDI interface,* an electrical connection between the computer and the synthesizer. Second, the musicians can buy an expensive sound card and a cheap keyboard. With this combination, the sound card produces the music, and the keyboard merely serves as a switch, sending on and off messages to the sound card as you tap different keys.

Both methods have their advantages. On the one hand, if you buy an expensive synthesizer, you can play it anywhere because it's producing the sounds. On the other hand, many new games support MIDI as a sound card option, so they create the soundtrack by using your synthesizer — the sound card merely passes the signals through to the synthesizer.

One last point: An expensive sound card is more compatible with games and other multimedia software, and expensive sound cards are still cheaper than expensive keyboards.

- ✔ If you've bought a computer primarily to create music, buy the expensive keyboard/synthesizer. You can find a cheap sound card with a MIDI interface for less than $100.

- ✔ When shopping for a MIDI card or sound card, make sure that it's MPU-401 compatible. These are the magic words most MIDI software requires.

✔ If you're a musician, be sure to give Turtle Beach's line of sound cards a listen — especially its Multisound Monterey. Next on the line comes Roland's Sound Canvas and its various incarnations. Finally, check out an AudiotrixPro or the Sound Blaster 16 with its Wave Blaster add-on module.

✔ For great sound on a budget, check out the Gravis UltraSound, known affectionately by its fans as the GUS. It has wavetable sound, is starting to be supported by game manufacturers, and is downright inexpensive.

Microphone and speakers

Don't bother using the cheap speakers that come with most sound cards. Hook the computer up to your home stereo (described in Chapter 13). Or buy a professional amp at a music store and run the whole thing through it. Either way, you can give the speakers to your little brother.

You don't need much of a microphone, either, unless you're interested in digital recording. If so, head for the music store and try out different microphones. Chapter 3 explains some of the terms you encounter when looking for a microphone. Try out the selection at the music store and let your ears be the judge.

MIDI instruments

MIDI cards merely provide a spot for you to plug in an instrument. But which one? The choices have expanded over the past few years, as described in the sections below.

Synthesizer keyboards

Most MIDI musicians use a *synthesizer,* an electric piano of sorts that can mimic an organ, trombone, drum set, and even weird instruments you've never heard of before. Some can even handle *sampling* — play a recording of a burp, for example, and the synthesizer will play burp sounds, changing the pitch as you press different keys.

Synthesizers cost between $200 to $3,000, depending on their features. Your ears as well as your wallet should be your guide.

✔ The expensive synthesizers have standard-sized keyboards and *weighted keys.* (When you push down on a key, it comes back up as if it were a real piano key, not a push button.)

✔ Not all synthesizers are MIDI compatible, especially the cheap ones sold in department stores.

✔ Some keyboards are simply *MIDI controllers*; they can't make any sounds on their own. When hooked up to a MIDI card, the keyboard sends on/off information as you tap its keys. These inexpensive keyboards are designed for use with a computerized synthesizer, either on a sound card or built into a separate box, like the Roland Sound Canvas.

Meddling with MIDI guitars

For years, guitar players who wanted MIDI had only one option: to learn how to play the keyboard. Now, a variety of MIDI gizmos let you connect your Les Paul to your computer's MIDI card.

Rave department. A company called Lyrrus sells a fantastic gizmo called a G-VOX, which is a little plastic bar with suction cups that fits onto your guitar, be it an electric, acoustic, or something in between. (It doesn't scratch the finish, either, if your guitar still has any finish left to scratch.)

The G-VOX software displays a guitar's neck on-screen. When you pluck a note on the guitar, a little dot appears on the neck on-screen, showing the exact spot you've plucked. When you play a chord, you see the same thing, but with more dots to show the fingering.

The killer part is the software libraries by Steve Morse and other guitarists. As they play a song, you can watch where their fingers are moving along the neck of the guitar. It's like having a private tutorial with Steve Morse, anytime you like.

Finally, the G-VOX can also serve as a plain ol' MIDI controller, just like a keyboard. When hooked up to your sound card, it lets your guitar sound like any instrument your sound card can emulate. For more information, call Lyrrus at 215-922-0880 or drop by your local music shop.

Tape recorder

MIDI works well when you feel like composing music. But because MIDI files simply tell synthesizers and sound cards when to play back certain notes, the files sound different on different equipment. If you want other people to hear your song — exactly as it sounds on your equipment — you need a tape recorder.

In fact, you should probably switch to a tape recorder rather than making digital recordings to your hard disk, because big, fast hard drives are too expensive, and because demo tapes are easier to hand out than hard drives.

- A company called Fostex makes a wide variety of tape recorders. You can get by with their less-expensive four-track models; MIDI already lets you mix 16 different channels. (Some software can squeeze in even more.)

- Sometimes a MIDI composition is perfect — if only it had a digitally recorded guitar track mixed in. Roland's RAP-10 sound card comes with a built-in Sound Canvas synthesizer as well as mixing software to add two digital audio tracks to your MIDI compositions. This system lets you add sounds — such as your voice, a real guitar, or alternative rock sounds that a synthesizer can't create, like a beer can being run over by a Renault.

Software You Need

Most sound cards come with a MIDI package tossed in for free. Although it's usually a stripped-down version of a company's real package, it's enough of a start to get you going. MIDI software comes in the following styles:

Sequencer: Designed mostly for composers, sequencers work like mixing boards in studios. They record notes as you play them and then let you edit out the mistakes and paste in new arrangements. As you keep adding new tracks and new instruments, a song eventually emerges from the mix.

Backgrounds: Some MIDI software lets you practice, not compose. Band in a Box, for example, comes with computerized musicians ready to play. Simply choose some chords, pick one of 75 styles, and then play along with the reggae band when the mood is right.

Clips: Just as desktop publishers can buy clip art — predrawn artwork — to use in their work, people can buy precomposed MIDI songs. MIDI files are small, and they adapt well to playback on different computers. Many people buy precomposed MIDI songs to use for their presentations (especially when they find out how much the record company wants in licensing fees for songs you hear over the radio).

Utilities: Because MIDI is a mish-mash of musical numbering schemes, MIDI editor/librarian programs tell synthesizers which sets of instrument sounds to use. Other utilities let you create your own sounds by editing the sounds your synthesizer can make.

Notation: Are you ready to print your masterpiece? Then look for notation software or see if it's a feature built into your regular MIDI package. It prints out sheet music of your song, ready to pass out to the band members.

✔ When you start to outgrow your sound card's MIDI software, look for Twelve Tone Systems' Cakewalk Professional, Passport's Master Tracks Pro, or Big Noise Software's Cadenza for Windows. These are professional-quality programs for people with enough time on their hands to figure out what MIDI is all about.

✔ MIDI programs that use *piano-roll* notation put a piano roll — a long piece of paper with dots and dashes — on-screen. A long dash stands for a long note; a dot is a mere tap.

✔ MIDI programs that use *staff* notation put sheet music — the same stuff you see sitting on the stands of musicians in the orchestra — on-screen.

What to Watch Out for

The French are difficult to talk to in pubs — until you learn French. The same holds true for MIDI. It's a completely new language, and you can't learn it overnight, much less in a strange pub. Expect to be confused when you first try to set things up. You're *supposed* to be confused.

To ease the confusion, you should know the following things:

- ✔ To edit music by using your sound card's synthesizer, you don't need any MIDI cables.

- ✔ If you don't have a musical keyboard, some software lets you play songs by hunting and pecking on your keyboard. If you're serious about MIDI, forget the computer's keyboard and buy a MIDI keyboard.

- ✔ Not all keyboards and synthesizers work with MIDI. If you're buying a synthesizer, make sure that it says it's MIDI compatible. If you found the item at a garage sale with no manual, look for two dime-sized jacks, one labeled IN, the other labeled OUT. These are MIDI ports, and you use them to connect the item to your computer.

- ✔ Have you hooked up an expensive synthesizer/keyboard, but the songs still play back sounding like your cheap sound card's synthesizer? You've probably reversed the IN and OUT cables. Switch them, and the sound should start coming from the keyboard, not the sound card.

Chapter 22
Building the Ultimate Game Machine

In This Chapter

▶ Computers

▶ Sound cards

▶ Joysticks

▶ Memory

▶ On-line services

Computer games aren't for kids anymore. After spending $2,500 for a multimedia computer setup, many parents are handing their kids the Nintendo and keeping the PC's joystick for themselves. This chapter covers what you need to build the ultimate game machine. (Good luck in keeping the kids away from it, too.)

Hardware You Need

A multimedia computer is like a hot-rod car: it's a basic stock model that has been souped up with a few enhancements. The next two sections describe the computer you need as well as the add-on accessories to make it scream.

The computer

Computer games drive a computer harder than most other programs. Don't be surprised to see the words *486 recommended* on the side of the latest game box. This recommendation means that the game still works on a 386, but it's too sluggish for you to enjoy to its fullest.

For example, Maxis' El-Fish lets you create (and breed) realistic little fish and watch them swim across your monitor to soothing background music. But the game doesn't run on anything less than a 386 with 4MB of RAM. For best results, Maxis recommends a *math coprocessor,* an extra bit of computer circuitry that's built into 486DX chips but left out of 486SX chips.

In addition to CPU power, you need a large hard disk. Leisure Suit Larry 6, for example, wants 10.5MB of hard disk space. Do you think that CD-ROM games have solved your hard disk problems? They've made them worse! The Return to Zork adventure game, for example, comes on a CD, but it recommends that you copy about 42MB of the game to your hard drive to "significantly speed up the performance." (I did. It did.)

✔ So what do you buy? The fastest computer you can afford. Sure, you can run most games on a 486SX. But some of the newest games run a lot better on a fast 486DX. The faster the computer you buy now, the more games it will play in the future.

✔ As for hard drives, 340MB isn't too large. You can get by with something smaller if you keep only one or two games on your computer at a time. If you're not running Windows, feel free to buy something even smaller. Beware, however, that many of the latest games are written specifically for Windows.

✔ Finally, make sure that the computer has at least 4MB of RAM. RAM is fairly easy to add to a computer later, in case you suddenly come across a killer flight simulator that wants 8MB.

✔ One of my other books, *Upgrading & Fixing PCs For Dummies*, explains how to add RAM. Actually, don't bother buying it; just head to the bookstore and read pages 168 to 173.

The sound card and CD-ROM drive

Without a sound card, you'll be missing half the game. In fact, even if you buy a new sound card, go back and play some of your older games to see what you've been missing.

Not all games work with all the cards on the market, so make sure that your card says it's *Sound Blaster compatible.* Game manufacturers are starting to include support for other cards, but Sound Blaster compatibility is always good to fall back on.

Finally, make sure that your CD-ROM drive says *double-speed* somewhere on the box. Triple-speed is even better. And for some real action, check out the NEC's quadruple-speed drive. When the troll walks across the bridge, he *walks* smoothly across the bridge — he doesn't start at one side and suddenly appear on the other. (Unless he's supposed to do that, of course.)

Check out Chapter 3 for sound card buying tips and Chapter 6 for CD-ROM drive information. Then buy the best ones you can afford. Both a sound card and a CD-ROM drive are integral for playing games.

Joystick overload

Joysticks seem to be on their way out. If you're going to be playing only Windows games, you may not need one because Windows games use the mouse, instead.

Don't give up on joysticks altogether, though; some of the best games still work under DOS, not Windows. Would you want to be a passenger in an airplane flown by a pilot who grew up using a *mouse* to play flight simulators?

- ✔ Joysticks take a lot of abuse. If you buy a pair, spend the extra money for some good ones. They work better, last longer, and make the game more fun.

- ✔ Joysticks plug in to a *joystick port*, also known as a *game port*, found on most sound cards. If you buy an expensive sound card for MIDI, though, it may not have a built-in joystick port. To play games, you have to buy an additional *game card*. (They're cheap.)

- ✔ The number-one cause of joystick problems is having two game ports in one computer. If your computer already has a game card, remove it before using the one on your sound card. If it's built in the computer, you'll have to pull out your computer's manual. See Chapter 16 for additional information.

- ✔ When playing a game, you're dealing with three different companies: the joystick maker, the computer maker, and the game maker. Because of this interaction, companies like Kraft, CH Products, and Advanced Gravis sell *adjustable* game cards. By turning a knob on these cards, you can fine-tune your joystick's performance, compensating for differing standards among manufacturers. If you buy a game card, be sure to disable the game port on your sound card, usually by removing a jumper — a tweezers-ridden object, illustrated in Chapter 16.

Potential potentiometer pretentiousness

An IBM computer's joysticks contain two devices called *potentiometers*, a very scientific term for *knobs that turn*. Moving the joystick up and down turns one knob; moving it to the left and right turns the other one; a quick diagonal movement turns both simultaneously. By watching the flow of electricity passing through the potentiometers, the PC knows how the joystick is being turned, and it can control the game accordingly.

If the potentiometers aren't rated at exactly the same capacity, they don't send accurate information to the PC. Cheaper joysticks have this rating problem, making it harder to control the game.

The joysticks used by most other brands of computers and game machines don't use potentiometers. They use *switches* — eight of 'em, in fact, so that you can move in only eight different directions (which is why they don't work on a PC).

Sneaky throttles

Joysticks for flight simulators often carry an additional throttle-control lever to control the plane's speed.

How does the throttle control send that extra information to the computer? It makes the computer think you've attached a second joystick. The movement of the throttle corresponds to the movement of that phantom second joystick. The result? If you're trying to use a throttle-control joystick in a two-player game, it may disrupt the second joystick's performance.

So either buy a pair of regular joysticks to play fair — or use the throttle joystick on the sly to totally annihilate your opponent.

✔ When buying a joystick, take it out of the box to see if it feels "right" in your hand. Is the stick's tension right? Is the tension adjustable? Most sticks come with calibration knobs for fine-tuning. Are the knobs in the way, where you can accidentally bump into them while maneuvering delicately between craters?

✔ All PC joysticks have at least two buttons, known as A or B. Most joysticks use one button atop the handle and a second button near the base. Other joysticks have a button as a trigger for the index finger and another button directly under the thumb. Make sure that the buttons are located conveniently for your grasp.

Memory Problems

Game software can be awfully picky about memory. Even if you have 12MB of RAM, the games still complain because they're looking for something called *conventional* memory. Conventional memory is like the first floor of a tall building. If it's filled up, you can't push your way to the elevator to access any of the floors above it.

A memory manager snatches some of the software that hogs the first floor — conventional memory — and stuffs it into some of the upper floors, known as *extended* or *expanded* memory. By clearing out everything but the software that has to live in conventional memory, the memory manager frees up enough room to keep all the software happy.

✔ DOS comes with a built-in memory manager of sorts, but it's a mere shovel compared to the bulldozer-powered memory managers on the market.

- If you're using DOS 6.2, quit Windows and type **MEMMAKER** at the DOS prompt. Follow the instructions on-screen, and DOS tries to organize your computer's memory.

- Check out the tips in Chapter 29: anything that makes your computer run smoother makes your games run better, too.

General-Purpose Tips

The following sections contain several tips that gamers need to know when trying to get their computers to cooperate.

Know your brand of sound card

Instead of determining what type of sound card you're using, most games lay the burden on you. You probably have to choose your sound card from a list when first installing the game. To make sure that you're setting up the game correctly, find out which card your sound card *emulates* — in other words, which card it mimics.

- When in doubt, choose the Sound Blaster setting first.

- Some games ask what IRQ and port number your card uses, so keep these numbers handy, as well. This gross stuff is covered in Chapter 16. (And after you figure out the numbers, write them down on the Cheat Sheet in the front of this book.)

- When in doubt, choose IRQ 5; if the game acts goofy, try IRQ 7.

Know how to change the volume

Sound cards can synthesize sounds as well as play back recorded sounds, and most games take advantage of this dual function. For example, many games play their musical sound track in the background by using the card's MIDI synthesizer. Then they play the characters' voices through the card's digital audio channel.

Unfortunately, the games rarely get the volume levels right. Either the music drowns out the characters, or the characters are shouting over barely audible music. To change the levels, you have to fiddle with your sound card's mixer program. Table 22-1 shows which setting controls what sounds in most mixers.

Table 22-1	Sound Controls in Mixers
This Setting	*Controls This Sound*
Main or Master	All the sounds simultaneously
VOC, WAV, or PCM	Digitally recorded sounds, such as grunts, shattering glass, or footsteps
CD	Sounds coming from the CD playing in an internal CD-ROM drive
MIDI, Synth, or Music	Music from the card's built-in synthesizer, used mostly for sound tracks
Line or AUX	Anything plugged into the card's Line or AUX jack; it usually controls sound levels from an external CD-ROM drive, tape recorder, or camcorder
Treble	Controls the high-frequency part of the sound but creates a background hiss if turned up
Bass	Controls the boomy, room-shaking part of the sound but creates a muddy sound when turned up
SPKR	The volume of the sound coming out of your PC's speaker

✔ By turning down the MIDI setting and turning up the VOC setting on a Sound Blaster 16, you can make the characters talk louder than the music. Do the opposite if you'd rather hear more music and less sound effects.

✔ Some mixer programs let you save the settings after changing them. If you finally find the correct volume settings for playing Nose Blasters, for example, save them as NOSEBLST or something similar. Then you can call up these settings in the mixer before playing the game and make sure that all the levels are set up right.

Using on-line services

Imagine being in a room with a bunch of people playing the same game. Think how easy it would be to call out hints to each other.

Now imagine a room that stretches across the world, with thousands of people playing games of every variety. You can find this big room on an *on-line service* — a big computer you can connect to your own computer through the phone lines. You need a *modem,* which is a translator that lets computers speak with each other over the telephone.

One service, CompuServe, has several sections devoted exclusively to game playing. People can dial up the service, usually with a local phone call, and select the gaming areas from the menus that appear on their computer screen. After they've reached the games forum, or *bulletin board*, they can type in messages. For instance, they can post the message, "How do I get past level seven in Prince of Persia?"

For serious gaming, make sure that you buy a modem and an account to an on-line service, such as CompuServe or America Online.

✔ Players swap not only hints but also technical information — such as how to make Nose Blaster II work with the PlatoSlaw sound card.

✔ Some companies give away free *demos*, which are short demonstration versions of the games found on store shelves. Demos usually offer the same sound and graphics as the games themselves. Gamers not only get a taste of the action, but they also get a test of whether their computers meet the game's technical requirements.

The 5th Wave **By Rich Tennant**

" I'M SORRY, BUT MR. HALLORAN IS BEING CHASED BY SIX MIDGETS WITH POISON BOOMERANGS THROUGH A MAZE IN THE DUNGEON OF A CASTLE. IF HE FINDS HIS WAY OUT AND GETS PAST THE MINOTAUR, HE'LL CALL YOU RIGHT BACK; OTHERWISE TRY AGAIN THURSDAY."

Chapter 23
Making Video Presentations

In This Chapter
▶ Understanding presentation software
▶ Choosing a presentation package
▶ Configuring a computer for presentations
▶ Making successful presentations

*B*ack in 1984, people needed a handy excuse when the neighbors asked why they bought that expensive computer. "Why, it's to keep track of the checkbook, of course," they said. "It's much easier to keep track of the household finances that way."

Ten years later, the neighbors are now asking people why they bought that expensive multimedia computer. The excuse? "Why, it's for presentations, of course," comes the reply. "It's easier to do presentations at the office that way."

Just as very few people wound up balancing their checkbooks with the original computers, very few people end up using their multimedia computers for presentations, either. But if you need a breather from multimedia computer games and encyclopedia browsing, this chapter on presentations is waiting.

After all, while writing out a check, you may run into the neighbors at the grocery store and need to tell them about all those presentations you've been making.

Using a Computer for Presentations

Presentations are fancy slide shows, created in the hopes of convincing important people that your project really is worth their money. With such a vague definition, presentations vary widely in content. A presentation can illustrate corporate finances at a board meeting or demonstrate how a floating country club can enhance the environment off the coast of Florida.

Although computers are starting to replace traditional slide shows and "flip-the-big-page" types of presentations, they've been slow in arriving. First, computers are whoppingly expensive compared to a slide projector or a large piece of paper. Second, they're difficult to set up and view. And third, they're slow when compared to old-technology slide projectors and videotape.

Multimedia computers are making inroads, however. Multimedia computerized presentations can take the following three forms:

Off-screen: Special overhead projectors can project a computer's screen onto a standard movie screen for easy viewing. Or when connected to a special converter card, computers can send video directly to a large television. Even easier, a presentation can be created on a computer and then transferred to videotape for later viewing. (It's easier to fit in a briefcase this way.)

On-screen: If you're watching the presentation directly on a computer monitor, it's considered on-screen. To be seen by more than a few people, these presentations require a large, expensive monitor.

Kiosk: Another form of on-screen presentation, kiosks give presentations from shopping malls, hotel lobbies, and trade shows. A kiosk is basically a computer monitor stuffed in a box, with a few buttons nearby — sort of like an ATM machine. By pushing buttons — or touching buttons directly on the kiosk's screen — you can tell the computer to dish up the information you're after.

Depending on your type of presentation, your budget, and your message, you need different types of computers and software, as described in the rest of this chapter.

Understanding Presentation Software

When presentation software first came to the PC, it didn't break much ground: it could display charts on-screen at the appropriate times and turn spreadsheets into pie charts. A few years later, presentation software could show fancy slide shows with special effects, letting one image blur into the next. Now a spreadsheet with boring carrot sales figures could leap off the screen, making a bar chart out of tall carrots.

Today, presentation software uses multimedia to jazz things up even further by adding sound and video. When looking for multimedia presentation software, keep the information in the next four sections in mind.

Multimedia isn't always better

When you're making a presentation, the object is to get a point across, not to wow people with computer technology. In fact, the very fact that you're using a computer can make some people suspicious right away: if your idea is so great, why can't you simply explain it in person rather than rely on slick computerized campaigning?

Look for a package that can handle video clips and sound because sound is one of the best ways to add power to a message. And some architectural firms, real estate agents, or developers may need video for before and after shots. But make sure that the package doesn't offer sound and video at the expense of the basics — you still need charts, tables, and graphs in a wide variety of easy-to-read styles.

Get the right package for the job

Presentation packages are designed for different jobs. Some are flexible; they let you stop in the middle of a presentation and move off in a slightly different direction to answer a question from the audience. Others create movies for presentations, designed for recording and playback from a VCR. Still others work mainly as slide shows, blending one picture into another to illustrate a point.

If you'll be making presentations in front of a wide variety of audiences, look for a package versatile enough to handle different jobs.

Is it easy to use?

Computers are supposed to make things easier. Can you really whip up a presentation more quickly using software than by drawing your charts by hand? Some software helps with organization and direction by including an outline program. Others toss complicated icons on-screen that are essential for developers but needlessly confusing for beginners.

Keep in mind how the presentation is to be played back, as well. Some software can compress your multimedia show into a single file, ready to be played back by a single viewer program. This feature makes it easy to move your show to different computers, without having to install a complete software package each time you want to play it back.

Does it come with clips?

Unless you have a camera, a camcorder, a music studio, and a lot of spare time, you need to come up with music, sounds, videos, and artwork to pack in your presentation. Many packages come with a wide variety of clips, ready for royalty-free use, that let you start working immediately. Others make you buy the clips separately or look for them yourself.

Setting Up a Computer for Presentations

Graphics always push a computer to its limit, and presentations are no exception. To create and deliver effective presentations quickly, you want a powerhouse computer, a high-quality sound card, and a clearly visible display.

Computer: You want a fast 486 computer to deliver and create presentations. To handle graphics smoothly, use an accelerated or local bus video card with at least 256 colors. Buy a 24-bit video card if you plan to use lots of photos or videos. Most multimedia programs run under Windows, so you want at least 8MB of RAM. Don't skimp on the hard drive, either — make sure that it's at least 340MB.

You probably don't need a CD-ROM drive while giving presentations, but you do need one while creating them. CDs are the easiest source of precreated sound, pictures, and video.

When giving a presentation, you want people to concentrate on your message, not your computer. The smoother the computer works, the less people will notice it.

Sound card: Sound is one of the easiest ways to add zip to your message, so don't skimp here. Get a wave table card and cables to plug in to the room's PA system. (Bring your own set of backup speakers, just in case the amplifier causes problems.)

Display: A standard computer monitor is much smaller than most television sets. For easy viewing by several people, buy a 20-inch (or larger) monitor or an overhead projector system. Neither option is cheap. In fact, the display is probably the most expensive part of your computer system.

- ✔ Have you ever glanced at the blank face of someone watching television? Don't use video in a presentation unless it is absolutely necessary. Video is distracting, leading the viewer's attention away from your main message.

- ✔ Use MIDI files for soundtracks instead of digital audio. They're smaller in size and can be looped endlessly without problems. Wave files, on the other hand, play back for a set number of seconds. If you stop the presentation to answer an unexpected question, a MIDI file can keep playing; a WAV file leaves the room in silence.

✔ Try using photos more than video. Kodak Photo CD offers a quick way to digitize images and then convert them to the format you need. A slide show with sound can be more effective than one with video, especially because it allows you to control the presentation's pace. Videos can't be sped up or slowed down to keep pace with the audience's interest level.

Are you using transparencies on an overhead projector? You can make them on your computer. Prepare your charts and text by using a word processor or presentation program and then print the transparencies by using your computer's laser printer. Most office-supply stores sell laser-printer-compatible transparency sheets.

Making Successful Presentations

Here are a few tips to keep in mind when creating or delivering multimedia presentations:

✔ When presenting concepts, use short words, incomplete sentences, and large fonts. Put a few words relating to your theme on-screen and spend time talking about them. Too many words on-screen look confusing, leading to a lack of interest.

✔ Keep a backup plan in mind. Computers can suddenly break down, but your presentation can go on if you keep a backup set of overhead transparencies for emergency situations.

✔ Keep your message in mind, not the multimedia presentation. The slides, photos, videos, and sound are less important than the message you want to give. If multimedia can help prove your point, use it. But don't add multimedia effects simply because your upgraded computer can handle them now.

✔ Before making a presentation, find out where it will be given, what computer will be used, and how many people will be watching. You need to adjust your presentation if any of these conditions change.

✔ Set up and test your equipment an hour before the presentation. Make sure that the sound levels are appropriate and that all the software is working correctly.

✔ All for contrast: If you use too much motion, your visuals don't stand out when you're using them to illustrate key points. Switch between still pictures and animation.

✔ The best presentations look easy to make, but they reflect hours of work and preparation time. Spend some time getting used to your package before relying on it for important work.

Part V
The Part of Tens

The 5th Wave   By Rich Tennant

Dave gets ready to install his new CD-ROM drive

In this part . . .

*J*ust like its predecessors in the . . . *For Dummies* series, none of the chapters in this part of the book contain exactly ten items. Some contain a lot less. Some contain a few more. And, if you're *really* counting, one chapter contains more than 30, so they all average out.

But because we're dealing with *multimedia* here, numbers don't matter — appearance does. That's why this part of the book contains neatly formatted lists, all arranged for your browsing pleasure. (Just don't start counting.)

Chapter 24

The Top Ten CDs (or Which Are the Good Ones?)

- -

In This Chapter

▶ Arthur's Teacher Trouble

▶ JFK Assassination: A Visual Investigation

▶ Your Own Photo CD

▶ Encarta 1994

▶ The San Diego Zoo Presents . . . The Animals

▶ The 7th Guest

▶ Street Atlas USA 2.0

▶ Musical Instruments

▶ Berlitz Japanese for Business

- -

*A*bout 8,000 compact discs currently fill the computer store shelves and back pages of computer magazines. Which are the *good* ones? This chapter narrows the masses down to the top ten.

Arthur's Teacher Trouble

The artwork and plot behind poor Arthur's school experiences would make this a great children's book. A multimedia computer breathes life into the book, however, by adding a narrator, fun sound effects, clever animation, and incredible attention to detail. As the narrator reads the book, the characters walk around on-screen with animation better than most TV cartoons, as shown in Figure 24-1.

But there's more — instead of merely watching the characters act out the story as it's being read, you can click on objects in the background: click on the cookies, for example, and they start singing and dancing. Click on a piece of paper, and it folds itself up into an airplane and takes off.

The program offers a bilingual mode, as well: clicking on the Spanish button changes the narration, as well as any on-screen words or background details; the tiny picture of the Lost Cat on the bulletin board changes to Gato Perdido; and the cookies lead off their doo-wop song with "Uno, Dos, Tres." I wish I'd had this program back in college.

If a sophisticated kid gets bored with "kiddie books," the background offers plenty of fun for the mischievous: click on the coffee cups in the kitchen to watch them shatter; click on the blender and it sucks in neighboring plants. It's easy to install, fun to play, and a top-notch way to introduce kids to computers.

For more information about this CD, contact this company:

Broderbund
500 Redwood Blvd.
Novato, CA 94948-6121
415-382-4600

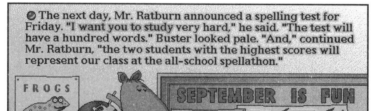

Figure 24-1:
Arthur's
Teacher
Trouble.

JFK Assassination: A Visual Investigation

A few years back, *Time* magazine set the multimedia standard with its Desert Storm: The War in the Persian Gulf CD. The CD chronicles the Persian Gulf war, complete with text, maps, charts, photographs, and recordings: a living example of multimedia's potential.

Now, Medio's JFK Assassination CD (see Figure 24-2) has upped the ante by adding video and computerized animation to its documentation of the JFK assassination. The CD includes the text of the Warren Report and two other books; photographs ranging from early pictures of Oswald to bullet fragments found in the limousine; four assassination videos, including the Zapruder film; maps showing the limousine's path near the Grassy Knoll; and computerized animations re-creating the assassination from a variety of viewpoints and situations.

This wide variety of information isn't simply shoveled onto the CD, however; careful design makes it easy to navigate. For example, what does the Warren Report mean by *triple underpass*? Click on that highlighted word to bring up a photo, along with the names of witnesses on the overpass. Click on the witnesses' names for descriptions of their statements. You could browse for hours.

Although sometimes as gory as its subject matter, the CD sets a new standard for multimedia, combining video, sound, text, animation, and photographs in a new way to shed new light on old material.

Contact the following company for details:

Medio Multimedia
2703 152nd Ave., NE
Redmond, WA 98052-5515
206-867-5500

Figure 24-2:
JFK
Assassination:
A Visual
Investigation.

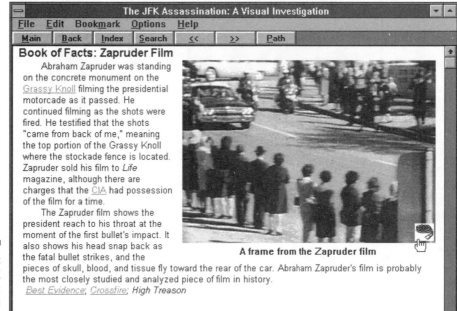

The JFK Assassination: A Visual Investigation

File   Edit   Bookmark   Options   Help

Main   Back   Index   Search   <<   >>   Path

Book of Facts: Zapruder Film

Abraham Zapruder was standing on the concrete monument on the Grassy Knoll filming the presidential motorcade as it passed. He continued filming as the shots were fired. He testified that the shots "came from back of me," meaning the top portion of the Grassy Knoll where the stockade fence is located. Zapruder sold his film to *Life* magazine, although there are charges that the CIA had possession of the film for a time.

The Zapruder film shows the president reach to his throat at the moment of the first bullet's impact. It also shows his head snap back as the fatal bullet strikes, and pieces of skull, blood, and tissue fly toward the rear of the car. Abraham Zapruder's film is probably the most closely studied and analyzed piece of film in history.
Best Evidence; *Crossfire*; *High Treason*

A frame from the Zapruder film

Descriptions of the Film:

Your Own Photo CD

Photo CDs don't cost any more than the other CDs in this chapter. Even when you grow tired of the other CDs in your collection, the Photo CD will still be near the top of the pile. After all, you created it.

With the disc, you can display several photos on the screen at once, or enlarge one to poster size, scanning the background for details you didn't notice when snapping the shutter. Use family members as Windows wallpaper. Figure 24-3 provides an example of Your Own Photo CD in action.

Plus, your pictures are locked safely on the CD, away from the ravages of shoe box land. Give Photo CD a try to see what your computer can do.

Call 800-235-6325 for a list of developers in your area.

Figure 24-3:
Your Own
Photo CD.

Encarta 1994

Encarta, the premier multimedia encyclopedia, has a little bit of everything. Listen to different countries' proverbs pronounced in 60 different languages. Click on a globe and start *zooming in*, starting with the continent of Europe and ending with a street map of Paris (or a picture of the inside of the Louvre).

Drop by the Timeline at 6,000,000 BC, look at cave paintings, the Shang dynasty, Socrates, feudalism, Vikings, Joan of Arc, Mozart, or the breakup of the Soviet Union.

Want some flash? Encarta's Gallery lets you listen to Louis Armstrong, examine Zulu beadwork, watch a video of a Venus Flytrap eating a small frog, see animations of the Doppler effect, examine climate maps of Australia, or study charts of household chemicals. Figure 24-4 shows a slimy example.

Writing a report on bicycles? The Find command automatically digs up 49 references, from history to hand signals. Encarta might not be as in-depth as a 20-volume set, but it's sure a lot more fun to search through — meaning it will probably be used a lot more often.

Contact Microsoft for more information:

Microsoft
1 Microsoft Way
Redmond, WA 98052-6399
800-426-9400
206-882-8080

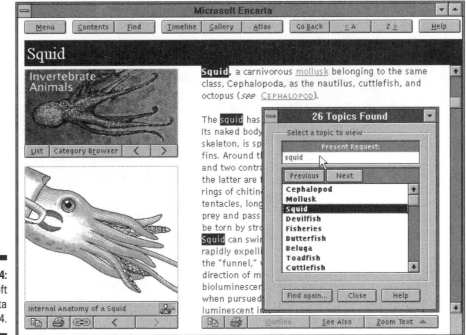

Figure 24-4:
Microsoft
Encarta
1994.

The San Diego Zoo Presents... The Animals

Almost two years old, The San Diego Zoo Presents . . . The Animals CD is starting to show its age. The animal pictures aren't full-screen, and the movies look a little smaller than some competing CDs. However, this best-seller shouldn't be passed by.

It includes more than 80 videos of animals at San Diego's world-famous zoo, nearly 100 animal sounds, and hundreds of pictures, from the aardvark to a zoo nursery's weigh-in of new arrivals.

The CD works several ways. You can take guided tours through different areas of the zoo; browse through hundreds of movies, sounds, and photos; search for animals by name (see Figure 24-5); explore animals by their habitat; or simply stroll through like a *real* zoo, pointing and clicking at things as they catch your eye.

If you want full-screen pictures, drop by the zoo, take your own, and put them on a Photo CD. But you'll still miss out on the movies, sounds, and wide variety of information packed on this CD.

For more information, contact the following:

The Software Toolworks, Inc.
60 Leveroni Court
Novato, CA 94949
415-883-3000

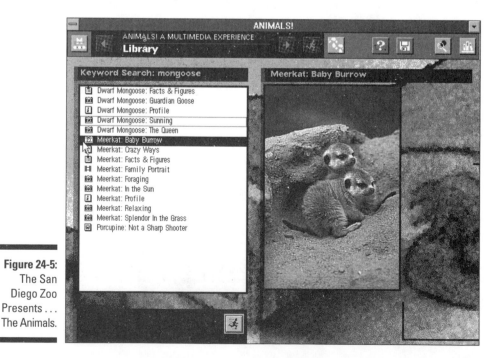

Figure 24-5:
The San
Diego Zoo
Presents . . .
The Animals.

The 7th Guest

The 7th Guest is a multimedia extravaganza, filling two CDs with soaring music, eerie special effects, and some of the best animation ever seen in a computer game. The plot's simple: you're dropped inside a haunted house, where you must solve puzzles in different rooms.

Because the game producers filmed a live cast of 23 actors, digitized a half-hour of full-motion video, and added the results to a computerized 3-D house, the game resembles a movie more than anything else. Much of the game is spent simply watching ghosts move around eerily on the screen (see Figure 24-6). Action-lovers will be impatient. Graphics lovers will consider it a tour-de-force.

It's a powerful multimedia production — too powerful, in fact, for many youngsters. You're watching *real* people in this game, not cartoon characters. The screams are intense (they woke my cat) and blood will flow as often as the knife stabs.

But if your last computer game was Pong, you'll be astounded at how far games have come. One last thing: all the advanced graphics and sound can push a computer pretty hard. Be prepared to spend some time fiddling with the sound card settings until everything is right.

Virgin Games can provide you with more information:

Virgin Games
18061 Fitch Avenue
Irvine, CA 92714
800-874-4607

Figure 24-6:
The 7th
Guest.

Street Atlas USA Version 2.0

By now, most people know that compact discs can hold an incredible amount of information. But get this — Street Atlas USA is a mammoth map containing *every* street in the nation.

You won't find any streets built after the CD and its maps were created, of course. But you'll find incredibly detailed layouts for every city in every state, including Alaska and Hawaii. See Figure 24-7 for an example.

Street Atlas starts by placing a map of the nation on the screen. You can zoom in — enlarge — different areas of the nation by clicking on them. Or simply search by name, ZIP code, or telephone area code. When you've narrowed your search to a specific area, type in the name of a street, and Street Atlas highlights it on the screen.

The uses? Quickly print out a map of your city for quick reference, using the exact amount of detail you want. Go ahead and write all over it — you can always print out another. Flying to a foreign city? Print a map showing the route you'll take from the airport to your destination.

Planning a cross-country road trip? Print out several maps: a large one with the freeway route and smaller ones showing each stop along the way.

Or simply browse, examining the roads circling the coast of Hawaii, running through Alaska, or leading to your friend's new ranch in Idaho.

For additional information, contact DeLorme Mapping:

DeLorme Mapping
Lower Main Street
P.O. Box 298
Freeport, Maine 04032
207-865-1234

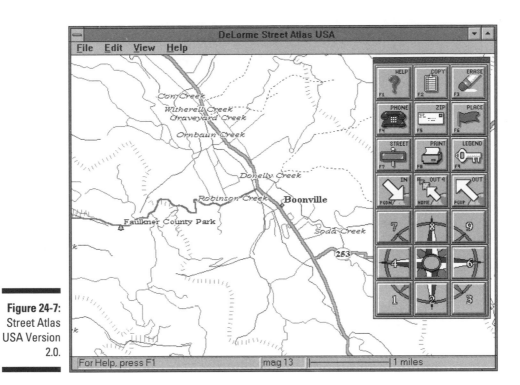

Figure 24-7:
Street Atlas
USA Version
2.0.

Musical Instruments

With billions of bucks in its big business bucket, Microsoft can afford to hire dozens of people for each of its multimedia creations. The results show it — Microsoft's Home series of CDs blows away the competition, both with Encarta 1994, described earlier, and Musical Instruments. (See Figure 24-8.)

Musical Instruments is the Big Expensive Coffee Table Book of CDs. It's a bit frivolous, but it's big, flashy, and sure to impress your friends when it's left lying around. In fact, it even has a "lying around" mode — push the Random button, and the program flashes colorful pictures of musical instruments on the screen randomly while playing back their sounds with rich clarity.

Like most of Microsoft's multimedia CDs, the richness comes through in the program's detail. The CD contains more than 200 instruments from around the world, from a nose flute to a Fender Stratocaster.

When it puts a picture of a sousaphone on the screen, for example, you can listen to the instrument's sound. But click on the little speaker next to the word *sousaphone*, and you'll hear how the word is pronounced, as well. Want a close-up of the mouthpiece or valves? Give 'em a click. Or click in the Views box to see photos at different angles.

The program lets you explore instruments individually, by their families, countries of origin, or use. Click on ensembles to hear how instruments are used in orchestras, wind bands, jazz bands, chamber groups, rock bands . . . well, you get the idea. There's a lot of detail here. (Check out the guitar solo from Les Paul, listed in Ensembles under Heavy Metal Bands.)

If you're interested, Microsoft can supply you with additional information:

Microsoft
1 Microsoft Way
Redmond, WA 98052-6399
800-426-9400
206-882-8080

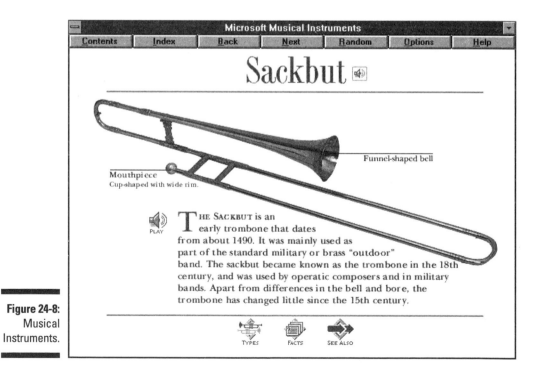

Figure 24-8:
Musical
Instruments.

Berlitz Japanese for Business

The kids get the best educational CDs, but adults aren't left out completely. Berlitz Japanese for Business (see Figure 24-9) teaches the language and culture of Japan to a newcomer faced with a business trip. Yet it never seeps into the "flash-card vocabulary" level of boredom.

For basic guidelines on making foreign sounds that Japanese people might be able to understand, begin in the program's Language Essentials section and start repeating the words. Why not rent a videotape? Because the CD graciously repeats the five vowel sounds endlessly, while a videotape makes you constantly fiddle with the rewind button.

And here's a new feature: talk into your sound card's microphone and the program records your voice as you practice. When it plays it back, you can listen to your voice and compare it with the on-screen tutor's pronunciations.

Other sections of the program offer some tips and necessary phrases you'll need upon arrival, while on the phone, at business meetings, when eating out, shopping, or at leisure. Want to know how to pronounce *saki*? Head for the on-screen bar and click on the saki bottle. While moving between sections, the program tosses in Japanese tips, so you'll know that laughing during a business meeting is *not* proper behavior.

This CD is a first-class production to picking up Japanese language and culture in a hurry. (Oh, and don't forget the animated tutorial on using chopsticks.) For more information, contact the following:

Bright Star Technology/Sierra Online
3380 146 Place Southeast, Suite 300
Bellevue, WA 98007
800-757-7707
206-649-9800

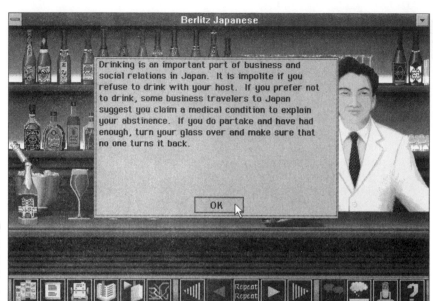

Figure 24-9:
Berlitz
Japanese
for Business.

Chapter 25

Ten Cheap Ways to Try Out Multimedia

● ●

In This Chapter

▶ Using a Speaker Driver for Windows

▶ Connecting your PC's speaker to a bigger speaker

▶ Buying a cheap sound card

▶ Spending a *lot* of time shopping

▶ Checking out a friend's machine

▶ Looking for free CDs

▶ Playing the sounds through your home stereo

● ●

*F*ace it, multimedia equipment isn't cheap. A lot of people have trouble budgeting an extra $300 just so the computer can say "Beam me up, Scotty" when it starts Windows. This chapter shows you some ways to try out multimedia computing without opening your wallet a quarter-inch more than necessary.

Using the Windows Speaker Driver

Microsoft really wanted Windows 3.1 to turn everybody's computer into a multimedia PC. But hardly anybody had a sound card back in 1992 when Windows came out. How could people hear the built-in chord and chime sounds? So Microsoft wrote some software to let Windows send sounds through the PC's built-in speaker — no sound card required. The software didn't work very well on everyone's computer, so Microsoft left it out of the final package.

However, Microsoft didn't run its failed software through the corporate shredder. Instead, Microsoft gave it away with a warning: "This may not work on your computer, but it's free, so don't complain."

You may be able to pick up a copy of Windows' Speaker Driver from a friendly salesperson at your local computer store. Or, if you have a modem, you can download it from Microsoft's BBS at 206-637-9009. If you're a CompuServe member, head to the Microsoft Software Library (GO MSL) and download SPEAK.EXE.

Connecting Your PC's Speaker to a Bigger Speaker

The speakers on an IBM clone were never supposed to do anything but beep when you hit the wrong key. So most computer manufacturers used the cheapest speakers they could find. Sometimes a speaker's connecting wires rub against the speaker's front, which muffles any sound. If you're a hands-on kind of person, with more time than money, consider bypassing the computer's speaker and using a speaker that is *designed* for sound.

Find a cheap radio at a garage sale and pull out its speaker. Next, unplug your computer, remove its case, and cut the two wires that attach to your computer's speaker. Finally, route these two wires to your new speaker, outside of the case. You may need a few feet of wire to complete the job. Either way, just twist the wires together and wrap them with electrical tape.

Mount your new speaker nearby, but away from any floppy disks — a speaker's magnet can erase the disks if it gets too close. Your newer speaker should sound much louder and clearer than the old one — too loud, in fact, especially if the computer ever goes haywire and locks up with the beep tone turned on continually.

But it's cheap. . . .

Starting with an Inexpensive Sound Card

A sound card goes a long way toward livening up a computer. Although the expensive $300 models sound great, feel free to start small. You can pick up a cheap sound card for about $50 these days. Sure, it doesn't sound like you're in Carnegie Hall, but at least you get a hint as to what multimedia computing is all about.

Or check out the classifieds. Because so many people are buying the fancier sound cards, you may be able to grab their old ones for a bargain.

Spending a Lot of Time Shopping

Most computer stores keep a multimedia computer set up and ready to go, usually near the door to attract customers. Before you buy your own multimedia computer, spend a lot of time shopping and sampling different computers at different stores.

After a while, you become familiar with the different levels of sounds and video a computer can offer. You not only get to play with a multimedia computer before buying one, but you know what quality sound and video you want for your own computer. Then when you know exactly what level of quality you want, you don't end up spending more money than you have to.

Checking Out a Friend's Machine

If you hear of a friend who has bought a new multimedia computer, see if you can wrangle an invitation to his or her house to check it out. It shouldn't be too hard to get in the door. After all, when you spend $3,000 on a computer, you'll be dying to show yours off, too.

And while you're there, see if your friend will give you a deal on the sound card from the *old* computer.

Looking for Free CDs

Some companies offer free multimedia magazines on CD. They hope to hook you into a subscription by giving away the first issue. Some paper magazines offer free multimedia compact discs as incentives for subscribing to the magazines.

Other magazines give away CDs filled with demonstration versions for bunches of programs. If you like a particular program, you can call their sales force for the program's code number. Type in the code number, and you've unlocked the program. You then can copy it to your hard drive and start using it.

It's a cheap way to start expanding your CD collection.

Hooking Up Your Sound Card to Your Stereo

Technology can be pretty redundant. For example, you need a TV and a computer monitor — yet both do pretty much the same thing. Your home stereo and multimedia computer both have CD players — and these do pretty much the same thing, too. Finally, your computer and your home stereo both have speakers. Why? That's two speakers too many.

In a few years, computers, televisions, VCRs, telephones, home stereos, and microwave ovens will merge into one technofried gadget. But until then, don't bother buying speakers for your multimedia computer. Instead, hook up your sound card to your home stereo, as described in Chapter 13. If your sound card came with cheap plastic speakers, you'll be amazed at how much better everything sounds.

Chapter 26
Ten Ways Manufacturers Try to Confuse You

● ●

In This Chapter

▶ Full-motion video doesn't always mean full screen

▶ Full-screen video doesn't always mean full screen

▶ Quarter-screen video doesn't always mean quarter screen

▶ Compact discs don't always contain multimedia programs

▶ Compact discs are rarely easy to open

▶ Your computer can talk and listen to you

● ●

*B*ecause the computer industry cannot even agree on what the word *multimedia* means, it's not surprising that manufacturers use rather loose definitions for other things, too. This chapter covers some of the spots where the industry tends to fudge a little bit. Don't let 'em fool you.

Full-Motion Video Isn't Always Full Screen

You may see the words *full-motion video* touted on the boxes of lots of software and hardware. Next to the words, you may then see a picture of a computer with a flashy video filling its screen.

But full-motion video is not the same thing as full-screen video. The term *full-motion* refers to the smoothness of the videos seen on TV or in movies. Technically, it means that 30 pictures flash by in one second — 30 frames per second — making the motion look lifelike.

When a computer plays full-motion video, however, it is rarely filling the screen with pictures — far from it, in fact. Full-motion video usually plays back in a postage stamp-sized square on-screen. This size is about the best that today's PCs can do without expensive upgrades.

If you want your video capture card to handle full-motion *and* full-screen video, you better budget at least $5,000.

Full-Screen Video Isn't Always Full Screen

In today's multimedia world, a *full-screen* picture or presentation means a screen with 640x480 resolution. If you're used to a 800x600 (bigger) screen and the traditional "full screen picture" is 640x480 (smaller than your 800x600), the "full-screen picture" won't fill your bigger screen.

To make the image full screen, you have to switch your resolution to the SuperVGA mode of 640x480. Otherwise, the full-screen picture only fills about half your screen.

Quarter-Screen Video Isn't Always Quarter Screen

Take a look at your 640x480 computer screen and imagine that it is divided into quarters, such as the screen in Figure 26-1. Wouldn't you think that one of these four blocks would qualify as quarter-screen video? Not so fast. . . .

When you divide 640x480 by four, you come up with a 160x120 resolution window. Some video capture cards say that 160x120 resolution qualifies as a quarter-screen video. But Figure 26-2 shows the true size of a 160x120 window, nestled in the upper-left corner. This figure sure doesn't look like the quarter screen described in Figure 26-1.

When a video capture card says it can capture quarter-screen video, see how the company defines the term *quarter screen*. If it's using the numbers 160x120, you know something is fishy.

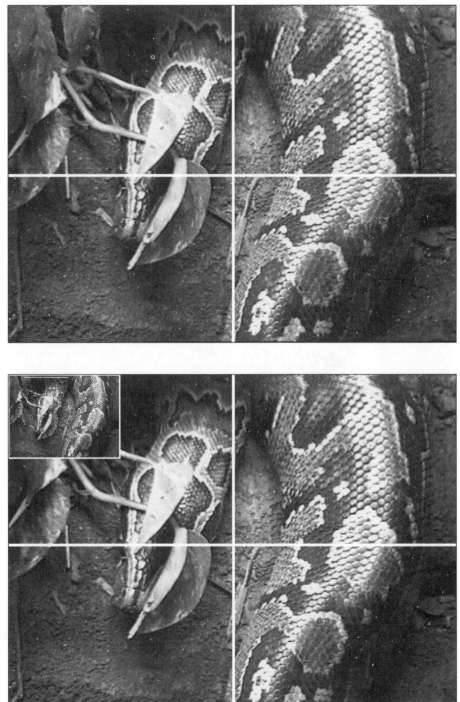

Figure 26-1:
Is this a
quarter
screen?

Figure 26-2:
Or is this a
quarter
screen?

CDs Aren't Always Multimedia

Today's compact discs are supposed to be fresh and exciting, packed with enough sound, animation, and videos to justify the expense of buying a CD-ROM drive and sound card.

Some of today's CDs are great — check out Chapter 24 for some of the winners. But others take the easy way out. Instead of packing their CDs with sound, graphics, and video, some companies simply shovel text on a CD, toss in a quick drawing or two, and call it a multimedia experience. It will be a real disappointment when you get it home.

When you're shopping, here are some warning signs of a boring CD masquerading as something exciting:

✔ Be skeptical of a CD that doesn't include a picture of the actual program on the box. Some sneaky CDs include pictures of programs — but of *other* programs in the same series, not the actual program you're holding in your hand.

✔ Some CDs list their contents on the box with a check mark next to Text, Pictures, Audio, and Video. Avoid the CDs that have only Text and Pictures checked off because they are probably yesterday's products. Sound and video are inexpensive to add to CDs these days, so all new programs should have them.

✔ One exception to the preceding rule: If you're buying a CD primarily for text — a phone book CD, for example, or the complete works of Shakespeare — don't look for sounds, pictures, or video. In fact, that stuff can slow you down when you're searching through big chunks of text.

✔ Be wary of CDs that contain bunches of games. Many companies shovel game software from yesteryear on a CD and then try to sell it again in repackaged form. The games are so old that they'll probably look terrible when running on your slick new multimedia computer.

✔ Don't be the first to buy a new CD. Wait a few months and see if people are still talking about it. For example, the boxes on some CDs look great but the disc itself is a disappointment. By waiting a few months, you can avoid the duds.

CD Boxes Aren't Easy to Open

Compact discs come packaged in one of two ways: inside a plastic box that is already broken or in a box that is wrapped with an impenetrable plastic wrap. The broken ones are easy to open — the cover just falls off. As for the broken cases, drop by your local music store. It usually sells replacements at a reasonable rate.

But the others are a hassle. Try dragging a fingernail down the side of the box to tear the plastic wrapper. If the wrapper is extra tough, use something sharp, such as a toothpick or garden trowel. After the plastic wrap is torn in a small area, the rest rips off pretty easily.

Finally, allot some extra time when trying to open the newfangled CD cases that pack two CDs into the space of one. These boxes open on both sides, doubling the confusion level.

Your Computer Can Talk and Listen to You

Some sound cards come with software that allows you to communicate directly with your computer: You simply tell your computer what to do. Bark a command into the microphone, and the PC carries it out. Throw away your keyboard! If you can't type very well, this feature can be handy. However, be prepared for some drawbacks.

First, the PC doesn't automatically recognize your voice. You have to train it, a process that can take several hours, depending on your microphone, your voice, and the number of words you want Mr. Computer to recognize.

For example, if you want the computer to open a file in your word processor, you need to repeat the words *open file* until the computer recognizes your voice — and knows you're not saying *poking Lyle* or something similar. You better learn how to keep your lips the right distance from the microphone, too. If you vary your position, the computer may vary its interpretation.

Second, the software doesn't recognize natural speech. You need to talk to the computer in the same tone of voice as the computer in the first Star Trek series — the one that always said "Working." If you speed up your voice, slow it down, or allow any emotion to seep in (including frustration), the computer doesn't recognize you.

If you're enthusiastic about talking with a computer, go the *other* way around — use software that makes the computer talk to you. In this way, the computer can read back the numbers you just typed into a spreadsheet so that you know if you typed in *47* rather than *46*. This type of software doesn't take much training, if any.

Chapter 27
Ten Thousand File Formats

● ●

In This Chapter

▶ Identifying a file's contents by looking at its name

● ●

*M*ultimedia programs mix text, sound, pictures, and video into a big pot. With all these different types of files, the user gets mixed up as well. To help you out, this chapter lists the most common file types.

Deciphering File Types

Table 27-1 shows some common file types and their identifiable tattoos that help you identify a file's contents by looking at the last three letters of the file's name (known as its *file extension*).

Table 27-1	Common Multimedia Files
The Filename	*The Contents*
AIF (Audio Interchange)	Sound. A leftover from Apple computers' heyday.
AVI (Audio Video Interleaved)	Video. Windows' preferred format for storing video; these files can be played through Microsoft's Video for Windows software or an updated Media Player.
BMP (Bitmap)	Graphics. Windows' main format for graphics; bitmap files can contain photos or illustrations.
CGM (Computer Graphics between Metafile)	Graphics. Files that can be transferred computers or resized without losing quality.

(continued)

Table 27-1 *(continued)*

The Filename	The Contents
CLP (Windows Clipboard)	Information. Windows' Clipboard, which can hold text, sounds, movies, illustrations, and photos; stores its stash in these files.
CMF (Creative Music Format)	Songs. A composition program packaged with some Sound Blaster cards saves songs in this format.
DIB (Device Independent Bitmap)	Graphics. Like a bitmap file, but more versatile.
ENC	Songs. MIDI file format used by Encore software.
EPS (Encapsulated PostScript File)	Information. Text or graphics to be printed on special PostScript printers; popular for exchanging graphics between different types of computers, such as Macs and PCs.
FLC	Animation. A series of illustrations from Autodesk's family of software or from one of dozens of other FLC-making packages.
FLI	Animation. A series of illustrations from Autodesk's family of software or from one of dozens of other FLC-making packages.
GIF (Graphics Interchange Format)	Graphics. Photos or graphics stored in a space-saving format started on CompuServe's on-line service; contains no more than 256 colors and can be transferred between different brands of computers.
ICO (Icon)	Graphics. Small files containing icons for Windows.
JPG (Joint Photographic Experts Group)	Photos. High-quality photographs stored by using a special compression format.
MCT	Songs. MIDI file format used by Musicator GS software.
MFF (MIDI file format)	Songs. A standard MIDI file compatible with most MIDI programs and sequencers.
MID (MIDI)	Songs. A slightly abbreviated version of the standard MIDI format; designed for Windows MIDI programs.

The Filename	The Contents
MOD (Module)	Songs. A file containing recordings of musical instruments and instructions for arranging them into a tune.
MOV (QuickTime)	Video. Movies originating from Apple's Macintosh computers.
MPG (Motion Pictures Expert Group)	Video. Highly compressed movies requiring special playback hardware and software.
MSP (Microsoft Paint)	Graphics. Old versions of Windows (before 3.0) stored graphics in these files.
MTS	Songs. MIDI file format used by Master Tracks Pro software.
PCD (Photo CD)	Photo. Photographs stored on Kodak's Photo CDs.
PCX	Graphics. A popular format for storing graphics; these files can be read by most major graphics programs, including Windows Paintbrush.
POW	Songs. MIDI file format used by Power Chords software.
RLE (Run-Length Encoded)	Graphics. A slightly compressed bitmap file in Windows.
ROL	Songs. The AdLib sound card's format for storing songs.
SEQ	Songs. MIDI file format used by Power Tracks Pro software.
SNG	Songs. MIDI file format used by Cadenza software.
TGA	Photos. File format used by Targa's line of high-resolution video products.
TIF (Tagged Image File Format)	Graphics. File format for moving pictures between types of software and computers; popularized by Aldus PageMaker and used by many scanners.
VOC (Creative Voice)	Sound. Sound Blaster format for storing recorded sounds.
WAV (Waveform)	Sound. Windows preferred format for storing recorded sounds.

(continued)

Table 27-1 *(continued)*

The Filename	The Contents
WMF (Windows Metafile Format)	Graphics. Widely used format for Windows applications.
WPG (WordPerfect Graphics)	Graphics. The format for WordPerfect's clip art.
WRK	Songs. MIDI file format used by Cakewalk Pro software.

Chapter 28

Ten Solutions to Common Problems

● ●

In This Chapter

▶ I need to move a 67MB file to another computer.

▶ My files are too big.

▶ I can't find all my clips.

▶ I switched video drivers in Windows, and now it doesn't work.

▶ The CDs look terrible on my $4,000 system.

▶ My video capture card doesn't record sound.

▶ All my captured videos are black and white.

▶ The people stutter in my videos.

▶ My videos don't play on other computers.

● ●

*B*ecause a multimedia computer can display videos, play sounds, and show pictures, it can dish out the same frustrations as a TV set, stereo, and slide projector. Add in the problems that a regular, nonsouped-up computer can have, and you understand the level of problems a multimedia computer can bring to your life. This chapter offers solutions to some of the most common multimedia computer problems.

I Need to Move a 67MB File to Another Computer

A 67MB file doesn't fit on an average floppy disk. If you're trying to move a large multimedia creation from one computer to another, you need something decidedly not average. Several companies have come up with their own mammoth floppy-drive substitute — the most popular options are described as follows:

SyQuest system: This system uses a hard disk enclosed in a special cartridge that slides in and out of a special contraption called a *removable cartridge disk drive.* The cartridges, sometimes called *platters,* are commonly found in 44MB and 88MB sizes.

Bernoulli system: Bernoulli drives cost a little more than the SyQuest system, but their disk/cartridges are more reliable. (In fact, the ads say they can survive an 8-foot drop, in case you want to try that at home.)

External hard drive: This system is a box with a hard drive inside. The hard drive plugs into your computer's printer port by using a thick cable.

High-capacity floppy disks: These floppy disks use more precise (and expensive) technology to stuff more information — up to 25MB — onto special floppy disks.

Tape backup units: If both systems have the same type of tape backup unit, you can use the Tape backup and Restore commands to move files from one computer to another. Or if you use a SCSI card, you can use a SCSI tape backup unit and use it on other computers.

Which system should you get? Call up the people you want to swap files with and buy the same system they have. Each type of system is incompatible with the others. Because SyQuest and Bernoulli have been around the longest, they're the most widely used, especially among desktop publishers.

✔ All of the options cost at least $500 to get set up, and the cartridges cost extra. Count on spending at least $100 for a Bernoulli or SyQuest cartridge that holds 88MB.

✔ In a pinch, a laptop can serve as a huge file transporter. Use Traveling Software's LapLink software and connect a cable between the parallel port of your computer and the laptop (the cable comes with the software). Then copy your big file to the laptop's hard drive. Take the laptop over to the other computer, connect the cable between the laptop and your other computer, and use LapLink to copy the file over. This is a slow process, but it's cheap if you already have the laptop.

The Files Are Too Big for My Hard Drive

A high-quality digitally recorded barf sound can easily fill a floppy disk. A 30-second video of decent size and quality can grab 25MB or more. These are facts of multimedia life.

Some people store their files on Bernoulli or SyQuest cartridges, described in the preceding section. This section suggests two other ways to deal with increasingly large files.

CD-ROM WORM drive

A few years ago, only a few people could afford the equipment needed to make a CD. Today, this same equipment costs less than $3,000. What a deal! Known as WORM drives, they let you Write Once Read Many times. (Get it?) One thing to keep in mind: the cheaper the price, the longer the equipment takes to create the CD.

If you only want a few CDs made, look in the Yellow Pages under "Data Storage Equipment." Most big cities have a CD mastering shop. Be forewarned, however — most shops have at least a hundred-disk minimum. If you want to put photographs on a single CD, your best bet is Kodak's Photo CD system, described in Chapter 19.

Tape-backup unit

A tape-backup unit works like a VCR. But rather than recording pictures, it records the files sitting on your computer's hard drive. People with tape-backup units try to remember to make a recording of their hard drives each night. Then if anything disastrous happens and the computer dies, they still have a copy of all their files on tape.

You can also copy large files to your tape-backup unit's tapes for safekeeping. In this way, you can store your huge files on a tape in the closet, not on your hard drive.

I Can't Find All My Clips

Can you remember what videos are in all those AVI files? How about that BMP named MODULE4.BMP? And which vacation pictures are stored on Kodak Photo CD 304110221231? If the size of your media collection has outpaced the size of your memory, it's time for a multimedia cataloging program.

For example, Kodak's Shoebox software stores a thumbnail-sized shot of all your pictures from all your Photo CDs and then lets you type in a few words about each of them. A few weeks later, when you're looking for the picture of Uncle Frank describing his military experiences in France, you simply type **France** and **Uncle Frank**, and Shoebox tells you which Photo CD to grab.

The program does a lot of other stuff, too, such as make slide shows and zoom in on pictures (that's why it costs so much).

✔ A Kodak Photo CD's 12-digit ID number appears in two places. It's in the lower-right corner of the *contact sheet* — the print with the little pictures on it — that comes with the disc. Or, if you've lost the contact sheet, the number is printed on the disc itself, right around the hole in the disc's center.

✔ More and more programs are becoming multimedia aware. For example, PC Tools not only lets you peek into spreadsheet and word processor files, but it also comes with viewers for quick peeks at most graphics files. It even tells you statistics about AVI files, MIDI files, WAV files, and some animations.

✔ If you don't want to buy anything extra, at least keep your clips in organized directories. For example, keep the AVI files in an AVI directory and the WAV files in a WAV directory. For a quick peek at the file's contents, drag the filename to a Media Player icon at the bottom of your screen, and Media Player starts playing it. (You find more on this quick and dirty Windows browsing in Chapter 29.)

I Switched Video Drivers in Windows, and Now It Doesn't Work!

Sometimes switching to a new video driver can irritate Windows. After you've switched drivers and Windows starts to load, it may suddenly stop short, toss a curse on-screen that flashes by too quickly to read, and then leave you stuck at the DOS prompt.

To correct the problem, try going undercover: use the DOS version of the Windows Setup program. First, type the following two lines at the DOS prompt, one after the other, pressing Enter after each one:

```
C:\>CD \WINDOWS
C:\WINDOWS>SETUP
```

The DOS version of Windows Setup pops up. Using this program, change the driver back to the old one — the one that worked. This process should bring Windows back to normal.

You don't know which Windows video driver was the *good* one? Then choose VGA from the Setup program's Display option. This step should get Windows back on its feet.

The Movies Don't Work Right

Because videos push your computer to the highest stress levels, they often cause the most problems. Try the following tips before giving up and pouring popcorn over the whole thing.

My video capture card doesn't record sound

Video capture cards do not record sound. You have to buy a sound card and route your camcorder's audio cables to the sound card's auxiliary input jacks (a process described in Chapter 14).

All my captured videos are black and white

First, check the Video Source option of your video capture software. If the software expects to receive NTSC standards and you're sending it S-Video (or vice versa), you can't see the right colors.

Or, if you're capturing in 256-color mode, tell your software to capture a *palette*. Otherwise, Windows doesn't know what colors to use, so it sticks with black and white.

If you're using Video for Windows, check out Chapter 20 for more information.

The people stutter in my Windows videos

A Windows video — an AVI file — has a sound track as well as moving pictures. Normally, the sound track and video end at the same time. But what if somebody's computer isn't fast enough to play back the video at the right speed? Microsoft has to make some decisions, fast.

So Microsoft tells Media Player to give priority to the *sound track*. If a computer starts huffing and puffing when playing back a video, it keeps playing the sound track and leaves out snippets of video. In this way, the movie and the sound track still end at the same time. But when people in the video start stuttering or the sound track keeps stopping and starting, Media Player isn't leaving out any video — and this is taking its toll on the sound track.

The temporary fix? Choose Configure from Media Player's Device menu and then click on the box next to the Skip video frames if behind option until an X appears. This technique fixes the currently playing video.

The permanent fix? Follow these steps to match the sound with the video:

1. **Click on the Drivers icon in Windows Control Panel.**

2. **When the box appears, click on the line reading** `[MCI] Microsoft AVI Video`.

   It's near the bottom of the screen.

3. **Click on the Setup button.**

4. **Click on the box next to the Skip video frames if behind option until an X appears.**

   This step is just what you did for the temporary fix, described in the preceding paragraph.

5. **Click on the Set Default button.**

   This is the clincher. You've just told Media Player to use the new video settings from now on. Click on the Close button, and you're through.

The sound and video look awful on my $4,000 system

Remember, there are two computers involved in multimedia software: your own computer and the computer that created the multimedia package to begin with. If the company that made the CD didn't pack it with high-quality sound and graphics, the CD won't look any better on your own computer — no matter how much money you've poured into it.

Most software companies build their discs for an average system, not the best one on the block. If they put super high-quality video on the CD, only people with the most expensive systems can use the disc, severely limiting its audience.

For example, more than half the CDs on the market still use 8-bit sound, complete with its hisses and pops. And until more people own 16-bit sound cards, the companies will continue to make 8-bit CDs.

Don't feel too bad, though. Your high-powered system will stay up-to-date longer than the cheap computer the neighbors bought at that half-price sale.

Nobody else can play my videos

Why can't other people play my videos? There could be two reasons. First, they may need a copy of Video for Windows *runtime* version, a piece of software that upgrades Media Player so that it can play video. The runtime version is packaged with most video capture cards, games, and software. If you belong to an on-line service, you can find it there as well.

The second reason is more complicated. Microsoft videos use a *codec,* a formula that compresses the movies to a manageable size. They also use the codec to decompress the movies while they're being played. If a computer doesn't have the codec used for the movie, it can't play it.

Some video capture cards come with runtime versions of Video for Windows that include their special codecs; others don't, and their manufacturers don't let you give away their codecs, either.

The solution? Create your movies by using one of the three codecs everybody has: Microsoft Video, Intel's Indeo, or Cinepak. All three are included with Video for Windows, so everybody has them.

Your best bet, however, is to give the other person a copy of the Video for Windows runtime version that came with your video capture card. This step ensures that they have an upgraded Media Player as well as the right codec and the latest drivers.

Chapter 29
Ten General-Purpose Tips

In This Chapter
▶ If it works, don't fix it
▶ Speeding up videos
▶ Making a permanent swap file in Windows
▶ Fine-tuning your AUTOEXEC.BAT and CONFIG.SYS files
▶ Defragment the hard drive
▶ Upgrade to PCI or local bus video
▶ Don't be intimidated by camcorders
▶ Buy plenty of caddies for your favorite CDs

*H*ere's a collection of general-purpose tips for making your flashy multimedia computer sing and dance a little bit better — without expensive lessons.

If It Works, Don't Fix It

If your current multimedia computer works fine, don't mess with it by installing new *drivers* — the software that lets your computer communicate with things like sound cards, video cards, printers, fax cards, and other goodies.

Manufacturers constantly release new drivers for their equipment, hoping that version 2.1, for example, will fix whatever problems people complained about in version 2.

But whenever a company changes its software to fix one person's problem, the changes can cause new problems on somebody *else's* computer. So if your computer is already working fine, don't feel that you have to change drivers simply because there's a new version out.

(If you ignore this and decide to install the new drivers anyway, be sure to keep a copy of your old drivers. You might need them again.)

Copy Favorite Files from Compact Discs

A lot of today's compact discs come with some great videos stored as AVI files. If you find a file you really like, copy it from the CD to your hard drive. Hard drives can spit out information more quickly than CD-ROM drives, allowing the video to play back much smoother.

If you're really into movies, however, you'll need a bigger hard drive. That cool Aerosmith MTV video — you know, the one where that cool gal gets a tattoo and karate kicks the guy who stole her purse — took up 50MB on the disc that Microsoft sent to Video for Windows programmers.

Make a Permanent Swap File in Windows

Windows needs lots of memory to keep track of multimedia song and dance routines. When a big Windows program asks for more memory than your computer can dish out, the program simply stops running.

But before opening your wallet, make sure you've opened a *permanent swap file* for Windows. This is a chunk of your hard drive that Windows can pretend is memory; when the real memory wears thin, Windows starts moving information back and forth to your hard drive. It's slower, but it works.

To make sure Windows has a permanent swap file, double-click on the 386 Enhanced icon from Windows Control Panel and click the Virtual Memory button. If you don't see the word *Permanent* listed on the next box, click on its Change button and change Temporary to Permanent in the Type box. Windows will shut itself down and reboot, graciously offering you a chance to save your work first.

If you haven't *defragmented* your hard drive for a while (covered in the next section), be sure to defragment it before changing your swap file. Otherwise, Windows might not be able to grab a big enough chunk of hard drive to make your efforts worthwhile.

Kodak's Access software wants 20MB of memory or more before it will open some of the higher-resolution images on a Kodak Photo CD. If your hard drive is big enough — and you can't resist looking at those high-resolution Kodak pictures — make your swap file at least 20MB.

Defragment Your Hard Drive

Your computer gets sloppy when storing files. It tends to break the files into little pieces and scatter the pieces around your hard drive. Then when you want the file, the hard drive runs around frantically collecting all the individual pieces and putting them back together. Another example of computer engineering. Sigh.

To keep your hard drive from huffing and puffing, use a disk *defragmentation* program. This program searches your hard drive, grabbing pieces of scattered files and writing them back onto the hard drive in one big piece. This lets your computer grab the files much more quickly. (And more quietly, too — your hard drive won't whir so much.)

If you're using DOS 6 or higher, Microsoft's Defrag program can do the job. Quit Windows and type the following at the DOS prompt:

```
C:\> DEFRAG
```

If you're not using DOS 6, you have to buy your own defragmentation program.

If your drive is in pretty bad shape, the process might take up to a half hour. But if you defragment your drive every week, the job won't take more than a few minutes each time.

If you're playing or capturing a lot of videos, be sure to run a disk defragmentation program frequently — perhaps every evening. Doing so keeps your hard drive running at its fastest, leading to the best-quality videos.

Quick and Dirty Windows Browsing

Some CDs come packed with sounds and movies. How can you sort through them all in Windows, watching or listening to them as quickly as possible? For some quick multimedia browsing, try the following little trick:

Load Media Player and minimize it to an icon at the bottom of the screen, right below your open File Manager window. Then drag the file's name from File Manager to the Media Player icon. When you let go of the mouse button, the file instantly begins to play, whether it's a movie, sound, music, or animation.

If one clip gets boring, drag another filename over to the Media Player icon and let go. Wham! Media Player stops playing the first file and starts playing the next.

Fine-tune your AUTOEXEC.BAT and CONFIG.SYS files

Keep this list handy in case a computer techie or the neighbor's kid drops by your house. Then tell them to give your computer a checkup, looking for the following items:

✔ Make sure Smartdrive is loaded.

✔ Running DOS 6.2? Then load the CD-ROM device drivers *before* Smartdrive.

✔ Load DOS high.

✔ Configure memory as *extended*, not *expanded* — unless you're certain a program needs it.

To *drag* something in Windows, point at it and hold down the mouse button. Then, without letting go of the mouse button, point at your target. When you're pointing at the target, let go of the button; the mouse then drops what you've just dragged.

Don't Use Programs Like Stacker or DoubleSpace

Stacker, DoubleSpace, and other compression programs let you cram twice as many files onto your hard drive. But you're paying a price in speed: the computer needs to compress all the information before writing it to disk and then decompress the information when it wants the information back.

This constant compressing and decompressing can slow down a hard drive's performance. A small delay may not be noticeable when you're loading a file from a word processor, but when you're playing back a video that looks more like a slide show, you'll notice.

For best results, ditch the compression programs and buy a bigger hard drive — and a fast one, too. "How fast?" asks the person in the back, looking for numbers. Anything under a 12ms access time is suitable, but hold out for 10ms if you can afford it.

Don't Be Intimidated by Camcorders

New equipment can be scary at first, especially camcorders. They have far too many buttons, and they make people look at you funny when you film in public. How do you come up with great videos? By ignoring the spectators' looks of hostility.

Instead of letting your camcorder gather dust in the old appliance graveyard, pretend you're a photojournalist on assignment from *National Geographic*, documenting part of your life for their next cover story. You'd better get some good stuff, or you'll lose that upcoming trip to Cabo San Lucas filming cocktail umbrellas for *Cosmopolitan's* travel section.

Afraid your videos won't look good? Then shoot pictures of *everything* to better your chances that something turns out. When you're ready to start editing your video, you'll have plenty of footage to work with.

Upgrade to PCI or Local Bus Video

Bad news. If your computer is a few years old, even a screaming-fast video card won't be able to keep up with the newer *local bus* or *PCI* video cards. The new technology in these cards has a better way of talking to the computer — a private telephone line, so to speak — and last year's technology just can't keep up.

Unfortunately, the only way to get local bus or PCI video is to buy a new computer (or a new *motherboard*, which is practically the same thing).

Multimedia depends on lightning-fast video. If you're starting to depend on multimedia, it's time you invested in a computer with local bus or PCI.

Buy Plenty of Caddies for Your Favorite CDs

CD-ROM drives feed on compact discs in two different ways.

Loading a *caddyless* drive is like putting a thin mint onto the tongue: the drive shoots out a plastic plate, you drop the bare CD onto the plate, and the drive sucks them both back in.

The other drives make you insert your disc into a *caddy* — a little plastic box — before putting the disc in the drive. These drives only come with one caddy, making it a pain to change to a new disc. You'll find yourself constantly pushing the CD-ROM drive's eject button, grabbing the caddy, opening it and removing the old CD, inserting the new CD, closing the caddy, and sliding the caddy back into the drive.

To cut down on caddy time, buy a few extra caddies for your favorite drives. This not only makes the CDs easier to load, but also keeps them cleaner. Because the disc lives inside the caddy, you'll never have to touch it, eliminating the possibility of wiping lunch remnants onto the disc.

Chapter 30
Ten Legal Do's and Don'ts

. . . .

In This Chapter

▶ Don't use things you don't own

▶ Do copyright your work

▶ Do understand public domain

▶ Do understand on-line law

▶ Do get model and property releases

▶ Do find out more information

. . . .

Standard disclaimer: I'm not an attorney, and I don't even play golf with one on TV. So please don't take this chapter as bona fide legal advice. The tips are merely simplified guidelines to use when making multimedia creations on your computer. Besides, think of the jokes the judge can make if you say, "But the author of *Multimedia & CD-ROMs For Dummies* said it was OK!"

If you have questions about copyright law, please consult an attorney. You should find his or her business card posted near every golf course.

Second disclaimer: These guidelines apply to the laws in the United States. If you're reading this chapter in another country, don't expect to find anything very useful.

Don't Fiddle with Things You Don't Own

By nature, computers make it easy to copy things. For years, they've been copying text and numbers. But now that they can copy video, pictures, and sounds, it's easier than ever to run into problems with the law. What stuff can you legally be playing with on your computer?

In the privacy of your own computer's hard drive, feel free to fiddle with just about anything. Go ahead and digitize guitar riffs from your favorite rock and roll CDs. Turn your favorite magazine cover into Windows wallpaper. Record your favorite game show host in a ten-second video clip. In other words, if you're fiddling around on your own home computer (not the one at the office) — and the things you're creating won't ever leave your own home computer — you're probably on the safe side of the law.

But if any of these files ever leave your computer — either through a floppy disk or the phone lines — you'd better think twice. If you personally didn't play that guitar riff, create that magazine cover, or host that game show, you're looking for trouble.

Finally, software is copyrighted, too. Even in the privacy of your own home, it's illegal to make copies of software and give it to friends or to accept copies of your friends' software. (Feel free to distribute *shareware*, however; people are supposed to give away shareware and then pay for it on the honor system if they decide to use it.)

Do Copyright Your Work

A copyright is a legal way to protect your creations. How do you copyright something? It's easy. If you created something after March 1, 1989, you have *already* copyrighted it — it's yours, it belongs to you, and nobody else has the right to take it. (Except your boss, of course. If you created something while on the job, it most likely belongs to your employer.)

There is an even stickier issue, however. Sometimes, the problem isn't proving that you created something but proving you were the *first* to create something. If somebody else says you've ripped off his or her multimedia poetry, how do you prove that it's the other way around?

For starters, put a copyright notice on your work. Somewhere in your picture or video, include the copyright symbol (c), the year, and your name. For example, if Zen Fendel made a video about grapes in 1993, he should have put the following information on the credits list at the front of his video: (c) Copyright 1993 Zen Fendel. Make sure to write out the word copyright. Some legal nitpickers don't know what (c) means.

If you're looking for serious copyright protection, contact the United States Copyright Office in Washington, D.C. (the address is listed at the end of this chapter). By filling out a form, paying a fee (usually less than $50), and mailing the office two copies of your work, you'll be *time-stamping* your work. In this way, if someone else copies your work and the whole thing ends up in court, the copyright office can pull up a copy of your work — complete with the time and date you sent it in.

(Copyright protection isn't necessarily automatic for things created before March 1, 1989, when the new copyright law went into effect. Earlier works should have a copyright notice on each copy, and they should be registered with the U.S. Copyright Office.)

Do Understand Public Domain

After a certain number of years, copyrights can expire. How many years? The number varies, depending on such things as the year the work was created, the number of years the author has been dead, and how strong the coffee was in the lawmakers' chambers the day they updated the copyright books again.

In any case, when the copyright expires, the work is somberly said to have "lapsed into the public domain." *Public domain* means anybody can do anything they want with the work. You've probably seen plenty of public domain videos: those old movies of even older airplanes that always fall apart on the runway, for example. No one has to pay the original creator to use public domain material — that's why it's so popular (and why you see those old movies so often).

Do Understand On-Line Law

A modem is a little box that lets computers talk to each other over the phone lines. The computers not only talk, but also swap files. In fact, huge computers out there known as *on-line services* let people call them up with their own computers and swap files with one another.

Although copyright law is notoriously complicated — and telecommunications is even more complicated — it boils down to two main rules: First, you can't *upload* (copy something to another computer) anything that you don't own. Second, you can't *download* (copy from another computer) any copyrighted images and try to make money from them.

Before uploading something you didn't create, you need permission from the person or company responsible for creating it. Or, if the creation is licensed — Barney the dinosaur, for example — you need permission from the agency responsible for licensing that character. (The agency almost always asks for lots of money.)

You simply aren't allowed to upload images gathered from magazines, newspapers, books, calendars, beer-bottle labels, or any other sources in your possession. You own only the *paper* versions of these items — you don't own the actual text or artwork or the right to make copies of the items and give or sell them to others.

Also, copyrighted images can be downloaded for your personal use only. They can't be sold. You can download a copyrighted image to use as Windows wallpaper, for example, but you can't give or sell that image to a friend to use as wallpaper.

Do Get Model and Property Releases

Are you planning to use somebody else's picture in your multimedia project? Whether it's a picture of a person or an object, you're safest if you get a signed release form first. A *release form* is like a parent's note to the teacher that gives the child permission to do something. For example, if you want to use a picture that somebody else snapped, have that person sign a statement saying the following things:

- ✔ Yes, I created the picture.
- ✔ Yes, I'm giving you the right to use my picture in your creation.
- ✔ Yes, I am receiving adequate compensation for my work.

Work out the financial details and then incorporate them into the release — even if you're just giving your friend a six-pack. Be sure to get a similar release from any models — posed people — in your work. Nothing is a guarantee for avoiding legal problems, but having a signed release can save you some grief down the road.

Do Find Out More Information

For more information on copyrights, contact the following office:

U.S. Copyright Office
Library of Congress
Washington, DC 20559-6000
202-707-3000

For information on using somebody else's songs or music in your work, contact the following office:

American Society of Composers, Authors and Publishers (ASCAP)
Licensing Department
1 Lincoln Plaza
New York, NY 10023
212-595-3050

Part VI

Glossary

In this part . . .

You'll find these words defined in the chapters covering sound, video, and compact discs. But they're repeated here for reference, anyway. After all, how many people would know to turn to the video chapter for help when stumped by the word *codec*?

Glossary

8-bit

An 8-bit card can display 256 colors; an 8-bit file contains up to 256 colors.

16-bit

A file or video mode containing up to 65,536 colors.

24-bit or True Color

A 24-bit card that can display 16.7 million colors, which is about the number of colors that the human eye can differentiate on a screen. A 24-bit file contains up to 16.7 million colors.

3DO

A compact disc-based console created by a bunch of corporations hoping to create The Ultimate Home Game Machine.

8514/A video card

A special variety of card that displays 1024x768 graphics.

Accelerated video card

A card with a special chip that helps your computer put pictures on the screen more quickly.

Access time

The number of milliseconds a drive takes to find and grab a piece of information.

ADC (Analog-to-Digital Converter)

A sound card that's able to record sound.

ADPCM (Adaptive Delta Pulse Code Modulation)

A way to pack more sound into a smaller file (although it won't sound quite as good). Chances are, you'll never have to deal with it.

Algorithm

The scientific formula used for a codec.

Aliasing

A fancy word to describe those yucky, jagged edges that make computerized pictures look, well, like they came out of a computer.

Analog

Natural things, like waves, sounds, and motion — things that computers have a hard time turning into numbers (see also Digital).

Antialiasing

Technology used to get rid of jagged edges found in computerized graphics.

Aspect ratio

A picture's proportions. (If you change a picture's height, some programs keep the *aspect ratio* by changing the picture's width, too, keeping things in balance.)

Automatic gain control

A sound card that automatically adjusts the volume to record or play at a comfortable level.

AVI

Audio Video Interleaved — the format that Windows uses for saving video with sound.

Bandwidth

The speed at which your card can send information to your monitor. The faster the speed, the better. Bandwidth is measured in *megahertz*, and 70 Hz is considered good.

Bitmap

A file format in Windows for storing graphics.

Blue Book

Format that CDs designed for laserdiscs use. (See also Laserdisc player.)

Caddy

A little plastic case that holds a CD so it can be inserted into a CD-ROM drive.

Cardioid microphone

Microphones that pick up sound mostly from in front of them. (See also Omnidirectional microphone.)

CD-DA

Compact Disc Digital Audio. Also known as Red Book or CD-Audio, this is simply a music CD.

CD Digital Audio (CD-DA)

A CD-ROM is in this mode when it's playing a musical CD. (Also called *Red Book*, for some corporate reason.)

CD+G

Compact Disc + Graphics. A standard for adding pictures to a regular music CD. (Very popular in Japan.)

CD-i

Compact Disc-Interactive. Yet another game machine console, this one by Philips. It can play music CDs, Kodak Photo CDs, and run special CD-i programs.

CD-Quality sound

A phrase describing sound recorded at 16 bits, 44 MHz. (That's the rate used to record your musical CDs.)

CD-ROM

Compact Disc Read-Only Memory. A fancy name for a CD.

CDTV

Yet Another Home Game Machine, this one by Commodore never took off.

CD-XA

Compact Disc Extended Architecture. An important new standard for packing different types of information onto a disc, such as computer data, sound, and pictures. Kodak Photo CD needs a CD-XA drive.

Codec

A way to compress video into a file and then decompress it when playing it back.

Compression

A way of making files take up less space.

Condenser microphone

These battery-powered guys work best when recording sensitive sounds like pianos and whispers.

Contrast

The range between a picture's lightest and darkest tones.

Coprocessed /Accelerated video

Cards with special computer chips for flinging pictures on-screen extra quickly.

DAC (Digital-to-Analog Converter)

A sound card that can play sounds stored in a file.

Data buffer

A way to temporarily store information, leading to smoother transfers. Most drives come with a 64K buffer (or *cache*). Bigger buffers are better.

Data transfer rate (DTR)

The number of kilobytes of information a drive can squirt into your computer in a second. Normal speed is 150K per second; double-speed drives can move 300K per second; triple-speed drives can move 450K per second; and quadruple drives . . . well, you get the idea.

Daughterboard

A small card that pops onto a sound card to give it new capabilities. For example, plugging a Wave Blaster daughterboard onto a Sound Blaster 16 adds wavetable sound.

DIB

Device-Independent Bitmap — a file format for graphics in Windows.

Digital

Computerized things; collections of numbers to represent pictures, sounds, text, or video (See also Analog.)

Distortion

Although electric guitarists spend hundreds of dollars trying to create it, most sound card owners consider it unwanted noise.

Dithering

A way to blur and change colors, making images look more realistic under different video modes and palettes.

DMA (Direct Memory Address)

A way for sound cards to talk to computers. If two cards try to talk on the same DMA, they'll argue, leading to hissing sounds or a frozen computer, especially when you're trying to access a disk.

Dot pitch

The distance between the little pixel dots on the monitor. The smaller the dot pitch, the clearer the picture.

Double-speed

A drive that reads information twice as fast as original, music CD players.

Drivers

Software that lets the computer talk to a specific part, like a sound card. Different parts need different drivers. (Your computer loads the drivers listed in a special file called CONFIG.SYS.)

Dropped frames

Skipping a particular image but picking up the next one down the line, when a computer can't keep up with the incoming information.

DSP (Digital Signal Processor)

A chip on your sound card that takes some of the workload off your computer, especially when fiddling with sound — adding echoes, reverb, and other effects.

Dubbing

Adding new pieces of video or audio to previously recorded stuff to touch it up.

Dynamic microphone

The best mike for recording loud, powerful stuff, such as heavy metal bands or arguments on Larry King's show.

Encoding

Compressing a file. (When you're translating home movies to computer files, you're encoding them.)

External

A part that lives in its own little box — not inside your PC.

FIFO (First In, First Out)

Information that lines up in order, with the first potato down the chute being the first to emerge from the bottom.

Filter

To remove an undesirable quality, such as removing a hiss from a recording or the wine stains from the picture of the carpet.

FM (Frequency Modulation) synthesis

An older technology to mimic musical instruments from computerized tones.

FPS

Frames per second — the number of pictures flashed in a second to give the video the illusion of motion. (NTSC uses 30 FPS; PAL/SECAM uses 25 FPS.)

Frame

A single picture that, when pieced together with other pictures and displayed in a certain order, creates movies. (Remember the flip-the-pages books where a cartoon guy would skip or jump?)

Frequency

Without getting complicated, an annoying mosquito whines at a *high* frequency; a fog horn rumbles at a *low* frequency.

Frequency response

The range of sound something can reproduce. If you listen to music on your CD-ROM drive, look for a frequency response close to 20 to 20,000 Hz.

Full-motion video

A computerized movie — not necessarily filling the screen — showing at either 30 frames per second (NTSC) or 25 frames per second (PAL/SECAM).

Full-screen video

A movie that fills the entire screen, not just a small box.

Full-screen video card

A way to run movies full screen, like a TV. Cards with special MPEG technology can display full-screen video.

GM (General MIDI)

MIDI files with all the instrument sounds lined up in a designated order; nobody's been futzing around, creating "new" instrument sounds. (See also MIDI, MT-32.)

Gradient

Having an area smoothly blend from one color to another, or from black to white or vice versa.

Gray scale

Images using shades of gray instead of color.

Green Book

The format for CD-i (Compact Disc-Interactive).

High resolution

Images with more pixels per square inch than low-resolution images, making them more realistic.

High Sierra

A format for placing files and directories on CD-ROM so that DOS can read them. Also known as *ISO 9660*.

Indeo™

Intel's codec for video.

Intel's Smart Video Recorder

Intel's video capture card with a special chip for capturing and storing videos on the fly. (See also Real-time compression.)

Interactive video

A program that lets people push buttons to control what videos they want to see.

Interlaced/Non-interlaced monitor

Technical stuff that's much too boring to bother with. Just remember that a *non-*interlaced display has less flicker and looks better.

Internal

A part that fits inside your computer, like a floppy drive.

IRQ (Interrupt Request)

A computerized "tap on the shoulder" used by sound cards when they need the CPU's attention. Your computer has only a few of these "shoulders," and cards trying to use the same IRQ won't work right.

ISO-9660

A format for placing files and directories on CD-ROM so that DOS can read them. Also known as *High Sierra*.

Jaguar

Yet Another Game Machine, this one by Atari. It can play audio CDs, display Kodak's new Photo CDs, and blow up aliens in 3-D.

Jewel box

The cheap little plastic box that CDs come packaged in. (See Fragile.)

JPEG

Joint Photographic Expert Group — a codec used mainly for still pictures, not movies.

Juke box

Large CD-ROM drives that hold several CDs, thereby letting you switch among discs easily and expensively.

Key frame

A video frame containing a complete picture, not just the changes from the previous frame.

Kodak Photo CD

A CD that stores photographs in a special format; requires a multi-session, Kodak Photo CD-compatible CD-ROM drive.

Laserdisc player

Similar to a VCR, this machine hooks up to a TV and plays back movies stored on discs. Some new specialized laserdisc players can play musical CDs as well.

Lossless compression

Computerized video containing all the original picture information (even the irrelevant parts).

Lossy compression

Computerized video with some of the stuff chopped out to save space.

Luminance

A video-geek's word for *brightness*.

MCI

Media Control Interface — a part of Windows that lets different brands of multimedia parts work together.

MIDI (Musical Instrument Digital Interface)

A way to store music as a series of computerized instructions; the resulting file can be played back on a wide variety of computers and electronic instruments.

MPEG

A way to compress movies so they fit on discs for quick and easy playback. An *MPEG chip* can play back movies full screen. (See also Full-screen video.)

MPEG and MPEG II

Motion Picture Expert Group — a group deciding how videos should be compressed. (The MPEG standard produces *consumer*-quality video; the MPEG II standard creates *broadcast*-quality video.)

MPU-401 interface

A MIDI standard created by Roland Corporation that is used by most professional musicians with their MIDI instruments.

MT-32

A MIDI standard with instruments arranged in a slightly different order than General MIDI. (See also GM.)

MTBF

Mean Time Between Failures. The higher the number, the more durable the drive.

Multiscan, multifrequency, or multisync monitor

Versatile monitors that can work in a wide variety of video modes.

Multi-session

A CD-ROM drive that can read CDs after they've been changed, like a Kodak Photo CD that has had some more photos added to it.

Multi-timbral

A sound creation technology with better-sounding instruments than FM synthesis; the technology is not as good as wavetable.

Multi-voice

Ability to mimic more than one instrument; found in most cards.

NTSC

National Television Standard Connection — the video standard used mostly in the United States, Canada, and Japan.

Omnidirectional microphone

Microphones that pick up sound from all around them, not just in front. (See also Cardioid microphone, Dynamic microphone.)

Optical storage unit

A fancy word for CD-ROM drive.

Orange Book

Standard for WORM format, also known as *Write Once Read Many* CDs. (Big companies use them to back up their boring computerized paperwork.)

Overlay

A way to superimpose computer graphics over a video; often used to add titles to video tapes.

Oversampling

A way to cut down noise and improve quality when reading a CD. The bigger the oversampling number, the better the quality.

PAL

Phase Alteration Line — video format used in most of western Europe and Australia.

Palette

The variety of colors contained in a video or graphics file.

Philips

A huge company that developed CD technology with Sony.

Phono cable

Cable used mostly for connecting stereo equipment but can also work for video equipment in a pinch. (Video-specific cables provide better pictures.)

Pixel

A tiny little dot on your monitor. (Put your nose against the glass and take a peek.)

Qsound

A new technology for making 3-D sounds so missiles sound like they're coming from *any* direction. (Packaged with the Sound Blaster 16.)

Quadruple-speed

A CD-ROM drive that reads information four times as fast as original music CD players.

QuickTime

Macintosh's equivalent of Microsoft's Video for Windows program for processing video.

RCA audio cable

Commonly found on most home stereos, this cable ends with a little round metal "hat" that slides onto a little round metal "head."

Real-time compression

A way to compress incoming movies or sounds as quickly as they come into the computer — also known as *one-step capture*.

Red Book

Nothing to do with the magazine, this term simply means a CD with music (like a Rolling Stones album) and no computer programs. Also means Compact Disc Digital Audio, or CD-DA.

Resolution

The number of columns and rows of pixels your monitor and card can display.

RIFF

Resource Interchange File Format — a format for storing sound or graphics files so they can be played by different brands of computer gear.

RLE

Run Length Encoding — Microsoft's codec for videos of no more than 256 colors.

Sampling rates

When computers listen to a sound or watch a video to stick the information into a file, they're *sampling* the information. The *higher* the sampling rate, the better the quality, the closer the computer pays attention to the information, and the bigger the resulting file. (It's measured in kHz — *kilohertz*.)

SCSI

Small Computer System Interface. A way to link several computer gadgets together.

SCSI port

A special connector required by most CD-ROM drives; found on a special SCSI *card*, as well as some sound cards.

SCSI/2

Same as SCSI but with a new and improved format.

SECAM

Séquential Couleur A Mémoire (Sequential Color with Memory) — a video format used mostly in France, as well as parts of eastern Europe.

Sound Blaster-compatible

This means the card works with any software written for the Sound Blaster card. (That's about 90 percent of the programs on the market.)

SVGA

A bantered-about term that generally means any video mode greater than 640x480 resolution with 256 colors or more.

S-VHS

Super-VHS — a high-quality videotape format sent through S-video cable.

S-Video

High-quality video used in Hi8 and S-VHS — also known as *Y/C Video*.

Synthesized

Sounds created by computer circuitry.

Teleconference

A phone meeting where callers can both see and talk to each other and nobody has to worry about the extra garlic bread he or she had for lunch.

TIFF

Tagged Image File Format — a file for storing high-quality graphics; especially handy for swapping files between PCs and Macintoshes.

Timing/Synchronization

Matching two things, like the sound of a voice to on-screen lip movements.

Triple-speed

A CD-ROM drive that reads information three times as fast as original music CD players.

True Color video card

A card able to display 16.7 million colors, which is about as many colors as the eye can differentiate on a monitor. (See also 24-bit.)

Tweaking

Fiddling with knobs until everything finally looks right.

VGA monitor or card

A resolution of 640x480 with 16 colors. (Also covers resolutions of 320x240 with 256 colors.)

Video conferencing

A way to talk to people and see them on a computer simultaneously. Requires special cameras, monitor, software, money, and patience with new technology.

Video memory

Memory chips that let a video card process pictures. The more memory, the higher the resolution the card can display. (See also VRAM.)

Video mode

A combination of resolution and color (for example, a combination of 640x480 resolution with 256 colors). There's no right or wrong mode. It all depends on personal preference and wallet width.

Voice

Another word for a musical instrument sound. A 20-voice synthesizer won't necessarily produce 20 instruments, however; many cards mix two or more voices when creating more complex instrument sounds.

Voice annotation

Adding snippets of sound to documents. Click on the Sound icon in the general manager's memo, for example, and hear him apologize personally for the budget cuts.

Voice command

Controlling the computer by voice, not keyboard. For example, say "Bold" and the computer will **boldface** a word. Fun! Unfortunately, you need to talk to your computer for several hours before the voice command software can recognize your voice. (Keep the door locked so bystanders won't watch in horror.)

VRAM

Especially speedy (and expensive) memory on fast video cards.

Yamaha OPL2 synthesizer

Found in older sound cards, it's a mono chip with 11 voices. Also called YM3812. (See also FM synthesis.)

Yamaha OPL3 synthesizer

Found in most mid-range sound cards, it's a stereo chip with 20 voices. Also called YMF262. (See also FM synthesis.)

Yamaha OPL4 synthesizer

A stereo chip with wavetable sound that's now appearing on the market. It works with all software written for the older OPL chips, too.

Yellow Book

A standard for compact discs containing computer programs and data.

Y/C

Video format used by S-VHS and Hi-8 — nerds say that the signal is broken into a separate chrominance (color) and luminance (brightness) channel.

Index

• Symbols •

16–bit ISA slot, 26
8–bit slots, 26

• A •

accelerated local bus video cards, 60
accelerated video cards, 58
access time
  CD–ROM drive, 85
  hard drives, 29
accessories, CD–ROM drive, 86–87
address conflicts, 155–156
album, Kodak Photo CD, 207–211
America Online, 245
Amiga computers, 103–104
amplifier, 43
Arthur's Teacher Trouble program,
    255–256
Atari computers, 105
audio output jack, 84
AUTOEXEC.BAT file, 292
AVI files, 167

• B •

backup units, tape, 282
Berlitz Japanese for Business program,
    265–266
Bernoulli system, removable hard drive,
    282
book
  how to use, 2
  icons, 4–5
  overview, 2–3
  purpose, 1
bulletin board, 245
bus mouse, 27

• C •

cables
  composite, 142, 147
  phono jack extension, 143
  RCA phono, 142
  S–video, 141, 147
  television connection, 147–149
  video, 142, 148
  video capture cards, 141–144
  Y–adapter, 136, 143
caddies, CD–ROM disk, 86–87
caddyless drive, 293–294
Cadenza for Windows program, 237
Cakewalk Professional program, 237
camcorders
  connecting to computer, 141–146
  multimedia, 34–35
  working with, 293
CANYON.MID file, 182
cards
  see also *controller cards, sound cards*
  accelerated video, 58
  sound, 24, 37–52
  Vesa Local bus, 26
  video capture, 65–78
cataloging program, 283–284
CD Mastering, 88
CD players, 35
CD–ROM controller, 121
CD–ROM discs
  buying tips, 274
  multimedia, 274–276
  opening boxes, 274–275
  free, 269–270
  use caddies, 293–294
CD–ROM drive installation, 122–127
  external, 122–124

internal, 124–127
sound cards, 121–122
CD–ROM drivers, 129–130
CD–ROM drives, 29, 79–92, 283
  access time, 85
  accessories, 86–87
  audio CD playback, 84–85
  audio output jack, 84
  buying tips, 80–82
  caddies, 86–87
  caddyless, 293–294
  CD Mastering shop, 88
  CD–XA disc format, 203–204
  cleaning, 90
  controller card, 82–84
  copying information to, 88
  data transfer rate, 85
  double–speed, 80
  game computer, 240
  glossary of terms, 90–92
  hypermedia, 89
  hypertext, 89
  installing, 121–130
  internal vs. external, 82
  jewel boxes, 87
  Kodak CD–ready, 86
  Kodak Photo CD compatibility,
    203–204
  MSCDEX.EXE program, 87
  multi–session compatible, 86
  multimedia packages, 93–98
  multimedia speed requirements, 81
  multisession, 203
  overview, 80
  proprietary vs. SCSI controller card,
    83–84
  quadruple-speed, 80
  Red Book–compatible, 88
  single–speed, 80
  sound routing, 88
  triple–speed, 80
  troubleshooting jerky playback,
    87–88
  writable, 88
  Yellow Book–compatible, 88
CD–ROM movies, jerky, 61, 87–88
CD–ROM programs
  Arthur's Teacher Trouble, 255–256
  Berlitz Japanese for Business,
    265–266
  El-Fish, 240
  Encarta 1994, 258–259
  JFK Assassination: A Visual
    Investigation, 256
  Musical Instruments, 263–264
  Street Atlas USA ver 2.0, 262
  The 7th Guest, 261
  The San Diego Zoo Presents...The
    Animals, 260
  Your Own Photo CD, 258
central processing unit (CPU), 18,
  22–23
CMS (Creative Music System), 40
codecs
  interframe coding, 70
  overview, 69–70
  types of, 71
  video, 69–71
colors, video mode, 57
combo drives, 82
compact discs, 29
composite cable, 142, 147
composite video vs. S–video, 74
CompuServe, 245
computers
  Amiga, 103–104
  Atari, 105
  connecting camcorder/VCR, 141–146
  connecting speaker to bigger speaker,
    268
  connecting to stereo, 135–140
  digital recording compatible, 234

game, 239–246
Macintosh, 104–105
MIDI compatible, 234
multimedia, 21–22
multimedia upgrade packages, 93–98
needed for multimedia, 18–19
new vs. multimedia upgrade, 97
Phillips CD–i (compact disc–interactive), 106–107
presentations, 247–252
removing dropped screws from, 119
Silicon Graphics Indy, 106
television as monitor, 99–102
types of, 103–108
voice recognition, 275
watching TV on, 101
CONFIG.SYS file, 292
contact sheet, Kodak Photo CD, 202, 204–205
Control Panel, Add option, 173
controller cards, 23–27
  accelerated video, 58
  CD–ROM drive, 82–84
  expansion bus/slot, 113
  game, 241
  I/O, 27
  installing, 114–118
  interface, 112–113
  interrupt conflicts, 153–155
  local bus, 58
  matching slots with, 113–114
  multimedia, 111–120
  SCSI, 33
  SCSI CD–ROM, 83–84
  Smart Video Recorder, 216, 227
  sound, 112
  troubleshooting problems with, 161
  VESA local bus, 26
  video, 27, 53–64, 111–112, 293
  video capture, 54, 112
  video memory, 60

controllers
  TV card, 101
  TV converter card, 100
conventional memory, 242
copyrights, 296–297
  additional information, 298
CPU (central processing unit), 18, 22–23

• *D* •

DAC (Digital-to-Analog conversion), 41
data transfer rate, CD–ROM drive, 85
defragment hard drive, 291
defragmentation program, 291
digital postcard, 184–187
digital sound recording, 233
DIP switch settings, 159–160
discs, copy files from, 290
discs, optical, 29
disks, high capacity, 282
disks, magnetic, 29
DMA channel conflicts, 155–156
dot pitch, 55
DoubleSpace program, 292
drive bay, 124
drivers
  CD–ROM, 129–130
  speakers, 267–268
  Windows, 171–173
drives
  CD–ROM, 79–92
  combo, 82
DX, CPU chip, 23

• *E* •

El–Fish program, 240
embedded files, 177
Encarta 1994 program, 258–259
equipment, movie processing, 66–67
events, Windows, 198–199

expanded memory, 242
expansion bus/slot, 23–27, 113
extended memory, 242
external CD–ROM drive
  installation, 122–124
  sound card, 128
External hard drive, 282
external modem, 27

• F •

family album, Kodak Photo CD,
  207–211
fax/modem, SatisFAXion400i, 28
fiddle factor table, 19
file extensions, 277–280
file formats, 277–280
  Kodak Photo CD, 203–204, 207
files
  AUTOEXEC.BAT, 292
  AVI, 167
  CANYON.MID, 182
  CONFIG.SYS, 292
  copy from CDs, 290
  embedded, 177
  Kodak Photo CD, 204
  MIDI, 46–47, 181–183
  moving large, 281–282
  MSCDEX.EXE, 87, 129–130
  sound, 48
  too large for hard drive, 282–283
  transporter, 282
  VFWRUN.EXE, 170–171
  VidCap capture, 215–216
  WAV, 195
FM (frequency modulation) synthesis,
  39–40
formats, file, 277–280
frame grabber, 65
frames, 22
  movie, 67
frames per second, 22

full–motion video, 271–272
full–screen video, 272

• G •

G–VOX program, 236
game computer
  CD–ROM drive requirements, 240
  game card, 241
  hard drive requirements, 240
  joystick port, 241
  joystick requirements, 241–242
  math coprocessor, 240
  memory managers, 242–243
  memory requirements, 242–243
  modem, 244–245
  on–line services, 244–245
  processor requirements, 240
  RAM requirements, 240
  sound card emulations, 243
  sound card requirements, 240
  volume adjustments, 243–244
  Windows compatibility, 240
game controller card, 241
game port, 44, 241
glossary, 301–310
  CD–ROM, 90–92
  hard drive, 30
  sound cards, 49–51
  television, 102
  video, 62–64
  video capture, 65–78
graphics accelerator chip, 58
guitars, MIDI compatible, 236

• H •

hard drives
  access time, 29
  CD–ROM WORM drive, 283
  defragmenting, 214, 291
  files too large, 282–283

size required for multimedia, 28
space needed, 28
terms, 30
hardware I/O address, 156
hardware requirements
  game computer, 239–246
  Kodak Photo CD, 203
  movie processing, 66–67
  presentations computer, 250–251
high capacity floppy disks, 282
hypermedia, 89
hypertext, 89

● I ●

I/O card, 27
icons, book, 4–5
interface cards, See *controller cards*
interframe coding, 70
internal CD–ROM drive installation, 124–127
internal modem, 27
interrupt conflicts, 153–155

● J ●

jewel boxes, CD–ROM disk, 87
JFK Assassination: A Visual
    Investigation, 256–257
joystick
  flight simulator, 242
  game computer, 241–242
  multimedia, 32
  potentiometers, 241
jumper settings, 156–159

● K ●

keyboard/synthesizer, 234–235
keyboards, MIDI controller, 235
kiosks, 248
Kodak Photo CD, 86, 201–212

Access program, 203–205
CD–ROM drive compatibility, 203–204
CD–XA disc format, 203–204
contact sheet, 202, 204–205
costs, 202–203
creating a family album, 207–211
editing prints, 202
file compression, 207
file formats, 203–204, 207
hardware requirements, 203
Kodak Pro Photo CD, 207
Lantern program, 204
mail order services, 206
overview, 201–202
Photo CD players, 204
photo finishing lab, 202
PhotoStyler, 204
Portfolio Disc, 207
presentations with, 251
processing, 205–206
resolution types, 206–207
Shoebox program, 205
software requirements, 203–205
storing on hard drive, 205
types of, 207
Kodak Pro Photo CD, 207

● L ●

Lantern program, 204
laptops
  huge file transporter, 282
  multimedia, 34–35
law, on–line, 297
legal questions, 295–298
  on–line law, 297
  public domain, 297
Leisure Suit Larry 6, 240
local bus
  cards, 58, 60
  slots, 26

• *M* •

Macintosh computers, 104–105
magnetic disks, 29
manufacturers tricks, 271–276
  full–motion video vs. full–screen,
    271–272
  quarter screen video, 272
Master Tracks Pro program, 237
math coprocessor, 240
MCA slots, 26
Media Player
  audio CD playback, 84–85
  AVI files, 167
  Border around object option, 178
  Caption option, 178
  CD Audio command, 166
  CD Audio driver, 172–173
  Configure option, 171
  Control Bar on playback option, 178
  control panel, 166–167
  customizing embedded clips, 178–179
  Device menu, 167
  Device option, 166–167
  Dither picture to VGA colors option,
    179
  enlarging pictures, 171
  File menu, 168
  file playback, 167–168
  Frames option, 170
  Full Screen option, 171
  media clip, 170
  media player reference, 169
  minimizing, 168
  Open command, 168
  Play button, 168
  Play in client document option, 178
  playing audio CDs, 172–173
  Scale menu, 170
  sizing window, 167
  Time option, 170

Tracks option, 170
  upgrading to play movies, 170–171
  Video for Windows, 170–171
  Video for Windows option, 167
  video playback, 169
  Zoom by 2 option, 171
megahertz (MHz), 23
memory
  conventional, 242
  expanded, 242
  extended, 242
  game computer problems, 242–243
  I/O address, 156
  multimedia requirements, 30–31
  video card, 60
MHz (megahertz), 23
microphones, MIDI compatible, 235
MIDI (Musical Instrument Digital Inter-
    face), 46–47
  files, 46–47, 181–183
  interface, 234
MIDI Mapper, 181–183
  basic standard, 181–182
  extended standard, 181–182
  sound card support, 183
MIDI music studio, 233–238
  backgrounds software, 237
  clips software, 237
  G–VOX program, 236
  guitars, 236
  hardware requirements, 234–237
  microphones, 235
  notation software, 237
  piano–roll notation, 237
  recording information, 233
  sequencer software, 237
  setup tips, 238
  software compatibility, 237
  sound card, 234
  sound interface, 234
  speakers, 235
  staff notation, 237

synthesizer, 234
tape recorder, 236
utilities software, 237
MIDI port, 44
model releases, 298
modems
  game computer, 244–245
  internal vs. external, 27
monitors, 53–64
  buying, 54–55
  dot pitch, 55
  installing, 131–134
  multiscan, 55, 134
  multisync, 55
  presentation compatible, 250–251
  scan rates, 134
  TV set as, 99–102
  vertical scanning frequency, 134
  video card configuration software, 133
  video port plug, 132
motherboards, 23
mouse, multimedia, 31–32
movies
  broadcast standards, 72–73, 101
  capture speed, 71–72
  codecs, 69–71
  file compression, 69–71
  frames, 67
  interframe coding, 70
  jerky, 61, 87–88
  MPEG (Motion Picture Experts Group), 74
  playback jerkiness, 72
  problems, 61
  processing, 65–78
  screen image requirements, 69
  tiny, 61
  troubleshooting, 285–287
  video hardware requirements, 66–67
MPC (Multimedia PC), 13–16
MPC/MPC2 Standards, 15–17
MPC2 (Multimedia PC II), 15–16

MPEG (Motion Picture Experts Group), 74
MSCDEX.EXE file, 87, 129–130
Multimedia PC (MPC), 13–16
Multimedia PC II (MPC2), 15–16
Multimedia PC Marketing Council, Inc., 14
multimedia, 9–19
  bundled packages, 93–98
  cataloging program, 283–284
  CD–ROM speed requirements, 81
  CDs, 274–276
  computer capabilities, 11
  computer role, 22
  controller card slot types, 113–114
  controller cards, 111–120
  copyrights, 296
  creating a family album, 207–211
  digital postcard, 184–187
  DMA channel conflicts, 155–156
  expansion bus/slot, 113
  free CDs, 269–270
  game computer, 239–246
  hypermedia, 89
  hypertext, 89
  installing, 94–95
  installing controller cards, 114–118
  interrupt conflicts, 153–155
  joystick, 32
  laptops, 34–35
  legal questions, 295–298
  memory requirements, 30–31
  mouse, 31–32
  parts, 17–18
  presentations, 248
  program elements, 12–13
  questions, 34–35
  refresh rates, 134
  shopping tips, 96
  sound cards, 24, 37–52, 112
  sound recording/playback, 189–200
  time shopping, 269

tips, 289–294
trying out, 267–270
TV card, 101
TV set as computer monitor, 99–102
upgrade pros/cons, 95–96
upgrade vs. new computer, 97
video capture cards, 112
video cards, 111–112
video mode switching, 173–176
multiscan monitors, 55, 134
multisync monitor, 55
Musical Instruments program, 263–264

• *O* •

Object Packager
  Add a label to any object's icon, 180
  Assign any icon to a command line
    option, 180
  Assign any icon to any data option, 180
  packing an object, 180–181
objects
  customizing embedded clips, 178–179
  embedding, 177–178
  linking, 179–180
off–screen presentations, 248
OLE (Object Linking and Embedding),
  176–181
on–line services, 297
  law, 297
  game playing, 244–245
on–screen presentations, 248
optical discs, 29
overdrive, 23

• *P* •

PCI slots, 26
PCMCIA card, 26
Phillips CD–i (compact disc–interactive)
  computers, 106–107
phono jack extension cable, 143

Photo CD players, 204
PhotoStyler program, 204
pixels, 56
ports, SCSI, 33
postcards, digital, 184–187
potentiometer, 241
presentations, 247–252
  clips, 250
  computer, 250
  creating, 251
  display monitors, 250–251
  hardware requirements, 250–251
  kiosk, 248
  off–screen, 248
  on–screen, 248
  software, 248–250
  sound card, 250
problems, 281–287
programs
  Arthur's Teacher Trouble, 255–256
  Berlitz Japanese for Business,
    265–266
  Cadenza for Windows, 237
  Cakewalk Professional, 237
  cataloging, 283–284
  DoubleSpace, 292
  El–Fish, 240
  elements of multimedia, 12–13
  Encarta 1994, 258–259
  G–VOX, 236
  JFK Assassination: A Visual
    Investigation, 256–257
  Kodak Photo CD Access, 203–205
  Lantern, 204
  Leisure Suit Larry 6, 240
  Master Tracks Pro, 237
  MIDI music studio, 237
  MSCDEX.EXE, 87
  Musical Instruments, 263–264
  PhotoStyler, 204
  presentations, 248–250
  Return to Zork, 240

Shoebox, 205, 283
SPEAK.EXE, 268
Stacker, 292
Street Atlas USA ver 2.0, 262
The 7th Guest, 261
The San Diego Zoo Presents...The
    Animals, 260
VidCap, 214
VidEdit, 214, 222–227
Video for Windows, 170–171
Your Own Photo CD, 258
property releases, 298
proprietary CD–ROM controller card,
    83–84
public domain software, 297

• *Q* •

quarter screen video, 272
questions
    legal, 295–298
    multimedia, 34–35

• *R* •

radio speakers, 258
RCA phono cable, 142
refresh rates, monitors, 134
releases
    model, 298
    property, 298
removable cartridge disk drives, 282
removable hard drives, 282
resolution, video mode, 56, 59
Return to Zork program, 240

• *S* •

S–video
    cable, 141, 147
    vs. composite, 74
sampling, 40
San Diego Zoo Presents...The Animals
    program, 260

SatisFAXion400i fax/modem, 28
scan rates, 134
SCSI (Small Computer System Interface),
    27, 33, 84
    sound cards & CD–ROM drive installa-
        tion, 122
SCSI CD–ROM controller card, 83–84
SCSI controller card, 33
    daisy chaining devices, 83
SCSI II ports, 33
SCSI port, 33, 44–45
    CD–ROM drives, 33
    sound cards, 33
Setup
    Change System Settings dialog box, 174
    Change System Settings option, 174
    Options menu, 174
    video mode switching, 174–175
Seventh Guest, The, 261
shielded y–adapter cable, 136, 143
Shoebox program, 205, 283
Silicon Graphics Indy computers, 106
SL, CPU chip, 23
slots, 23–27
    freeing up, 27–28
Smart Video Recorder, video capture
    card, 216, 227
software
    see also *programs*
    Kodak Photo CD compatible, 203–205
    public domain, 297
solutions to problems, 281–287
sound cards, 24, 37–52
    8–bit vs. 16–bit, 47
    accessories on, 43–45
    amplifier, 43
    buying guide, 38–46
    CD–ROM drives, 121–122
    CMS (Creative Music System)
        technology, 40
    Digital-to-Analog conversion, 41
    DMA channel conflicts, 155–156
    FM synthesis, 39

game computer, 240
game port, 44
glossary of terms, 49–51
hooking up to stereo, 270
inexpensive, 268
information from external CD–ROM, 128
interrupt conflicts, 153–155
MIDI compatible, 234–235
MIDI files, 46–47
MIDI port, 44
mixers, 193, 244
physics of sound, 42
playing stereo through, 138–139
presentation compatible, 250
RCA phono plugs, 137
record/playback, 40–43
sampling, 40
SCSI port, 44–45
shielded y–adapter cable, 136
sound file types, 48
stereo connections, 135–140
synthesizing sound, 39–40
upgradable, 40
uses for, 38
volume adjustments, 243–244
volume knob, 190
wavetable, 39–40
sound files, 48
Sound Recorder, 190–191
control panel, 194
editing sounds, 195–196
home stereo recording/playback, 138–139
sound recording, 192–195
special effects, 195–196
sound track, 285–286
sounds
8–bit vs. 16–bit recording, 191
adjusting volume, 190
bad, 286
digital recording, 233
editing, 195–196
kHz modes, 191
matching with video, 286
mono vs. stereo recording, 191
recording/playback, 189–200
special effects, 195–196
SPEAK.EXE program, 268
speaker drivers, 267–268
speakers
connecting, 268
MIDI compatible, 235
radio, 268
Stacker program, 292
stereo
connecting computer to, 135–140
playing through sound card, 138–139
sound cards, 270
still image grabber, 65
Street Atlas USA Ver 2.0 program, 262
swap files, Windows, 290
SX, CPU chip, 23
synthesizer, 39–40
MIDI compatible, 234–235
Syquest system, removable hard drive, 282

• T •

Tape backup units, 282–283
tape recorder, MIDI compatible, 236
television
broadcast standards, 101, 149
cabling, 147–149
connecting computer to, 147–152
glossary of terms, 102
TV converter card, 100
using as computer monitor, 99–102
viewing computer programs on, 149–150
watching TV on computer, 101
Windows presentation hints, 151
terms, 30, 301–310

CD–ROM, 90–92
hard drive, 30
sound cards, 49–51
television, 102
video, 62–64
video capture, 75–78
The 7th Guest program, 261
tips, 289–294
copy favorite files from compact discs, 290
defragment hard drive, 291
don't use file compression programs, 292
enjoy camcorders, 293
if it works, don't fix it, 289–290
permanent swap file in Windows, 290
quick windows browsing, 291–292
upgrade to PCI or local bus video, 293
use CD caddies, 293–294
troubleshooting, 281–287
see also *problems*
files too large for hard drive, 282–283
movies, 285–287
moving large files, 281–282
video capture card, 285
video drivers, 284
videos won't play, 287
TV card, 101
TV converter card, 100

• V •

VCR
connecting to computer, 141–146
watching TV on computer, 101
vertical scanning frequency, monitors, 134
VESA Local Bus card, 26
VFWRUN.EXE file, 170–171
VidCap program, 214
audio format adjustment, 216–217
Audio Format dialog box, 217

Audio Format option, 217
broadcast format, 219
Capture Audio option, 221
capture file, 215–216
Capture menu, 218, 220–222
capture method, 221
Capture Video Sequence dialog box, 221
capturing options, 220–222
capturing video to memory, 221
color limitations, 218
Colors option, 218
composite video source, 219
Directly to Disk option, 221
Edit Capture Video option, 221
Enable Capture Time Limit option, 221
File menu, 215–216
Frame Rate option, 218–221
Frames option, 220
Level button, 217
MCI control of source video option, 221
memory requirements, 221
Options menu, 217
overlay, 219
Overlay Video option, 219
Palette option, 218
palettes, 218
picture adjustment, 219
Preview video option, 219
previewing video, 219
Quality option, 217
recording videos, 214–222
S–video source, 219
Save Captured Video As option, 215–216, 222
Single Frame option, 220
Size option, 217
VCR as video source, 219
Video Display option, 219
video format adjustment, 217–218
Video Format option, 217
Video option, 220–221

video source adjustment, 219
Video Source option, 219
VidEdit program, 214, 222–227
   Audio Offset option, 224
   Compression Options button, 225
   Compressor Settings Quality option, 226
   Data rate option, 226
   Delete option, 224
   deleting frames, 224
   Details button, 225
   Edit menu, 224
   editing videos, 224
   file compression, 222
   File menu, 223, 225
   Insert option, 224
   inserting frames, 224
   Interleave audio every: option, 226
   Key frame every: option, 226
   Mark Out button, 224
   Open option, 223
   opening files, 223
   overwrite mode, 224
   Pad frames for CD–ROM playback:, 226
   Play button, 224
   Preview button, 225
   redrawing screen, 224
   Save as default option, 226
   Save As option, 225
   saving videos, 225–227
   Synchronize option, 224
   synchronizing sound/video, 224
   Target option, 225
   Use Default option, 226
   Video Compression Method option, 225
   Video menu, 224
   View menu, 224
   Zoom option, 224
   zooming, 224
video cable, 142, 148

video capture card, 54, 65–78
   broadcast standards, 72–73, 101
   cabling, 141–144
   capture speed, 71–72
   codecs, 69–71
   editing movies, 67–69
   file compression, 69–71
   frame editing, 67–69
   frame grabber, 65
   glossary, 75–78
   half–screen, 67
   image sizing, 67–69
   interframe coding, 70
   interrupt conflicts, 153–155
   MPEG (Motion Picture Experts Group), 74
   one–sixteenth screen, 67
   playback jerkiness, 72
   quarter–screen, 67
   S–video vs. composite, 74
   screen image requirements, 69
   shortcomings, 66
   Smart Video Recorder, 216, 227
   still image grabber, 65
   troubleshooting, 285
   types of, 65
   Video for Windows, 214
video card, 27, 53–64
   configuration software, 133
   local bus video, 293
   memory, 60
   not in computer, 61
   PCI, 293
   updating, 61
Video for Windows program, 170–171, 213–230
   compressing videos, 225–226
   creating/editing videos, 227–230
   file compression, 214
   overview, 213–214
   runtime version, 214

upgrading, 214
VidCap program, 214–222
VidEdit program, 214
video capture card, 214
video grabber, See *video capture card*
video mode, 56–58
 choosing, 58
 colors, 57
 pixels, 56
 resolution, 56, 59
 switching through controller card
  software, 176
 switching Windows, 173–176
 troubleshooting Windows startup
  problems, 175
video port, monitor plug, 132
videos
 bad appearance, 286
 black and white, 285
 broadcast standards, 72–73, 101
 capture speed, 71–72
 capturing, 214–222
 codecs, 69–71
 creating/editing, 227–230
 file compression, 69–71
 full–motion vs. full–screen, 271–272
 full–screen, 272
 hardware requirements, 66–67
 interframe coding, 70
 matching sound, 286
 movie editing, 67–69
 MPEG (Motion Picture Experts Group),
  74
 not playing, 287
 playback jerkiness, 72
 quarter screen, 272–273
 screen image requirements, 69
 terms, 62–64
voice recognition, 275
volume knob, 190

• *W* •

WAV files, 195
wavetable, 39–40
Windows, 165–188
 adding drivers, 171–173
 adjusting sound volume, 190
 browsing, 291–292
 CD Audio driver, 172–173
 Control Panel, Add option, 173
 digital postcard, 184–187
 dragging files, 168
 Drivers dialog box, 172
 events, 198–199
 exploding, 197–198
 make a permanent swap file, 290
 Media Player, 84–85, 165–171
  AVI files, 167
  Border around object option, 178
  Caption option, 178
  CD Audio command, 166
  Configure option, 171
  Control Bar on playback option, 178
  control panel, 166–167
  customizing embedded clips,
   178–179
  Device menu, 167
  Device option, 166–167
  Dither picture to VGA colors option,
   179
  enlarging pictures, 171
  File menu, 168
  file playback, 167–168
  Frames option, 170
  Full Screen option, 171
  media clip, 170
  media player reference, 169
  minimizing, 168
  Open command, 168
  Play button, 168

Play in client document option, 178
playing audio CDs, 172–173
Scale menu, 170
sizing window, 167
Time option, 170
Tracks option, 179
upgrading to play movies, 170–171
Video for Windows option, 167
video playback, 169
Zoom by 2 option, 171
MIDI Mapper, 181–183
  basic standard, 181–182
  extended standard, 181–182
  sound card support, 183
Object Packager
  options, 180
  packing an object, 180–181
objects
  customizing embedded clips,
    178–179
  embedding, 177–178
  linking, 179–180
OLE (Object Linking and Embedding),
  176–181
Setup
  Change System Settings dialog box,
    174

Change System Settings option, 174
  Options menu, 174
  video mode switching, 174–175
sound playback, 195
Sound Recorder, 138–139, 190–191
  control panel, 194
  editing sounds, 195–196
  sound recording, 192–195
  special effects, 195–196
speaker driver, 267–268
television presentation hints, 151
troubleshooting video mode settings,
  175
video drivers, 284
Video for Windows program,
  170–171, 213–230
video mode controller card software,
  176
video mode switching, 173–176
videos, 285–286
Write, digital postcard, 184–187

• *Y* •

Y–adapter cable, 136, 143
Y–C video, See *S–video*, 74
Your Own Photo CD program, 258

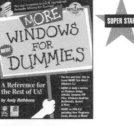

Title	Author	ISBN	Price
INTERNET / COMMUNICATIONS / NETWORKING			11/11/94
CompuServe For Dummies™	by Wallace Wang	1-56884-181-7	$19.95 USA/$26.95 Canada
Modems For Dummies™, 2nd Edition	by Tina Rathbone	1-56884-223-6	$19.99 USA/$26.99 Canada
Modems For Dummies™	by Tina Rathbone	1-56884-001-2	$19.95 USA/$26.95 Canada
MORE Internet For Dummies™	by John R. Levine & Margaret Levine Young	1-56884-164-7	$19.95 USA/$26.95 Canada
NetWare For Dummies™	by Ed Tittel & Deni Connor	1-56884-003-9	$19.95 USA/$26.95 Canada
Networking For Dummies™	by Doug Lowe	1-56884-079-5	$19.95 USA/$26.95 Canada
ProComm Plus 2 For Windows For Dummies™	by Wallace Wang	1-56884-219-8	$19.99 USA/$26.99 Canada
The Internet For Dummies™, 2nd Edition	by John R. Levine & Carol Baroudi	1-56884-222-8	$19.99 USA/$26.99 Canada
The Internet For Macs For Dummies™	by Charles Seiter	1-56884-184-1	$19.95 USA/$26.95 Canada
MACINTOSH			
Macs For Dummies®	by David Pogue	1-56884-173-6	$19.95 USA/$26.95 Canada
Macintosh System 7.5 For Dummies™	by Bob LeVitus	1-56884-197-3	$19.95 USA/$26.95 Canada
MORE Macs For Dummies™	by David Pogue	1-56884-087-X	$19.95 USA/$26.95 Canada
PageMaker 5 For Macs For Dummies™	by Galen Gruman	1-56884-178-7	$19.95 USA/$26.95 Canada
QuarkXPress 3.3 For Dummies™	by Galen Gruman & Barbara Assadi	1-56884-217-1	$19.99 USA/$26.99 Canada
Upgrading and Fixing Macs For Dummies™	by Kearney Rietmann & Frank Higgins	1-56884-189-2	$19.95 USA/$26.95 Canada
MULTIMEDIA			
Multimedia & CD-ROMs For Dummies™, Interactive Multimedia Value Pack	by Andy Rathbone	1-56884-225-2	$29.95 USA/$39.95 Canada
Multimedia & CD-ROMs For Dummies™	by Andy Rathbone	1-56884-089-6	$19.95 USA/$26.95 Canada
OPERATING SYSTEMS / DOS			
MORE DOS For Dummies™	by Dan Gookin	1-56884-046-2	$19.95 USA/$26.95 Canada
S.O.S. For DOS™	by Katherine Murray	1-56884-043-8	$12.95 USA/$16.95 Canada
OS/2 For Dummies™	by Andy Rathbone	1-878058-76-2	$19.95 USA/$26.95 Canada
UNIX			
UNIX For Dummies™	by John R. Levine & Margaret Levine Young	1-878058-58-4	$19.95 USA/$26.95 Canada
WINDOWS			
S.O.S. For Windows™	by Katherine Murray	1-56884-045-4	$12.95 USA/$16.95 Canada
MORE Windows 3.1 For Dummies™, 3rd Edition	by Andy Rathbone	1-56884-240-6	$19.99 USA/$26.99 Canada
PCs / HARDWARE			
Illustrated Computer Dictionary For Dummies™	by Dan Gookin, Wally Wang, & Chris Van Buren	1-56884-004-7	$12.95 USA/$16.95 Canada
Upgrading and Fixing PCs For Dummies™	by Andy Rathbone	1-56884-002-0	$19.95 USA/$26.95 Canada
PRESENTATION / AUTOCAD			
AutoCAD For Dummies™	by Bud Smith	1-56884-191-4	$19.95 USA/$26.95 Canada
PowerPoint 4 For Windows For Dummies™	by Doug Lowe	1-56884-161-2	$16.95 USA/$22.95 Canada
PROGRAMMING			
Borland C++ For Dummies™	by Michael Hyman	1-56884-162-0	$19.95 USA/$26.95 Canada
"Borland's New Language Product" For Dummies™	by Neil Rubenking	1-56884-200-7	$19.95 USA/$26.95 Canada
C For Dummies™	by Dan Gookin	1-878058-78-9	$19.95 USA/$26.95 Canada
C++ For Dummies™	by Stephen R. Davis	1-56884-163-9	$19.95 USA/$26.95 Canada
Mac Programming For Dummies™	by Dan Parks Sydow	1-56884-173-6	$19.95 USA/$26.95 Canada
QBasic Programming For Dummies™	by Douglas Hergert	1-56884-093-4	$19.95 USA/$26.95 Canada
Visual Basic "X" For Dummies™, 2nd Edition	by Wallace Wang	1-56884-230-9	$19.99 USA/$26.99 Canada
Visual Basic 3 For Dummies™	by Wallace Wang	1-56884-076-4	$19.95 USA/$26.95 Canada
SPREADSHEET			
1-2-3 For Dummies™	by Greg Harvey	1-878058-60-6	$16.95 USA/$21.95 Canada
1-2-3 For Windows 5 For Dummies™, 2nd Edition	by John Walkenbach	1-56884-216-3	$16.95 USA/$21.95 Canada
1-2-3 For Windows For Dummies™	by John Walkenbach	1-56884-052-7	$16.95 USA/$21.95 Canada
Excel 5 For Macs For Dummies™	by Greg Harvey	1-56884-186-8	$19.95 USA/$26.95 Canada
Excel For Dummies™, 2nd Edition	by Greg Harvey	1-56884-050-0	$16.95 USA/$21.95 Canada
MORE Excel 5 For Windows For Dummies™	by Greg Harvey	1-56884-207-4	$19.95 USA/$26.95 Canada
Quattro Pro 6 For Windows For Dummies™	by John Walkenbach	1-56884-174-4	$19.95 USA/$26.95 Canada
Quattro Pro For DOS For Dummies™	by John Walkenbach	1-56884-023-3	$16.95 USA/$21.95 Canada
UTILITIES / VCRs & CAMCORDERS			
Norton Utilities 8 For Dummies™	by Beth Slick	1-56884-166-3	$19.95 USA/$26.95 Canada
VCRs & Camcorders For Dummies™	by Andy Rathbone & Gordon McComb	1-56884-229-5	$14.99 USA/$20.99 Canada
WORD PROCESSING			
Ami Pro For Dummies™	by Jim Meade	1-56884-049-7	$19.95 USA/$26.95 Canada
MORE Word For Windows 6 For Dummies™	by Doug Lowe	1-56884-165-5	$19.95 USA/$26.95 Canada
MORE WordPerfect 6 For Windows For Dummies™	by Margaret Levine Young & David C. Kay	1-56884-206-6	$19.95 USA/$26.95 Canada
MORE WordPerfect 6 For DOS For Dummies™	by Wallace Wang, edited by Dan Gookin	1-56884-047-0	$19.95 USA/$26.95 Canada
S.O.S. For WordPerfect™	by Katherine Murray	1-56884-053-5	$12.95 USA/$16.95 Canada
Word 6 For Macs For Dummies™	by Dan Gookin	1-56884-190-6	$19.95 USA/$26.95 Canada
Word For Windows 6 For Dummies™	by Dan Gookin	1-56884-075-6	$16.95 USA/$21.95 Canada
Word For Windows For Dummies™	by Dan Gookin	1-878058-86-X	$16.95 USA/$21.95 Canada
WordPerfect 6 For Dummies™	by Dan Gookin	1-878058-77-0	$16.95 USA/$21.95 Canada
WordPerfect For Dummies™	by Dan Gookin	1-878058-52-5	$16.95 USA/$21.95 Canada
WordPerfect For Windows For Dummies™	by Margaret Levine Young & David C. Kay	1-56884-032-2	$16.95 USA/$21.95 Canada

Fun, Fast, & Cheap!

CorelDRAW! 5 For Dummies™ Quick Reference
by Raymond E. Werner

ISBN: 1-56884-952-4
$9.99 USA/$12.99 Canada

Windows "X" For Dummies™ Quick Reference, 3rd Edition
by Greg Harvey

ISBN: 1-56884-964-8
$9.99 USA/$12.99 Canada

Word For Windows 6 For Dummies™ Quick Reference
by George Lynch

ISBN: 1-56884-095-0
$8.95 USA/$12.95 Canada

WordPerfect For DOS For Dummies™ Quick Reference
by Greg Harvey

ISBN: 1-56884-009-8
$8.95 USA/$11.95 Canada

Title	Author	ISBN	Price
DATABASE			
Access 2 For Dummies™ Quick Reference	by Stuart A. Stuple	1-56884-167-1	$8.95 USA/$11.95 Canada
dBASE 5 For DOS For Dummies™ Quick Reference	by Barry Sosinsky	1-56884-954-0	$9.99 USA/$12.99 Canada
dBASE 5 For Windows For Dummies™ Quick Reference	by Stuart J. Stuple	1-56884-953-2	$9.99 USA/$12.99 Canada
Paradox 5 For Windows For Dummies™ Quick Reference	by Scott Palmer	1-56884-960-5	$9.99 USA/$12.99 Canada
DESKTOP PUBLISHING / ILLUSTRATION/GRAPHICS			
Harvard Graphics 3 For Windows For Dummies™ Quick Reference	by Raymond E. Werner	1-56884-962-1	$9.99 USA/$12.99 Canada
FINANCE / PERSONAL FINANCE			
Quicken 4 For Windows For Dummies™ Quick Reference	by Stephen L. Nelson	1-56884-950-8	$9.95 USA/$12.95 Canada
GROUPWARE / INTEGRATED			
Microsoft Office 4 For Windows For Dummies™ Quick Reference	by Doug Lowe	1-56884-958-3	$9.99 USA/$12.99 Canada
Microsoft Works For Windows 3 For Dummies™ Quick Reference	by Michael Partington	1-56884-959-1	$9.99 USA/$12.99 Canada
INTERNET / COMMUNICATIONS / NETWORKING			
The Internet For Dummies™ Quick Reference	by John R. Levine	1-56884-168-X	$8.95 USA/$11.95 Canada
MACINTOSH			
Macintosh System 7.5 For Dummies™ Quick Reference	by Stuart J. Stuple	1-56884-956-7	$9.99 USA/$12.99 Canada
OPERATING SYSTEMS / DOS			
DOS For Dummies® Quick Reference	by Greg Harvey	1-56884-007-1	$8.95 USA/$11.95 Canada
UNIX			
UNIX For Dummies™ Quick Reference	by Margaret Levine Young & John R. Levine	1-56884-094-2	$8.95 USA/$11.95 Canada
WINDOWS			
Windows 3.1 For Dummies™ Quick Reference, 2nd Edition	by Greg Harvey	1-56884-951-6	$8.95 USA/$11.95 Canada
PRESENTATION / AUTOCAD			
AutoCAD For Dummies™ Quick Reference	by Bud Smith	1-56884-198-1	$9.95 USA/$12.95 Canada
SPREADSHEET			
1-2-3 For Dummies™ Quick Reference	by John Walkenbach	1-56884-027-6	$8.95 USA/$11.95 Canada
1-2-3 For Windows 5 For Dummies™ Quick Reference	by John Walkenbach	1-56884-957-5	$9.95 USA/$12.95 Canada
Excel For Windows For Dummies™ Quick Reference, 2nd Edition	by John Walkenbach	1-56884-096-9	$8.95 USA/$11.95 Canada
Quattro Pro 6 For Windows For Dummies™ Quick Reference	by Stuart A. Stuple	1-56884-172-8	$9.95 USA/$12.95 Canada
WORD PROCESSING			
Word For Windows 6 For Dummies™ Quick Reference	by George Lynch	1-56884-095-0	$8.95 USA/$11.95 Canada
WordPerfect For Windows For Dummies™ Quick Reference	by Greg Harvey	1-56884-039-X	$8.95 USA/$11.95 Canada

FOR MORE INFORMATION OR TO ORDER, PLEASE CALL ▶ 800. 762. 2974

For volume discounts & special orders please call
Tony Real, Special Sales, at 415. 312. 0650

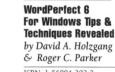

11/11/94

IDG BOOKS

Order Center: **(800) 762-2974** *(8 a.m.–6 p.m., CST, weekdays)*

Quantity	ISBN	Title	Price	Total

Shipping & Handling Charges

	Description	First book	Each additional book	Total
Domestic	Normal	$4.50	$1.50	$
	Two Day Air	$8.50	$2.50	$
	Overnight	$18.00	$3.00	$
International	Surface	$8.00	$8.00	$
	Airmail	$16.00	$16.00	$
	DHL Air	$17.00	$17.00	$

*For large quantities call for shipping & handling charges.
**Prices are subject to change without notice.

Ship to:

Name _____

Company _____

Address _____

City/State/Zip _____

Daytime Phone _____

Payment: ☐ Check to IDG Books (US Funds Only)

☐ Visa ☐ Mastercard ☐ American Express

Card # _____ Expires _____

Signature _____

Subtotal _____

CA residents add applicable sales tax _____

IN, MA and MD residents add 5% sales tax _____

IL residents add 6.25% sales tax _____

RI residents add 7% sales tax _____

TX residents add 8.25% sales tax _____

Shipping _____

Total _____

Please send this order form to:

**IDG Books Worldwide
7260 Shadeland Station, Suite 100
Indianapolis, IN 46256**

*Allow up to 3 weeks for delivery.
Thank you!*

Learn to Use Video-Capture/Playback!

Add Music and Voice-Overs to Your Presentations!

Dazzle 'Em with Animation!

The World of Multimedia at Your Fingertips!

Welcome to the First CD-ROM that Uses Multimedia to Teach You about Multimedia!

Inside, you'll find over 20 hours of fact-packed, interactive multimedia information for beginners and professionals.

You'll Interactively Explore:

- The basic fundamentals of multimedia
- In-depth information about multimedia technology
- What kind of hardware and software you'll need
- Easy steps to creating multimedia presentations
- Vast clip libraries of video, graphics, animations, and sounds
- An interactive Table of Contents, Glossary, and Index

System Requirements:
386SX PC or better, Windows 3.1 or 3.0 with extensions, 2MB RAM, 4MB recommended, 30MB hard disk, VGA display, 256 colors, CD-ROM drive, sound board recommended

Order Your Copy of
The Guided Tour of Multimedia Today!
Only $14.95 — see other side for order form!

CD Presented in Association with

Order Form

Order Center: (800) 762-2974 (8 a.m.-5 p.m., PST, weekdays) or (415) 312-0650

For Fastest Service: Photocopy this order form and FAX it to: (415) 358-1260

Quantity	ISBN	Title	Price	Total
	1-56884-558-8	*The Guided Tour of Multimedia* CD	$14.95	

Shipping & Handling Charges

Subtotal	US	Canada & International	International Air Mail
Up to $20.00	Add $3.00	Add $4.00	Add $10.00
$20.01-40.00	$4.00	$5.00	$20.00
$40.01-60.00	$5.00	$6.00	$25.00
$60.01-80.00	$6.00	$8.00	$35.00
Over $80.00	$7.00	$10.00	$50.00

In U.S. and Canada, shipping is UPS ground or equivalent.
For Rush shipping call (800) 762-2974.

Subtotal _____

CA residents add
applicable sales tax _____

IN and MA residents add
5% sales tax _____

IL residents add
6.25% sales tax _____

RI residents add
7% sales tax _____

Shipping _____

Total _____

Ship to:

Name _____

Company _____

Address _____

City/State/Zip_____

Daytime Phone _____

Payment: ❏ Check to IDG Books (US Funds Only)　❏ Visa　❏ Mastercard　❏ American Express

Card# _____ Exp._____ Signature_____

Please send this order form to: IDG Books, 155 Bovet Road, Suite 310, San Mateo, CA 94402.

Allow up to 3 weeks for delivery. Thank you!

IDG BOOKS WORLDWIDE REGISTRATION CARD

RETURN THIS REGISTRATION CARD FOR FREE CATALOG

Title of this book: MULTIMEDIA & CD-ROMs FOR DUMMIES

My overall rating of this book: ❑ Very good [1] ❑ Good [2] ❑ Satisfactory [3] ❑ Fair [4] ❑ Poor [5]

How I first heard about this book:

❑ Found in bookstore; name: [6] _____

❑ Advertisement: [8]

❑ Word of mouth; heard about book from friend, co-worker, etc.: [10]

❑ Book review: [7]

❑ Catalog: [9]

❑ Other: [11]

What I liked most about this book:

_____

_____

What I would change, add, delete, etc., in future editions of this book:

_____

_____

Other comments:

_____

Number of computer books I purchase in a year: ❑ 1 [12] ❑ 2-5 [13] ❑ 6-10 [14] ❑ More than 10 [15]

I would characterize my computer skills as: ❑ Beginner [16] ❑ Intermediate [17] ❑ Advanced [18] ❑ Professional [19]

I use ❑ DOS [20] ❑ Windows [21] ❑ OS/2 [22] ❑ Unix [23] ❑ Macintosh [24] ❑ Other: [25]_____
(please specify)

I would be interested in new books on the following subjects:
(please check all that apply, and use the spaces provided to identify specific software)

❑ Word processing: [26] _____

❑ Data bases: [28] _____

❑ File Utilities: [30] _____

❑ Networking: [32] _____

❑ Other: [34] _____

❑ Spreadsheets: [27] _____

❑ Desktop publishing: [29] _____

❑ Money management: [31] _____

❑ Programming languages: [33] _____

I use a PC at (please check all that apply): ❑ home [35] ❑ work [36] ❑ school [37] ❑ other: [38] _____

The disks I prefer to use are ❑ 5.25 [39] ❑ 3.5 [40] ❑ other: [41] _____

I have a CD ROM: ❑ yes [42] ❑ no [43]

I plan to buy or upgrade computer hardware this year: ❑ yes [44] ❑ no [45]

I plan to buy or upgrade computer software this year: ❑ yes [46] ❑ no [47]

Name: _____ Business title: [48] _____ Type of Business: [49] _____

Address (❑ home [50] ❑ work [51]/Company name: _____)

Street/Suite# _____

City [52]/State [53]/Zipcode [54]: _____ Country [55] _____

❑ **I liked this book!** You may quote me by name in future
IDG Books Worldwide promotional materials.

My daytime phone number is _____

IDG BOOKS

THE WORLD OF
COMPUTER
KNOWLEDGE

❏ YES!

Please keep me informed about IDG's World of Computer Knowledge.
Send me the latest IDG Books catalog.

SECRETS™

...FOR DUMMIES™
COMPUTER
BOOK SERIES
FROM IDG

MACWORLD
MW
AUTHORIZED
EDITION

AUTHORIZED
PC WORLD
EDITION